Designing and Implementing Effective Professional Learning

for Krissy, Emma, and Claire,
who inspire me to give my best
every single day

Designing and Implementing Effective Professional Learning

John Murray

CORWIN

A SAGE Company

FOR INFORMATION:

Corwin
A SAGE Company
2455 Teller Road
Thousand Oaks, California 91320
(800) 233-9936
www.corwin.com

SAGE Publications Ltd.
1 Oliver's Yard
55 City Road
London EC1Y 1SP
United Kingdom

SAGE Publications India Pvt. Ltd.
B 1/I 1 Mohan Cooperative Industrial Area
Mathura Road, New Delhi 110 044
India

SAGE Publications Asia-Pacific Pte. Ltd.
3 Church Street
#10-04 Samsung Hub
Singapore 049483

Acquisitions Editor: Dan Alpert
Associate Editor: Kimberly Greenberg
Editorial Assistant: Heidi Arndt
Permissions Editor: Karen Ehrmann
Marketing Manager: Stephanie Trikay
Project Editor: Veronica Stapleton Hooper
Copy Editor: Terri Lee Paulsen
Typesetter: C&M Digitals (P) Ltd.
Proofreader: Wendy Jo Dymond
Indexer: Karen Wiley
Cover Designer: Gail Buschman

Printed in the United States of America.

A catalog record of this book is available from the Library of Congress.

ISBN: 9781452257792

This book is printed on acid-free paper.

13 14 15 16 17 10 9 8 7 6 5 4 3 2 1

Contents

List of Figures

Preface

Nothing has promised so much and been so frustratingly wasteful as the thousands of workshops and conferences that led to no significant change in practice when teachers returned to their classroom.

—Michael Fullan

A friend of mine has a rare kidney disease. Her prognosis is good as she goes in for treatments and meets with her doctor regularly to examine her progress. Her doctor meets with other physicians to discuss her test results and they share their perspectives, insights, and approaches in treating cases like hers. Her doctor is confident that she is receiving quality care based on the combined knowledge and experience of their team. These doctors dedicate a half day every week to review cases, look at new information emerging from research, and determine the most promising treatments for their patients. By focusing on consistent collaboration and communication, rather than functioning as solitary practitioners, the physicians improve their individual and collective practices.

We expect our doctors to regularly evaluate and monitor our health and to select the best available plan for improvement—and we demand that they eliminate treatments that don't work and replace them with more effective ones. But we rarely make the same demands of our schools and our teachers. Professionals in other fields, from medicine to financial management to law, engage in ongoing learning opportunities. The time has come for schools to engage teachers in learning the way other professions do—continuously, collaboratively, and on the job.

Fortunately, examples of how to do this already exist, as many countries are working to improve their education systems by investing in teacher learning as a major engine for student achievement. The highest-achieving countries on international measures, such as the Programme for International Student Assessment (PISA) and the Third International Math and Science Study (TIMSS), have been particularly focused on developing teachers' expertise both before and after they enter the profession and throughout their careers (Stigler & Hiebert, 1999).

Noted educational researchers Linda Darling-Hammond (2003) and Vivien Stewart (2011) have studied the professional learning opportunities provided for teachers in the high-achieving nations of Finland, Sweden, Japan, South Korea, and the United Kingdom and have found that their teacher learning programs share many features, including

- teacher learning opportunities sustained over time;
- time for teacher professional learning embedded into the school day;
- teacher learning opportunities involving active learning and collaboration;
- professional learning activities embedded in context and focused on specific content to be taught to specific grade levels; and
- teachers who are involved in decisions about curriculum, assessment, and professional learning content and activities.

In these countries, professional development is not something that is done to teachers. It is a process focused on improving student learning, and it requires teacher engagement and active teacher learning.

Unfortunately, while there is understanding about what constitutes effective teacher professional learning, multiple studies (Birman et al., 2007; Blank & de las Alas, & Smith, 2008; Murray, 2011; Wei, Darling-Hammond, & Adamson, 2010) have demonstrated that American teachers do not receive the kind of high-quality teacher professional development common in many other nations. For too long, teacher professional development practices have treated educators as passive recipients of information and schools have expected little change in classroom practices. In-service training, consisting of workshops, speakers, and short-term courses, remains the dominant mode of teacher professional learning in most schools in this country. Often called "one-shot" or "drive-by" professional development, traditional in-service training has been criticized by researchers and school teachers and leaders as ineffective in bringing about substantive improvements in teacher knowledge, teacher instructional practices, and student learning. Traditional in-service professional development has consumed tremendous resources over the past two decades, with few corresponding results for teachers and students.

Not only do most schools continue to rely upon fragmented, ineffective one-day or two-day activities; few learning opportunities for teachers also feature the intense emphasis on content, repeated chances for practicing what is learned, and meaningful ongoing conversations about instruction that positively influence teacher learning, classroom practice, and student achievement. Schools lack the structures or cultures to support the kind of job-embedded, sustained, contextual, collaborative teacher professional learning that leads to substantive improvements in teaching and learning. What we all want for our students—a variety of learning opportunities that engage them in experiencing and solving real-world problems, using their own experience, and working with others—is often denied to teachers when they are learners.

For our schools to achieve on a wide scale the kind of teaching that has a substantial impact on student learning, much more intensive and effective professional learning than has traditionally been available is required. If we want all students to possess the higher-order thinking skills they need to succeed in the 21st century, we need educators who possess higher-order teaching skills and deep content knowledge. In this book, I explore how school leaders can work to create meaningful, effective professional development programs in their schools to develop the structures and capacity needed to bring about real change. Professional development is supposed to contribute to change in the classroom, and when it doesn't we waste time and resources and compromise teachers' trust that time engaged in professional development is well spent. Workshops, speakers, and conferences can raise awareness and enthusiasm, and can impart knowledge, but they rarely provide the opportunities for reflection, discussions with colleagues, and continued support that are needed to bring about real instructional change.

In many ways teacher professional learning is more important now than ever before. As both Thomas Friedman (2007) and Tony Wagner (2008) have powerfully argued in recent years, students need to learn more complex material in preparation for further education and work in the 21st century. Teachers, therefore, must learn instructional approaches that develop the knowledge and skills students need to succeed in an increasingly diverse and interconnected world. Ensuring student success necessitates new types of instruction, conducted by teachers who understand content, learning, and pedagogy; who can adapt to the diverse needs of their students; and who can build powerful connections between students' experiences and the goals of the curriculum. These types of transformations demand significant learning on the part of teachers and will not occur without support and guidance. Efforts to improve student achievement can succeed only by building the capacity of teachers to improve their instructional practice and the capacity of schools to promote teacher learning. If teachers are not engaged throughout their careers in learning experiences that enable them to better serve their students, both teachers and students suffer.

Realizing the magnitude and importance of the challenge, the public, politicians, and educators have made high-quality professional learning opportunities for school teachers a priority in modern educational reform proposals (Fishman, Marx, Best, & Tal, 2003). For example, the No Child Left Behind (NCLB) Act of 2001 requires states to make "high-quality" professional development available for all teachers and this has led to substantial resources being devoted to teacher professional development at the local, state, and federal levels; for example, in 2007–2008 the federal government spent almost $2 billion on professional development for teachers (Desimone, 2009). In addition, The Teaching Commission (2006) has cautioned that "targeted professional development is essential to help teachers meet the demands of recent reforms" (p. 11). Finally, both President Obama and Secretary of Education Arne Duncan have made professional development a priority in their Education Agenda (Darling-Hammond, 2010).

Teachers are not just born; they can be developed. Enhancing the effectiveness of professional learning is the leverage point with the greatest possibility for strengthening the knowledge and teaching practices of educators. For most teachers, professional learning is the most accessible avenue they have for developing the knowledge and skills required to better meet the needs of their students. If teachers are not engaged throughout their careers in new learning experiences that enable them to better serve their students, both teachers and their students suffer. It is the responsibility of every school and every school leader to make teacher growth and development a priority. All school leaders, from superintendents to principals to department heads, must possess a strong resolve to create and maintain the conditions and culture needed to build capacity in the individual and the school. Effective professional learning is learning from the work teachers do. It involves reflective dialogue, observing and responding to one another's teaching, collaborating to implement new strategies, sharing effective teaching approaches and materials, and engaging in research focused on common issues of practice. It not only involves dialogue and collaboration among teachers within a specific school, but also includes teachers connecting with and learning from educators from around the world through the creation of personal learning networks.

The information, ideas, and recommendations in this book are purposely aligned with Learning Forward's revised Standards for Professional Learning (2011). The seven standards, developed from the literature on best practices for effective teacher professional learning, serve to guide the decisions and practices of all educators charged with designing, managing, implementing, and evaluating professional learning in schools:

- **Learning Communities**—Professional learning that improves teaching practices and results in enhanced student achievement occurs within adult learning communities committed to continuous improvement.
- **Leadership**—Professional learning that improves teaching practices and results in enhanced student achievement requires skillful leaders who develop organizational capacity and implement designs to support professional learning.
- **Resources**—Professional learning that improves teaching practices and results in enhanced student achievement requires prioritizing, monitoring, and coordinating resources for teacher learning.
- **Data**—Professional learning that improves teaching practices and results in enhanced student achievement uses a variety of data to plan, develop, and assess teacher professional learning.
- **Learning Designs**—Professional learning that improves teaching practices and results in enhanced student achievement uses research-based learning strategies to achieve its intended goals.
- **Implementation**—Professional learning that improves teaching practices and results in enhanced student achievement applies research on change and sustains support of implementation of professional learning for long-term change.
- **Outcomes**—Professional learning that improves teaching practices and results in enhanced student achievement aligns its outcomes with educator performance and student curriculum standards.

While this book is a balance of research, theory, and practice, it is primarily intended to be a practical resource that educators can use as they work to create meaningful, effective professional learning programs in our schools. For the school principal, it can serve as a comprehensive resource to help them extend and refine their ability to lead effective professional learning. For the superintendent and other central office leaders, it can provide the information needed to give them a sense of the complexity of professional learning and the factors that influence its effectiveness. For the director of professional development, it has the necessary detail and practical information to serve as a guide in creating an effective professional learning plan for the district. And for the teacher-leader, it emphasizes the importance of teachers taking ownership of their own learning and provides practical details regarding how teacher-leaders are an essential part of designing and implementing effective professional learning programs. Finally, most graduate programs in educational leadership, educational administration, or supervision and curriculum have entire courses or sections of courses devoted to leading professional development programs, and this book has excellent potential for use in these settings.

Chapters 1 through 5 provide the foundational knowledge practitioners need to design, implement, evaluate, and sustain effective professional learning in schools. In Chapter 1 I discuss why global and societal shifts make teacher professional learning particularly important today, and reflect on why conventional professional development methods are inadequate in addressing the learning needs of schools and teachers. In Chapter 2 I present current models of professional learning action and examine the characteristics of effective professional learning activities.

The revised Learning Forward Standards for Professional Learning "describe the context, content, and processes for effective professional learning" (Learning Forward, 2011, p. 19), and it is essential that each school leader focus on these three areas to create and sustain an effective teacher professional learning program. While the context, process, and content emphasis are not as prominent in the 2011 Standards as in the 2001 Standards, "they remain a foundation for the seven 2011 standards" (Learning Forward, 2011, p. 19). Learning Communities, Leadership, and Resources standards define the essential context for effective teacher learning and are examined in Chapter 3. Without the appropriate context in place, even the most thoughtfully planned and implemented professional learning activity will fail. Content—establishing the goals of professional development activities and how to assess them—is the focus of Chapter 4. Content, which encompasses the Data and Outcomes standards, refers to the "what" of professional learning and consists of the learning needs of students, and the specific knowledge, skills, and teaching approaches to be acquired by teachers to better meet those student needs. Process—the "how" of professional learning—is the topic of Chapter 5. Process encompasses the Learning Designs and Implementation standards and involves the types of professional learning activities, and the way those activities are planned, organized, implemented, and followed up.

With a foundational understanding established, I proceed to discuss eight powerful professional learning strategies in Chapters 6 through 13: lesson study, Critical Friends, action research, school rounds, mentoring, peer coaching, online professional learning, and personal learning networks. Many professional learning approaches exist; I have intentionally limited my discussion to just the eight listed earlier for four reasons. First, each of the eight strategies is consistent with research-based principles of effective teacher professional learning. Second, practitioners have found these strategies to be effective in bringing about improvements in instructional practices and student learning, the very outcomes that are the goals of professional learning activities. Third, these strategies are representative of a variety of approaches with some being group approaches (lesson study, Critical Friends, action research, and school rounds), some being individual or pair approaches (mentoring and peer coaching), and some being approaches leveraging technology (online professional learning and personal learning networks). Finally, by limiting the focus to eight strategies I am able examine each one in detail rather than just provide the cursory descriptions found in other works on the subject.

Each strategy chapter provides the detail and guidance school leaders need to use the approach in their schools. Specifically, every strategy chapter includes the rationale behind the strategy, the essential features of the strategy, suggestions for implementing the strategy, resources for learning more about the strategy, and examples of the strategy in action. Some designs will appear more daunting than others, particularly if your school is in the early stages of becoming a learning community. However, we can't wait to implement the strategies presented in this book. Our students will be more engaged, and will learn more, when we create and sustain a context supportive of adult learning, when we intentionally focus the content of professional learning on student needs, and when we carefully choose strategies that help teachers meet those needs.

Following the eight chapters on strategies, I devote Chapter 14 to the very practical concern of how school leaders can overcome the teacher resistance involved in moving to new professional learning practices. Finally, in Chapter 15 I summarize the take-home messages from the book and emphasize the urgency educators must have in making teacher professional learning a priority. I hope this book will serve both as a source of information about teacher professional learning and a "how-to" manual that can be adapted to the particular characteristics and circumstances of individual schools. We are unlikely to seek the services of mechanics, surgeons, or plumbers who are not current with the latest knowledge, products, and procedures in their fields. Our students deserve the same from the educators who serve them. Effective teacher learning programs in our schools are a necessity, not a frill. It is time to engage all teachers in a lifelong process of professional growth. The stakes are too important to ignore: our schools, our children, and our future.

Acknowledgments

I am fortunate to be able to work on a daily basis with dedicated principals and teachers. They are committed equally to teaching, understanding their students' learning, and developing their practice. It is because of them and teachers like them that I am able to illustrate the principles of building and sustaining effective teacher professional learning opportunities. Particular thanks go out to the following educators who inspired me to believe that teachers, and their students, deserve more than occasional traditional drive-by professional learning opportunities: David Mallery, Kerry Brennan, Toby Jones, Stephanie Perrin, Ben Gregg, Julie Faulstich, and Lisa Kensler. I also express my deep gratitude for the service rendered by Lisa Kensler and Cynthia Reed in their honest appraisal of several draft chapters and for Dan Alpert, senior editor at Corwin, who believed in this book from the very beginning. Finally, I have had the great benefit of patient and loving support from my wife, Krissy, and my daughters, Emma and Claire, particularly when I was thoroughly distracted by the work of seeing this project to fruition.

Publisher's Acknowledgments

Corwin gratefully acknowledges the contributions of the following reviewers:

Kathy Gross
Director of Professional Learning
Springfield Public Schools
Springfield, Missouri
Nancy Kellogg
Education Consultant
Boulder, Colorado

About the Author

 **John Murray** is an educational consultant and presenter on effective teacher learning practices in American schools. He has also been a classroom teacher, science department head, high school principal, and university instructor in his more than 20 years as an educator. His previous book was titled *Effective Teacher Learning Practices in U.S. Independent Schools*, and he has published more than a dozen articles on effective teacher professional learning. He holds a PhD in educational leadership from Auburn University, an MA in private school administration from Teacher's College at Columbia University, and both an MEd and a BA from the University of Virginia.

1

The Need for Change

Using the same ineffective approach again and again while expecting different results may not be the definition of insanity, but it sure isn't smart.

—Unknown

Traditional Approaches to Teacher Professional Learning

In the United States, every K–12 educator participates in some form of professional learning each year. My experiences with professional development at the start of my career as a high school science teacher more than 20 years ago may not be so different from what many teachers experience today. As a new teacher, I was often confused about why a lesson fell flat or how to connect with a difficult student. I wanted and needed professional learning that was relevant and useful but little was forthcoming. My principal observed me once each year and provided feedback in the form of a checklist, my department head never visited my classes, and school cultural norms made teachers visiting one another's classes taboo. I made incremental improvements in my teaching by trial and error, guided by my instincts about what worked and what didn't. Several times each year we had professional development days, during which an outside "expert" would speak on an educational topic chosen by school administrators. The focus of each professional development day was different, and there was never any follow-up or opportunities for reflective dialogue with colleagues. These days seemed to be based on the premise that learning happens as a direct result of exposure to new information, as if upon hearing new information we would learn it. We usually competed for seats in the back of the room where we could grade student assignments, plan for classes, or think about how to best support a challenging student.

Schools in the United States historically have been dominated by an egg-crate culture in which teachers are isolated from one another in separate classrooms as well as insulated from the need to demonstrate their own learning and growth. Richard Elmore (2002), professor of educational leadership at Harvard, argues that many schools in the United States are "hostile and inhospitable places for adult learning" (p. 4) because there are few mechanisms by which new knowledge about teaching and learning can enter schools; few structures and processes in place to help teachers adapt, practice, and polish new practices; and few sources of assistance for teachers struggling to make improvements. Teacher learning is often pushed aside in schools as teachers and administrators race through the day meeting all of their other duties.

Perhaps at least partially due to the fact they are easier to schedule, and interfere less with other responsibilities and obligations, professional learning opportunities for teachers typically have consisted of workshops, speakers, conferences, and short-term courses. These approaches have been to shown to be ineffective in bringing about improvements in teacher knowledge, classroom instruction, and student learning and have been criticized for being disconnected from the real issues and challenges teachers face on a daily basis (Blank, de las Alas, & Smith, 2008).

Why is this? First, these approaches rarely address specific teacher needs, student needs, or school needs. Professional development programs are meant to improve the classroom practices of teachers and enhance student learning, but these goals are almost impossible to achieve without tailoring them to specific teacher and student needs. Yet teacher and student needs often are not considered when schools select professional learning activities—a sure recipe for teacher cynicism and resistance. We expect teachers to assess student needs and design learning activities to address them, yet many schools continue to ignore these fundamental principles of instructional design when selecting professional learning opportunities for their teachers.

Second, teachers are often passive recipients of information in traditional professional learning rather than being engaged in the design and delivery of the activity. In the traditional paradigm, professional development is seen as something that is done to teachers rather than as a process requiring teacher participation. However, when teachers actively involve students in activities rather than just lecture to them, students are more engaged and their learning is enhanced. Educators know this learning principle but often fail to apply it when considering professional learning experiences for their teachers.

Third, opportunities for follow-up on the ideas presented are rare and poorly organized. A teacher once told me a story about how she spent several days in workshops focusing on differentiated instruction, received no follow-up instruction or support, and then was asked to demonstrate at the end of the semester how she had implemented differentiated instruction principles with her students. Again, good teachers do not expect student learning to occur without reinforcing concepts and skills, but follow-up for professional learning activities is frequently fragmented or nonexistent.

Fourth, teachers have few opportunities to collaborate with colleagues on the skills and ideas presented. When teachers can collectively reflect on what they have learned, share insights about what it means, and share thoughts about potential applications to their instruction, they are much more likely to add what they have experienced in a professional learning activity to their instructional repertoire. But because school culture has favored teacher isolation and few structures exist to encourage collegial sharing, collaboration among colleagues remains rare in our schools.

Finally, opportunities to develop and practice new lessons and approaches based on what is presented are rare, and opportunities to receive feedback on attempts to practice new methods are even more unusual. Teachers and coaches expect that multiple opportunities for practice, with accompanying feedback, will be needed for significant improvements in learning and performance to occur. No professional learning experience can lead to significant improvements in teaching and learning without building in regular opportunities for teacher practice and feedback, and yet this rarely happens in our schools.

Despite multiple studies demonstrating the ineffectiveness of traditional forms of teacher professional learning (Darling-Hammond, Wei, Andree, Richardson, & Orphanos, 2009; Desimone, Porter, Garet, Yoon, & Birman, 2002), and despite teachers and school leaders criticizing them for wasting time and resources, research indicates that professional learning opportunities in U.S. schools continue to consist primarily of traditional workshops, speakers, and conferences

(Murray, 2011; Wei, Darling-Hammond, & Adamson, 2010). This reliance on traditional methods of professional learning is consistent across school divisions, with few differences between elementary schools, middle schools, and high schools. Further, research indicates no significant differences in professional development practices across schools with different professional development budget sizes (Darling-Hammond et al., 2009; Murray, 2011). So having more funding for professional development does not lead to more effective professional development practices.

Why does such a large gap exist between research-based best practices of teacher professional learning and current practices? Professional issues such as time pressures and stress at work play a role. Many teachers feel overextended and may not have the additional time and energy needed to invest in more effective methods of professional growth and learning. Related to this are structural obstacles that make it difficult for teachers to engage in more effective ongoing, job-embedded forms of teacher learning. The schedule of the day must be restructured to provide teachers with focused opportunities to engage in the type of work called for by research on effective professional development.

In Finland, Sweden, and Germany, three countries noted for both their high student achievement and effective teacher professional development, time for teacher professional learning is built into the regular teacher work day (Jaquith, Mindich, & Darling-Hammond, 2011). They have developed creative scheduling to carve out dedicated time during the day for teacher collaboration and learning. It is clear that time must be restructured to allow U.S. schools to adopt more effective professional learning practices.

Another issue is the problem of introducing change in a climate replete with failed change initiatives. As Rob Evans (2002) observes, "even in cases where schools have tried to implement changes in how their teachers learn, the effect has been minimal because teachers are often cynical and resistant from the many prior initiatives that went absolutely nowhere" (p. 128). Teachers are hesitant to commit time and energy without some understanding of the reasons for their efforts and some confidence that the work will lead to some positive result. Teachers must be convinced that "this change initiative will be different" for more effective methods of professional learning to take hold.

Two even more culturally embedded and intractable reasons best explain the current gulf between best practices and reality (Jaquith et al., 2011). First, professional development programs in schools are typically based on the false assumption that significant teacher insight and learning requires external direction. This leads to teachers being sent to conferences to learn from experts, and bringing the experts to the school to speak and conduct workshops. Because formal follow-up to these events is rare and because informal avenues for sharing and discussing what is learned are typically absent, these "outside" professional development events do not influence teacher instruction or student learning. More damaging, though, is that this false assumption leads to a reduction in collaboration and conversation among teachers, the very things schools most need to establish sustained effective professional learning.

Second, and perhaps of even greater importance, American schools have long been characterized by a culture in which teachers work in isolation and are insulated from opportunities to engage in and demonstrate professional learning and growth. The professional learning activities that do exist typically are not even built into the regular work day, disconnecting them from the daily issues faced by teachers and communicating in a not so subtle way that professional learning is far down the list of priorities schools have for their teachers. Efforts to close the gap between research-based best practices and current practices begin with creating a culture that supports continuous, job-embedded professional learning.

New Demands Require Change

There are three reasons why teacher professional learning matters more today than ever before and why schools must focus on improving their current professional development practices. First, research over the past 20 years has led to multiple discoveries about learning and learners and the accompanying "best practice" teaching strategies that are too compelling to ignore (Bransford & Brown, 2002). A reliance on the "stand-and-deliver" or "sage on the stage" model of teaching, with the teacher at the center of everything, is not the most effective method of instruction for helping students understand concepts on a deep level. Teachers need to use more varied strategies founded on research about how children learn. Unless teachers actively pursue innovative advances in the profession, traditional professional development methods are not likely to help them develop the best practice instructional approaches that are transforming some U.S. and many international schools. Among these are multiple intelligences instruction, differentiated instruction, "backward design" planning and assessment, project-based instruction, personal student learning networks, instruction based on cognitive neuroscience, and inquiry science instruction. This list is only a sample of the research-based best practices available to assist teachers and schools, and while many schools are already helping their teachers implement these strategies in their classrooms, many others have not yet changed.

Second, as both Mel Levine (2003) and Rob Evans (2005) have emphasized, cultural and demographic changes in our society mean that today's students come with more learning challenges now than ever before. The students attending schools today are more likely to use English as a second language, face more personal difficulties and learning differences, and have more dysfunctional family lives than in the past. The changing needs of students require teachers to learn new methods to reach a more diverse group of students, to expand their repertoire beyond being distributors of information to become facilitators, coaches, and guides. Professional learning opportunities are essential to help teachers effectively work with diverse learning styles and disparate needs. As Cheryl Johnson (2007) puts it, "it is an issue of equity and we must provide rich learning opportunities for our teachers so they can connect with the variety of students they are charged with teaching" (p. 638).

Finally, and both Thomas Friedman (2007) and Tony Wagner (2008) would argue most importantly, the changes described earlier are taking place against a backdrop of the shift from an industrial economy to a knowledge economy based on the instantaneous, global transmission of information. Our students must compete and succeed in a "flat world" that has been and will continue to be transformed by rapidly evolving technologies and the incredible economic growth of China, India, Singapore, and many other countries. These changes are powerful and demand that we rethink what our students need to know, understand, and be able to do—and how they are best taught. The traditional model of teachers dispensing pieces of information disconnected from other subject areas is largely obsolete as a way to prepare our students for the realities of a modern world where critical thinking, problem solving, collaboration, adaptability, oral and written communication, and imagination are critical survival skills. For teachers to recognize these changing dynamics and determine how to address them through instructional change is a daunting task that can't be accomplished with traditional methods of teacher professional learning.

Many of us teach as we were taught; however, the world is not the same as it was when we were students in the classroom. Teachers today must help an increasingly diverse group of students develop a new set of knowledge and skills needed to thrive in our modern "flat world." To meet these demands they must have opportunities to learn about, adapt, and implement research-based, practitioner-proven new approaches to teaching and learning. Regrettably, most U.S. schools are not currently providing professional learning opportunities that significantly improve the knowledge, skills, and attitudes of teachers, and that lead to new types of instruction that develop the essential skills students most need to succeed and thrive in college and beyond.

If teachers are not supported and encouraged to continuously seek new knowledge and skills, it is not only their instructional practices that suffer over time. Their ability to adapt to change also erodes, their self-confidence declines, and they become less able to have a positive influence on their colleagues and their students. This is why it is so crucial that all teachers engage in effective professional learning activities, regardless of their current instructional proficiency and the relative abilities of their students.

In this chapter I have examined the current state of professional learning in American schools, specified why current approaches are ineffective, emphasized why teacher professional learning matters more today than ever, and discussed structural and cultural obstacles that must be addressed before professional learning in schools can be improved. In Chapter 2 I focus on the characteristics of effective professional learning, and in Chapter 3 I discuss how to build school capacity (culture) to support a professional learning program with these characteristics.

2

Effective Teacher Professional Learning

We always tell our students that we want them to be lifelong learners. Before we can realize that goal with students we must first get our teachers to learn continuously throughout their careers.

—David Mallery

When asked, teachers report that workshops, speakers, and conferences—even when engaging and informative—rarely bring about changes in their instructional practices or student learning. This ineffectiveness of traditional teacher professional learning has led to extensive research on what constitutes effective professional development—and a consensus is emerging about the essential characteristics of professional development that are critical to increasing teacher knowledge and skills and hold promise for increasing student achievement (Darling-Hammond et al., 2009; Webster-Wright, 2009). "High-quality" or "effective" teacher professional learning is defined as that which results in improvements in teachers' knowledge and instruction and improvements in student learning. While the impact on student achievement is frequently viewed as the key indicator of the effectiveness of professional development (Learning Forward,

2011), the influence of professional development on teacher knowledge and classroom instructional practice is also essential, as these are results that must precede increased learning for students.

The primary purpose of this chapter is to explain the specific characteristics of effective teacher professional learning programs. However, because theoretical models are important tools in helping educators understand how and why specific professional development programs and activities are more or less effective than others, the first section of this chapter briefly outlines how such models can be useful to school leaders.

Theoretical Models of Professional Development Action

I recently spoke with a high school principal who was frustrated that her professional development programs never seemed to "stick" with her faculty. In an unusual move, she not only asked teachers whether or not they liked the professional learning opportunities provided for them, but also examined the extent to which the activities enhanced teacher knowledge and instructional practice. Assessments (paper-and-pencil tests and videotapes of classroom teaching) consistently revealed positive changes in teacher knowledge and classroom instruction in the weeks and months following a professional learning activity, but teachers invariably reverted to their previous classroom methods. She wondered why her faculty was particularly resistant, and wanted to know what she could do to help make the changes in teaching practices more permanent.

While teacher resistance is a significant concern in leading a change in professional learning methods, and is discussed in detail in a later chapter, something else was at work here. Further discussions with this principal revealed that she had never asked teachers about the influence of the instructional changes on student learning and/or student attitudes and behaviors. When she investigated further with her faculty, she learned that the instructional changes did not stick because teachers did not see any changes in students learning. Even though teachers initiated new instructional practices, they saw no corresponding improvements in student learning—and gradually reverted to their previous approaches. Understanding theoretical models of professional development action helped this principal make sense of why her professional learning programs were not resulting in the permanent changes she desired, and helped her consider how to redesign her programs to achieve the intended goals.

The current theoretical model of the action of professional development recognizes that quality professional development is influenced by multiple factors, and emphasizes the interactive nature between professional development activities, teacher learning, and student learning (Desimone, 2009; Guskey, 2000). The model (see Figure 2.1) follows these steps:

1. Professional learning activities consist of three major components. *Context* characteristics refer to the "who," "when," "where," and "why" of teacher professional learning, and includes the traits of the specific educators involved in the professional learning, the context in which they work, and the students they teach (Guskey & Sparks, 2004). *Content* characteristics refer to the "what" of professional learning and consist of the new knowledge, skills, and understandings to be acquired by teachers. *Process* characteristics are the "how" of professional learning and concern the types of professional learning activities, and the way those activities are planned, organized, implemented, and followed up.

2. Teachers actively participate in the professional learning activities, rather than merely being passive recipients of knowledge.

3. The professional development improves teachers' knowledge, skills, and attitudes. This is a significant departure from earlier models that did not recognize the internal transformation that must precede any changes in instructional practice.

4. Teachers use their new knowledge, skills, and attitudes to improve their instruction and their pedagogy. Time for both individual and collaborative reflection is considered to be an important part of making instructional changes.

5. The instructional changes lead to improved student learning. The changes, or lack of changes, in student learning serve as feedback, which impacts the development of future professional learning activities. Student learning outcomes also influence whether an instructional change will "stick." In addition, student learning outcomes provide feedback, which can lead to additional changes in teacher knowledge, skills, and attitudes, and further changes in classroom teaching.

Figure 2.1   Theoretical Model of Professional Development Action

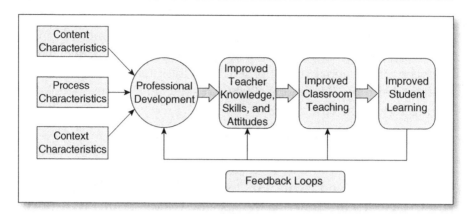

There are several important distinctions between this current model of professional development action and earlier models. First, by specifying that professional learning activities include content, process, and context features, the current model brings greater understanding about the key variables to consider when designing effective professional development programs. In addition, the current model illustrates the importance of a systemic approach to professional development by including feedback loops where student learning outcomes influence changes in classroom teaching; changes in teacher knowledge, skills, and attitudes; and future professional development activities.

This aspect of the model helped the principal described above understand why her professional development opportunities were not resulting in long-lasting changes in classroom practices. The current theoretical model emphasizes that for professional development efforts to succeed they must take into account the factors that interact to influence the relationship between professional development and student learning.

Characteristics of Effective Professional Development

Researchers have used the current theoretical model of professional development in their search for the defining characteristics and qualities of effective teacher professional learning. Grounded in sound principles of adult learning (see Figure 2.2), this research has resulted in considerable agreement that the key characteristics of effective

Figure 2.2 Adult Learning Principles

Adult Learning Maxims	Approaches for Adult Learners
1. Adults are internally motivated to learn and need to direct their own learning. They want to be involved in diagnosing, planning, implementing, and evaluating their own learning.	1. Provide learning experiences that are hands-on, active, and connected to real-life challenges. Give adults opportunities to apply what they learn.
2. Adults seek knowledge that relates to their current situation and helps them address current challenges. They want learning experiences that are sustained and intensive and are supported by coaching and modeling.	2. Involve them in the design and implementation of the learning experience. Give them significant control over their own learning.
	3. Provide ongoing support in the form of coaching and mentoring during the learning process.
3. Adults prefer collaborative learning involving the sharing of ideas and perspectives.	4. Provide multiple opportunities for them to reflect, analyze, and practice in a collaborative setting.

Source: Adapted from Roberts and Pruitt (2003).

teacher professional learning include an emphasis on pedagogical content knowledge, a focus on student learning, implementation over time, alignment with school goals, a connection to teacher needs, and ongoing teacher collaboration (Goldschmidt & Phelps, 2010; Wei et al., 2010). Transitioning to these research-based characteristics of effective teacher professional learning will require a significant shift in focus for many schools (see Figure 2.3).

Focus on Student Learning and Specific Content

Traditionally, designers of teacher professional learning activities have emphasized improving general teaching practices, such as cooperative learning or classroom management, separate from distinct academic disciplines. They have typically not addressed teachers' knowledge of the subjects they teach or instructional strategies within particular subject areas. However, research suggests that professional development is most effective when it addresses the daily challenges of teaching and learning specific subject matter, rather than emphasizing abstract educational maxims or teaching methods disconnected from context (Desimone, 2009).

For example, teachers are more likely to implement instructional practices that have been modeled for them in professional learning activities. In addition, teachers themselves report that professional

Figure 2.3 The Shift From Traditional PD to Research-Based Effective PD

From workshops and speakers . . .	to learning that is part of the daily work of teachers.
From infrequent professional development days . . .	to ongoing learning over time.
From one-size-fits-all programs for entire faculties . . .	to team-based learning focused on specific teacher needs.
From passive "sit and get" learning . . .	to learning by doing, interacting, and applying.
From isolated learning . . .	to learning collaboratively.
From privatization of practice . . .	to open, ongoing sharing and examination of instructional practices.
From infrequent and cursory assessments of PD effectiveness . . .	to planned assessments examining evidence of improved student outcomes.
From fragmented exposure to many concepts and approaches . . .	to sustained commitment to focused initiatives that are connected to teacher and school goals.

Source: Adapted from Dufour, Dufour, and Eaker (2008).

development is most valuable when it provides multiple opportunities to actively participate in work that builds their understanding of academic content and how to best teach it to their students. Lee Schulman (1986) coined the term "pedagogical content knowledge" to describe the special kind of subject-matter understanding that enables teachers to best support the learning of their students. Teachers with high pedagogical content knowledge "anticipate common misconceptions held by students, know how to lead them into different conceptual understandings, help students see and understand relationships between and among ideas and concepts, and encourage students to apply and transfer knowledge" (Sparks, 1998, p. 100).

Professional development that leads teachers to develop specific pedagogical content knowledge improves teacher instruction and student outcomes (Goldschmidt & Phelps, 2010). One way to do this is to put teachers in the position of studying the very material that they teach their own students. For example, one school I know had their middle school science teachers participate in a 100-hour summer program, during which they engaged in a learning cycle that included exploring a phenomenon, generating a theory that explained what had occurred, and applying it to novel situations. After going through this process, the teachers developed their own units and taught them to one another before returning to their classrooms in the fall. It also is useful for groups of teachers to collaboratively analyze and discuss student work such as projects, tests, and essays to identify common student errors and difficulties, reach common understanding of the criteria for mastering a given concept or skill, and determine which instructional approaches are or are not effective, and for whom.

Evidence accumulated over the past decade points to the strong link between professional learning activities that focus on subject-matter content and how students best learn that content with increases in teacher knowledge, skills, improvements in practice, and student achievement (Hill, 2010). As Coalition of Essential Schools founder Ted Sizer (1999) once said, "the most powerful professional learning experiences are active learning opportunities embedded in teachers' work where they experience for themselves the learning they want their students to do" (p. 8).

Extended Over Time and Connected to Practice

A common criticism of traditional professional learning activities is that they are too short and offer limited opportunities for follow-up with teachers. As in previous decades, much of professional development today consists of occasional workshops, typically lasting less than a day, each one focusing on discrete topics that have little direct connection to teachers' classrooms. However, such fragmented, episodic workshops do not provide teachers the needed time for serious study of specific subject matter or for applying new ideas in the classroom and reflecting on the results.

Teachers need professional development that extends over time and is linked with their classroom teaching, allowing for multiple cycles of practice, feedback, and reflection (Guskey, 2000). Professional development of longer duration is more likely to contain the kinds of learning opportunities necessary for teachers to integrate new knowledge into practice. For example, longer activities are more likely to allow for deep discussion of content, student conceptions and misconceptions, instructional strategies, and assessment strategies (Johnson, Kahle, & Fargo, 2006). In addition, activities that extend over time are more likely to cause teachers to try out new practices in the classroom and receive feedback on their teaching. Many studies confirm that intellectual and instructional change requires professional learning activities to be of long duration, including both the span of time over which the activity is spread and the number of hours spent in the activity (Johnson & Marx, 2009).

Professional learning time has the greatest influence when it is built into the regular work day and week of teachers (job embedded). Job-embedded professional learning supports the kind of context-specific teacher learning that is most effective in bringing about teacher, student, and school improvements. Importantly, these findings are confirmed by studies showing that teachers view professional development activities as most effective when they happen daily or weekly over the course of an entire school year. While duration of the professional learning is not the only variable that matters, there is substantial evidence that teacher learning, and associated student learning, are enhanced with intensive, ongoing professional development (Hill, 2010).

Align With School Priorities and Goals

Many school leaders are familiar with Peter Senge and his work on learning organizations and the importance of "systems thinking" when working to bring about change in schools. Senge (1999) argues that all the people and structures in a school are connected to one another and that positive change can be created and sustained only by recognizing and nurturing these interconnections. Yet a common frustration of many teachers is that professional learning activities often are disconnected from the people, structures, and educational philosophies of their schools. A teacher once told me, "Our superintendent says we should be focused on one thing, our principal says our school goals for this year are another thing, and our in-service activities seem completely unrelated to both of them." Not only are professional learning activities often disconnected from a school's mission and specific goals, but they are also rarely designed and selected to address specific teacher and student needs.

Professional development is more effective when the activities are part of a coherent program of teacher and school improvement (Penuel, Fishman, Yamaguchi, & Gallaher, 2007). A coherent professional development program is connected to student needs, teacher needs, school goals, school curriculum, and the school mission. Professional development will have little impact when teachers see a disconnect between what they are guided to do in a professional learning activity and the other realities of their current school experience. For substantial change in teaching practices to occur, curriculum, school goals, teacher needs, student needs, and professional learning activities must be closely linked to connect what teachers learn in professional development with school initiatives and the daily challenges they face in the classroom.

Build Strong Collaborative Working Relationships

Impeded by the traditional model of isolated classrooms and the resulting norm of privacy, U.S. schools historically have offered few opportunities for collective teacher work. Therefore, early efforts at developing occasions for teacher collaboration were often ineffective, as both teachers and educational leaders did not have clear images of how teachers could work and learn well together.

Studies have found that when schools create productive working relationships within academic departments or grade levels, across them, or among teachers schoolwide or districtwide, the benefits can include improved classroom instruction, enhanced student learning, and transformed school cultures (Supovitz & Turner, 2000; Webster-Wright, 2009). Despite cultural norms of teacher isolation and frustration associated with attempts at teacher collaboration, interest has been growing in professional development designed for groups of teachers from the same school, department, or grade level.

A necessary prerequisite to breaking down teacher isolation, but one which rarely occurs in schools, is for teachers to have time in their work day to plan lessons together, share instructional practices, assess student work together, and observe each other's teaching. It is often difficult for teachers to open their classrooms to one another and talk about those instances when their instruction needs improvement. This is why teachers need to meet regularly so they can establish the trust needed to have productive collaborative discussions.

Educational researchers and teachers have identified four potential advantages of professional development designed for groups of teachers (Jaquith et al., 2011). First, teachers who work together are more likely to discuss concepts, skills, and problems that arise during their professional learning experiences. In direct contrast to the passive learning associated with traditional professional development, actively engaging teachers in collaborative work is much more likely to lead to instructional improvements. Second, teachers who are from the same school, department, or grade are likely to share common curricular materials, course offerings, and assessments. Through engaging in collective professional learning, they will be better prepared to integrate what they learn with other aspects of their instructional environment. Third, teachers who share the same students can discuss students' needs across classes and grade levels. Finally, collaborative professional development may help create a shared professional culture, in which teachers in a school or district develop a common understanding of instructional goals, methods, problems, and solutions.

Perhaps the best way to encourage collaboration and break down isolation is for teachers to observe and critique one another's teaching. Teachers also can record their teaching to make their practice less private, open their teaching to peer review, learn new instructional approaches, and analyze aspects of their practice that may be difficult to capture otherwise. The benefits can include improved classroom instruction, enhanced student learning, and transformed school cultures.

Summary

In Chapter 1 I reviewed the current state of professional learning in American schools, discussed why traditional professional learning approaches are ineffective, and argued that teacher professional learning matters more today than ever. In this chapter I explained the current theoretical model of professional development action and examined the research-based characteristics of effective teacher professional learning. With this foundation in place, we are now ready to explore how school leaders can work to develop meaningful, effective professional development programs in their schools and how they can develop the structures and capacity needed to bring about real change in how their teachers grow and learn in the teaching profession.

The school leader must attend to the critical lenses of context, content, and process to create and sustain an effective teacher professional learning program. Learning Communities, Leadership, and Resources standards define the essential context for effective teacher learning and are examined in Chapter 3. Without the essential conditions in place, even the most carefully planned and executed professional learning activity will fail. Content, establishing the goals of professional development activities and how to assess them, is the focus of Chapter 4. Content, which encompasses the Data and Outcomes standards, refers to the "what" of professional development and consists of the learning needs of students, and the specific knowledge, skills, and teaching approaches to be acquired by teachers. Process, the "how" of professional development, is the topic of Chapter 5. Process encompasses the Learning Designs and Implementation standards and involves the types of professional development activities, and the way those activities are planned, organized, implemented, and followed up.

3

Context

Building an Atmosphere
to Support Teacher Learning

Real, substantive teacher professional development is needed in American schools but for that to happen contexts and cultures supportive of adult learning in our schools must first be developed.

—Paul Tough

As Paul Tough says in the epigraph at the beginning of this chapter, creating and sustaining a context supportive of teacher professional growth is a necessary component of building an effective teacher professional development program. A supportive context, or school culture for teacher professional learning, will not happen by accident. It must be created intentionally to allow learning activities to flourish. Professional learning activities are much more likely to result in improvements in teacher knowledge and instructional practices, and student learning, when school leaders have worked to create a supportive environment. The Learning Forward standards of Learning Communities, Leadership, and Resources provide a useful guide for schools and school leaders as they work to build and maintain the necessary conditions for effective teacher professional learning. This chapter examines each of these standards and the roles they play in establishing an environment where effective teacher learning can take off.

Learning Communities

A teacher I know told me a story about his school's efforts to develop a professional learning community (PLC). His new principal wanted to create a school culture focused on student learning, one where teachers regularly shared their challenges, experiences, and teaching approaches with one another; where all teachers would continue to grow and develop; and where there was a spirit of curricular and instructional innovation. The principal had distributed articles about professional learning communities to her teachers to help them understand the concept, had created time for teachers to meet in groups to discuss their teaching approaches, and had communicated goals to be accomplished in these group meetings. When the attitudes, skills, and behaviors of the faculty did not change, both the principal and her faculty became frustrated that the improvements described in the articles they had read had not materialized in their school. Why didn't the desired transformations occur?

The idea of improving schools by developing PLCs has grown in popularity over the past decade. But while the term *professional learning community* has become commonplace, the actual practices of PLCs are rarely found in American education. The story related above is an all-too-familiar example of what I see happening in many schools seeking to establish a professional learning community. The initial enthusiasm of the principal was coupled with misunderstanding about the fundamental concepts behind the initiative, which led to implementation difficulties, frustration that efforts led to no changes, and the eventual decision to search for another way to bring about the desired change. Despite the popularity of the term, transforming the culture of a school to reflect PLC principles remains a challenging and elusive task.

The PLC model can be useful for school leaders working to establish such a supportive context, but only if leaders reflect critically on the merits of the model and work to apply it to their unique situation. What are the core principles of professional learning communities? How do these principles guide school leaders' efforts to sustain the professional learning model so that it creates the needed environment to support effective teacher learning? This section focuses on answering these questions.

American schools historically have been dominated by a culture in which teachers are not only isolated from one another in separate classrooms, but also are insulated from the opportunity to be professionally observed and from the need to demonstrate their own learning and growth. The construct of the professional learning community can help school leaders in their efforts to make classroom practice less private and create a culture where faculty members regularly share the challenges and successes of teaching with one another so that all become better teachers and learners. Richard Dufour (2004) has defined a professional learning community as a "community of educators committed to working collaboratively in ongoing processes of collective inquiry and action research to achieve better results for the students they serve" (p. 10).

In a PLC, the faculty and school leaders as a whole consistently operate along five dimensions (Hord, 1997):

1. Supportive and shared leadership

2. Shared values and vision

3. Collective learning and application of learning

4. Shared personal practice

5. Results orientation

Establishing a professional learning community within a school takes time, patience, and commitment. It requires dedicated and intentional effort on the part of everyone, but the school leaders in particular must possess great resolve to facilitate and sustain the processes needed to bring about substantive change. Each dimension develops at its own pace, many times overlapping with other dimensions.

Supportive and Shared Leadership

Research findings and anecdotal evidence confirm that a school organization can be transformed into a PLC only with the active commitment of school leaders. Principals historically have had a significant amount of power and authority to make decisions for their school. They have been expected to be wise and competent in all aspects of their school, something Lucianne Carmichael (1995) calls "omnicompetence." This expectation of omnicompetence has made it difficult for principals to admit that they need professional learning opportunities or to recognize and seek out the potential of faculty contributions to decision making. Simultaneously, with the authority of the principal so dominant, it has been difficult for teachers to volunteer ideas about how to improve some aspect of the school (Hord, 1997; Morissey, 2000).

But for a professional learning community to develop and thrive, the traditional omnicompetence of the principal and traditional top-down hierarchical conceptions of leadership and decision making need to be replaced by a more democratic approach. Principals can set the tone by actively participating in their own professional learning, becoming what Peter Senge (1999) calls "the head learner." The typical pattern needs to change so that principals become learners too and work with teachers to question, investigate, and seek solutions to school challenges. This new relationship between principals and teachers leads to shared and collegial leadership (termed distributed leadership) in the school, where everyone grows professionally and comes to see him- or herself working with others to develop a better school (Hord & Sommers, 2008).

Supportive distributed leadership is one of the necessary elements in building a school-based PLC. A willingness to share decision making, the capacity to facilitate the work of teachers, and the ability to participate without dominating characterize this approach. Rather than being top-down change agents, principals attend to teacher learning and development, moving faculty members from passive participants to active decision makers (York-Barr & Duke, 2004). They come to understand that they cannot do it alone, that leading a school and building a learning community are too complex for them to be the sole problem solvers.

Some have misinterpreted the concept of distributed leadership, thinking that strong leadership from the principal is not required to build a PLC. Nothing could be further from the truth. Strong principals are crucial in creating and maintaining a professional learning community—but they lead from the center instead of the top. They recognize that the task of building a learning community is less about command and control and more about learning, delegating, and orchestrating. Shirley Hord (2008) has described principals who exhibit the distributed leadership necessary to establish PLCs as "post-heroic" leaders, who view themselves not as the architects of school effectiveness but as facilitators of teacher and school growth (Morissey, 2000).

Shared Values and Vision

Professional learning communities operate through shared values and vision. As Senge (2006) has emphasized, "you cannot have a learning organization without a shared vision, without a commitment to what you collectively stand for and where you are collectively going" (p. 43). While the shared values and vision typically embody an unwavering focus on student learning, the specific details can and should be tailored to the specific realities of each school.

The importance of a shared vision in establishing a PLC is accepted and recognized, but the process for actually developing the vision often is given far too little attention. For the vision to have the intended result of building a culture of professional learning and galvanizing the efforts of teachers, it can't be dictated to the faculty. As Ken Blanchard (2007) emphasizes, "the process used to develop a shared vision is as important as the vision itself" (p. 233). Principals establishing a learning community work with their faculty in the co-creation of shared values and a shared vision. The process of co-creating the vision may not be the most efficient way, but it is the strategy most likely to result in the shared vision needed to drive a learning community (Dufour, DuFour, & Eaker, 2008). Wise principals recognize that a vision will have no impact unless it is understood, accepted, and connects with the educators in a school.

Rather than selling a personal vision to the faculty, principals establish a focus on shared values and vision by creating ongoing processes through which all teachers can speak from the heart about what really matters to them and be heard (Dufour, 2004; Hord, 1997). Principals listen to the interests, values, ideas, and goals of faculty members, and they facilitate consensus building and conflict resolution to find a common set of values and a shared vision to guide everyone moving forward. Shared values and a vision that are owned, supported, and endorsed by the faculty can serve as the foundation for them to work together productively in a learning community, and can serve as guideposts for school decisions about teaching and learning (Dufour et al., 2008). Rather than turning to rigid rules and procedures, principals can use the shared values and vision to guide the efforts of teachers. Building a truly shared vision is an energizing experience for teachers and principals, it provides direction to teachers and principals, and it fosters trust and respect between the principal and faculty, and among faculty members, that will be needed to create and sustain a learning community.

Collective Learning and Application of Learning

Working together to build shared knowledge on the best way to meet goals and address the needs of clients is what professionals in all fields are expected to do, whether it is curing patients, designing a building, or helping all students learn. Professional learning communities are characterized by collective inquiry, in which teachers and school leaders relentlessly question current methods and structures, search for better ways to do things, test new approaches, and reflect on the results of these tests—all in the pursuit of enhancing student learning (Dufour, 2004; Hord, 1997). The benefits of collective inquiry are not just enhanced teaching practices and improved school structures, but also the resulting collegial relationships and strengthened commitment to improve the school (Harwell, 2003).

Collective inquiry helps teachers overcome the differences caused by the specialization of grade level and subject matter. Collective inquiry forces debate among teachers about what is important and promotes understanding and appreciation for the work of others. Finally, collective inquiry binds school leaders and teachers together as a group committed to searching for ways to improve the teaching and learning in their school. Ultimately, it is this commitment to searching together that leads teachers to view themselves, their colleagues, and their school differently, and results in significant changes in the culture of the school.

Shared Personal Practice

Unfortunately, despite compelling evidence about the benefits of teacher collaboration, teachers in many schools continue to work in isolation. Separated by their classrooms and packed teaching schedules, teachers in many schools rarely discuss student learning and instructional practices together. Also problematic is that many schools stop short of full collaboration. Teachers may come together to discuss operational procedures such as how to respond to tardiness, when to hold parent conferences, and what grade book software to adopt, but that collaboration stops at the classroom door (Dufour, 2004; Hord, 1997). Coming together to reach consensus about these operational issues is important, but it doesn't rise to the level of collaboration needed to form a true PLC.

At the most basic level, professional learning communities work together to realize a shared vision about student learning in their school. Dufour and colleagues (2008) call the kind of collaboration present in a learning community *shared personal practice*—and it requires a paradigm shift from the traditional teacher role in schools. When teachers share personal practice, they meet in teams to share ideas, discuss common professional challenges, analyze student work, and plan lessons. They also open up their classrooms and their teaching to review by colleagues. Collaboration on this level requires teachers to make public what historically has been private: learning goals, teaching strategies, classroom materials, pacing, questions posed to students, frustrations and concerns about student learning and behavior, assessment strategies, and student results (Dufour et al., 2008; Hord & Sommers, 2008). This type of powerful teacher collaboration builds trust, leads to greater willingness to innovate and take risks and learn from mistakes, and share successful strategies and approaches with colleagues. All of these results, in turn, are likely to lead to greater student engagement and achievement.

To establish collaboration on the level of shared personal practice requires school leaders and faculty to eliminate the all-too-common excuses. Few principals or teachers would assert that working in isolation promotes improved teaching and learning in their schools, yet I continue to hear reasons for why they do not regularly work together. Typical comments include "We just can't find time to do it," "We can't create consensus on the idea," and "We need training in how to collaborate." These are legitimate, but not insurmountable, challenges and many schools have been able to navigate through them to form successful learning communities. In the end, creating a culture characterized by shared personal practice is a question of commitment and will. Meaningful collaboration must be systematically embedded into the daily life of the school. A principal and faculty working together will find a way.

Results Orientation

In a true PLC, teachers and school leaders recognize that all of their efforts in these areas—supportive and shared leadership, shared values and vision, collective learning and application of learning, and shared personal practice—must be evaluated on the basis of results rather than intentions. As Peter Senge (2006) emphasizes, "the purpose behind building a learning community revolves around the premise that such organizations will produce dramatically improved results" (p. 44). Of course, the result educators in a PLC are seeking is improved student learning. For educators in a PLC to stay focused on results (enhanced student learning), they must collectively inquire into three critical questions (Dufour et al., 2008):

1. *What do we want our students to learn? What specific things do we want our students to know, understand, and be able to do as a result*

of each course and grade level? Schools with established PLCs maintain a results orientation by having a process (discussed in detail in Chapter 4) in place to ensure that teachers work together to determine what they want students to learn and how they will structure their curriculum and instruction to help students reach the learning goals they have set.

2. *How will we know if our students are meeting the learning goals we have set for them? Have our students acquired the knowledge, understanding, and skills we have deemed most essential for each course and grade level?* When teachers in a PLC engage in collaboratively asking and answering these questions, they focus on assessing student learning in the most authentic and beneficial ways and gain a clear picture about existing gaps between the learning goals they have set for students and current levels of student achievement.

3. *How should we respond when students do not meet the learning goals we have established? What processes and structures will we put in place to help these students reach our student learning goals?* Historically, what typically happens when a student does not meet learning goals depends on the practices of his or her individual teacher. In a true PLC there is a coordinated, collective response when students do not meet learning goals, and teachers and school leaders collectively share the responsibility to help weaker students improve. This collective response and shared responsibility decreases the uneven and inequitable student support found in many schools.

In schools with true PLCs there is no lack of commitment to student learning. Too many schools seem to operate as if their primary purpose is to ensure that topics are covered and children are taught. PLCs are built on the premise that schools exist to ensure that all students learn essential knowledge, understandings, and skills. All characteristics of PLCs flow from this unwavering commitment to the result of improved student learning.

Leadership

A professional learning community exists when each of the five dimensions—supportive and shared leadership, shared vision and values, collective learning and application of learning, shared personal practice, and a results orientation—are in place and working together. The five dimensions are deeply interconnected (Hord, 1997; Hord & Sommers, 2008). The strength of the relationships between school leaders and faculty, and among faculty members, is the foundation of all five dimensions of professional learning communities. Transforming a school to engage teachers in operating this way is challenging and takes time. Progress is made when school leaders and teachers find ways to go beyond the traditional structures and norms of schools by learning together and working together toward the common goal of increasing student learning. The principal's role is a critical one, orchestrating a delicate balance between support and pressure, helping teachers to take on new roles while they themselves work to dispose of old paradigms about the role of principal (Dufour, 2004; Dufour et al., 2008). When I interviewed principals in schools where PLCs flourished about how they were able to create and support such a culture, they suggested the following approaches.

Clarity of Purpose

Principals today are bombarded daily with demands from a variety of constituencies: teachers; students; parents; local, state, and federal requirements; community organizations; and local businesses. To establish and sustain a culture of adult professional learning, principals must be clear about their primary responsibility: to help create and maintain the conditions that help the teachers in their building enhance their knowledge and instructional practices so they can better help all students acquire the knowledge, understandings, and skills deemed essential for their success. To create a culture of adult professional learning, principals must move school conversations from "What was taught?" to "Was it learned?" and "How can we improve our instructional practices?" In schools with contexts supportive of ongoing teacher learning, principals are relentlessly focused on supporting the professional learning of teachers and do all in their power to align policies and guidelines to ensure effective professional learning within their schools (Dufour, 2004).

Communicate Expectations

School leaders must clearly articulate the essential connection between student learning and teacher professional learning. "I walked into our opening faculty meeting and told them that the workshops were over, that we were going to work together to pool the collective expertise, experience, and passion in the room to make sure that every teacher and administrator was learning how to more effectively support student learning," says one principal. Principals in schools with thriving professional learning programs involve the entire faculty in co-creating a shared vision for the school, and they also communicate clearly and frequently that all of the adults in the school are expected to work together to enhance student learning and growth. They communicate that they expect all of the adults in the school (including themselves) to be true professionals and continually work together to improve their knowledge and skills (Dufour & Eaker, 2004). Their actions and expectations model the attitudes and behavior they expect from their faculty and set the stage for learning by all of the adults in the school.

Attend to the Foundation

Co-creating shared values and a shared vision that people buy into, and that guide the actions of the adults in the school, is a messy, time-consuming process, but one that forms the foundation in building a culture supportive of teacher learning. Principals encourage effective teacher learning through engaging the entire faculty in the process of establishing shared values and vision.

Educational researchers Shirley Hord (1997) and Melanie Morrisey (2000) suggest an exercise that principals can use to build shared values and a shared vision:

1. Give a pad of sticky notes to every teacher. Each teacher thinks of what he or she most values in a school and what he or she hopes the school will become and writes one idea per sticky note.

2. Teachers work in small groups (purposely arranged to include a variety of grades and academic disciplines). Each group is given a big piece of chart paper, and group members post their notes on the paper.

3. Each group arranges their notes into categories and collectively writes a statement that best summarizes or describes its collective vision for that category.

4. A writing committee (composed of faculty volunteers) collects the statements from each group and crafts a list of short statements based on the common themes identified by the groups.

5. Each small group meets again to critique the draft of the writing committee, and proposes revisions, additions, and deletions.

6. The writing committee reviews the proposals and makes changes suggested by the groups.

7. The second draft is presented to the entire faculty for review and discussion. The faculty members are asked if they can "own" the list of statements and, if not, what changes still need to be made.

The challenge of this process is to build support and unity without compromising the substance, meaning, and clarity of the list. Each faculty member should have the opportunity to present his or her views, and respect for differences must be supported and nurtured. When disagreements occur, individuals should be encouraged to explain their reasoning to see if there is a way to identify common ground. Consensus does not mean unanimity. Even at the end of this process, differences of opinion will remain, but it is important that everyone has had the opportunity to express his or her ideas and is prepared to support the vision statement. As Dufour (2004) has said, "if the vision is widely shared and is sufficiently compelling, it will serve to establish an environment supportive of adult learning and a true learning community" (p. 78).

Begin With a Problem or a Goal

When I asked one principal how he initiated the process of building a culture supportive of teacher learning, he replied that "the most critical component is de-privatizing practice to get groups of teachers discussing, debating, and planning together on a regular basis, so you must get faculty engaged in this right from the start." One proven way to do this is to identify a "problem to be solved" or a "goal to be achieved" with faculty members and then dedicate time to bring them together (both as a whole and in small groups) at regular intervals to learn together how to deal with the problem or goal and engage in dialogue about that learning (Dufour & Eaker, 2004). Doing this begins the process of sharing leadership, breaking down teacher isolation, and learning how to share personal practice, and it can even contribute to the construction of shared values and a shared vision.

Teach Collaboration Skills

Noted educational researcher Seymour Sarason (1996) has called creating a collaborative environment "the single most important factor in sustaining the effort to create a school culture of adult learning" (p. 340). However, it is unrealistic and unwise to expect teachers who are used to working in isolation to be able to seamlessly engage in productive collaborative discussions with colleagues. Simply providing time for teachers to collaborate will not ensure that they will engage in meaningful discussions about how they can adjust instruction to more effectively address student learning goals. Without proper training, the time set aside for teacher collaboration can actually deter efforts to build a context supportive of teacher professional learning as teachers may simply reinforce negative aspects of school culture (Dufour, 2004).

Principals who have successfully built cultures supportive of ongoing teacher learning report those teachers must be supported to develop skills in talking and making decisions together. Specifically, teachers must understand and develop skills in dialogue and discussion (Garmston & Wellman, 2009). In dialogue, teachers must "seek first to understand, then be understood" as knowledge, ideas, feelings, biases, and assumptions are shared among them. The goal in dialogue is to understand one another so that groups are better able to work and learn together. Discussion is preferable when the goal is to make a decision about a course of action. In this case, group members state and support their reasons for adopting a particular action, before finalizing decisions through voting or consensus building. When teachers are provided guided practice in using dialogue and discussion to conduct productive conversations, conflict is appropriately managed, effective decisions are made, and the trust needed to fuel ongoing group learning is built.

Develop the Leadership Capacity of Teachers

Creating and sustaining a context supportive of effective teacher professional learning often means shaping a new school culture, and that daunting task requires more than one leader. Effective teacher learning occurs when schools are democratic and participatory. McLaughlin and Talbert (2006) emphasize that "a culture of effective teacher learning develops when principals learn to relinquish a measure of control and help teachers participate in building leadership throughout the school" (p. 81).

Recognizing this, principals in schools with successful professional development programs take steps to build the leadership capacity of their teachers (York-Barr & Duke, 2004). They understand that expertise is widely distributed throughout a school, and they work to draw upon and develop the capacity of others to assume leadership roles. While principals may take the lead in the beginning, over time they urge faculty members to assume prominent roles. For

Figure 3.1   Four Cost-Effective Ways to Create a Context Supportive of Teacher Professional Learning

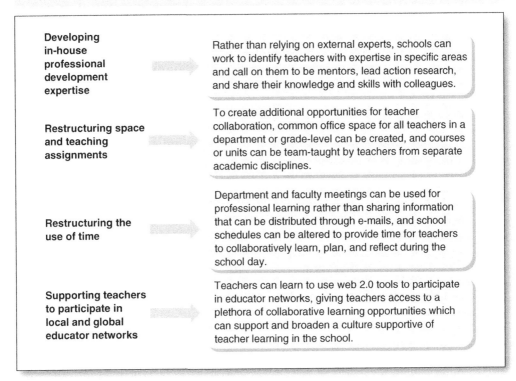

Developing in-house professional development expertise	Rather than relying on external experts, schools can work to identify teachers with expertise in specific areas and call on them to be mentors, lead action research, and share their knowledge and skills with colleagues.
Restructuring space and teaching assignments	To create additional opportunities for teacher collaboration, common office space for all teachers in a department or grade-level can be created, and courses or units can be team-taught by teachers from separate academic disciplines.
Restructuring the use of time	Department and faculty meetings can be used for professional learning rather than sharing information that can be distributed through e-mails, and school schedules can be altered to provide time for teachers to collaboratively learn, plan, and reflect during the school day.
Supporting teachers to participate in local and global educator networks	Teachers can learn to use web 2.0 tools to participate in educator networks, giving teachers access to a plethora of collaborative learning opportunities which can support and broaden a culture supportive of teacher learning in the school.

example, they encourage teachers to assume leadership roles in the development of new programs and activities and involve teachers in decisions on issues such as departmentalization, schedules, and faculty study topics. These actions not only expand the leadership capacity of individuals within the professional staff, but they also expand the capacity of the school to successfully solve problems.

Resources

Creating a context supportive of teacher professional learning necessitates prioritizing, monitoring, and coordinating essential resources. Specifically, important human, time, technology, and monetary resources are needed to establish conditions supportive of effective teacher learning. Decisions about how, when, and where these resources are applied require a clear understanding of student and teacher learning needs, a deep commitment to equitable resource allocation, and careful consideration of priorities to achieve the intended student and teacher outcomes.

Human

Human resources—the teachers and leaders in a school—are perhaps the most valuable, and underutilized, resource available in efforts to create and sustain a culture of professional learning. Professional development programs in American schools are typically based on the false assumption that significant teacher insight and learning requires external direction. This assumption leads to teachers being sent to conferences to learn from experts, and bringing the experts to the school to speak and conduct workshops. Because formal follow-up conversations to these events are rare, and because informal avenues for sharing and discussing what is learned are typically absent, these "outside" professional development events do not influence teacher instruction or student learning. More damaging, though, is that this false assumption leads to a reduction in collaboration and conversation among teachers, the very things schools most need to establish a culture of teacher learning. The assumption that teacher learning must be externally driven must be challenged and changed for progress toward quality professional learning in schools to occur.

Often, the expertise and knowledge needed to address staff learning needs can be found within the school itself. Principals and other school leaders must work to identify faculty members with expertise in specific areas and call on them to be mentors, lead action research, and share their knowledge and skills with colleagues in a variety of formats. Drawing upon "in-house" professional development expertise in this way promotes the collective learning and application of learning and shared personal practice that are so important in creating a culture of adult learning in a school.

There are two additional things school leaders can do with their human resources (faculty) to help establish a context supportive of adult learning. First, they can rearrange the physical proximity of teachers to one another. For example, a common office space for all teachers in a department or grade level reduces isolation and leads to informal discussions about teaching and learning. These interactions not only improve teaching practice, but also advance the trusting, collaborative relationships that are so important in building a community of learners. Second, teaching roles can be redefined to make teachers more interdependent. Entire courses, or at least individual units or lessons, can be team-taught by teachers from separate academic disciplines. This practice leads to rich discussions among teachers about how to best design and deliver instruction and how to most accurately assess student learning, deepens student learning, and once again builds the relationships that form the heart of a learning community.

Time

Time must be found when teachers can regularly collaborate to do the learning, decision making, problem solving, and creative work that characterize a PLC. Time is a resource and time—or, more properly, a lack of it—is a common barrier impeding the development of professional learning cultures in schools. Formally rearranging the use of time so that teachers are supported in their interactions is one of the most important resources school leaders can supply as they work to build an environment supportive of teacher learning. There are several strategies school leaders can employ to carve out the time needed to establish a context supportive of teacher learning.

First, school schedules can be structured to include time, preferably during the school day, for teachers and school leaders to collaborate, reflect, and plan. Professional learning embedded into the workday in this way increases opportunities for teachers to learn as individuals and teams and promotes a culture of continuous improvement. Consistent job-embedded learning time for teachers emphasizes the importance of ongoing learning as a professional responsibility of all teachers and connects the focus of teacher learning to the learning needs of their students.

Second, structures and time should be established to support open, frequent communication among faculty members and between the principal and teachers. For example, instead of using faculty meetings to disseminate information that can be distributed by e-mail, they can be used as professional learning opportunities where in-house faculty experts present on topics, where department or grade-level teams share instructional ideas with the faculty, or where individual teachers report on action research they are conducting in their classrooms. In addition, faculty meetings can also be used to give teachers the opportunity to express concerns and ask questions. This practice reduces harmful rumors and misinformation, and it builds the trust and respect that helps teachers take the risks needed to work productively in teams.

Technology

Modern technology is another important resource in creating a context supportive of teacher professional growth and learning. High-speed broadband and web-based technologies are essential parts of facilitating collective teacher learning and application of learning, and shared personal practice among teachers within the school building. However, learning management systems and modern digital tools and applications (discussed in detail in later chapters) have become important resources that expand the context for effective professional learning beyond the school building. Web applications give teachers access to just-in-time learning and make it possible for them to participate in local or global learning networks during their workday, which increases opportunities for job-embedded learning.

Money

The amount of money available for professional development varies considerably across schools and school districts (Odden & Archibald, 2002), but what professional development funds are spent on has been remarkably similar for all schools over the past two decades (Murray, 2011):

1. Educational consultants and facilitators for on-site and off-site workshops

2. Expenses related to staff attending conferences

3. Materials (e.g., books, journals, and software) connected to mandatory in-service days

4. Costs for substitutes for teachers engaged in professional development

5. Mentors and instructional coaches hired from outside the school

The recent economic downturn has led many American school systems to reduce their professional development budgets (Christie, 2010). This is in direct contrast to many other countries, where teacher professional development is valued so highly that reducing investments in it is not seen as an option (Darling-Hammond et al., 2009). Teacher professional learning is more important now than ever before, and the limited funds earmarked for professional development in schools must be maintained or even increased, rather than being cut.

Even with a reduced professional development budget, though, schools can do a better job of creating a context supportive of teacher professional learning by spending their money in different ways. Professional development consisting primarily of workshops and outside experts has been ineffective in establishing the culture of professional learning needed to bring about improvements in instructional practices and student learning. It is more effective, and less costly, to build a context supportive of teacher professional learning through drawing upon and developing in-house professional development expertise, restructuring space and teaching assignments to foster teacher collaboration, restructuring the use of time to create opportunities for job-embedded teacher learning, and helping teachers use digital tools to participate in educator learning networks (see Figure 3.1)

Summary

When you enter a school that has established a culture of teacher professional learning, you sense that people understand what is important, recognize what the goals and priorities are, and are working together in a collaborative way to advance the school toward them. When a school has built a context supportive of teacher professional learning, you can walk around the building on any given day and see teachers talking to one another, discussing learning goals, and discussing what activities they are going to engage in. There is an attitude of cooperation and innovation, an absence of fear in seeking help and opening one's classroom to colleagues, and it is obvious that the support teachers feel is systemic. In short, when you walk into such a school you know, understand, and feel that a context or culture is in place that fully supports the ongoing learning of both the adults and students in the building.

This chapter focused on the importance of establishing a school context or culture to support professional learning and discussed how the Learning Forward standards of Learning Communities, Leadership, and Resources can assist school leaders in creating a culture where educators collaborate to improve the teaching and learning in their schools.

I explained that a learning community operates along five interconnected dimensions—supportive and shared leadership, shared visions and values, collective learning and application of learning, shared personal practice, and a results orientation—and emphasized that the leadership of the principal plays a crucial role in helping teachers learn new ways of interacting with each other and the principal. I also emphasized that principals can help to lead the creation of a culture of teacher professional learning by keeping a consistent focus on student learning; by communicating their expectations for teacher learning clearly and frequently; through engaging the entire faculty in the process of establishing shared values and vision; by helping teachers learn collaboration skills; by getting groups of teachers discussing, debating, and planning together on a regular basis; and by developing the leadership capacity of faculty members. Finally, I outlined the essential human, time, technology, and monetary resources needed to establish a culture of teacher learning in a school.

In addition to working with faculty in the ongoing process of creating and sustaining a context to support teacher professional growth, the principal must also attend to the lenses of content and process in building an effective teacher professional learning program. Content—specifying the goals of professional development activities and how to assess them—is the focus of Chapter 4, while process—the "how" of professional development—is the topic of Chapter 5.

4

Content

Specifying the Goals of Professional Learning Activities

The content of professional learning activities must be based on student needs that are defined through data analysis and professional opinion.

—Lois Brown Easton

A principal and curriculum director had spent the summer crafting a two-year plan for professional development in their school. The best consultants had been hired to make presentations and lead workshops for their professional development days. Faculty members had been scheduled to attend conferences connected to their area of teaching. Weekly grade-level or department meetings were planned, and topics were selected to give each meeting a focus. Time was reserved in scheduled faculty meetings for teachers to report on their grade-level and department meeting discussions. The plan was well organized and would lead to every faculty member participating in professional learning activities on a weekly basis. The topics for the professional development days and weekly grade-level and department meetings were carefully chosen and were based on research and discussions with other schools.

The problem with their plan, though, is that it was based on research alone, without considering staff needs and school data. The principal and curriculum director neglected several key content issues in the development of their plan: student needs, teacher needs, and ways to assess the effectiveness of the professional development program. Decisions about the content of professional learning activities should be founded upon what students need to know, understand, and be able to do and, therefore, what knowledge and skills teachers need to have to help students achieve. It is remarkable how often schools neglect important principles of learning when selecting and implementing professional learning opportunities for teachers. We expect our teachers to "begin with the end in mind" when designing instruction for their students; to carefully consider student needs, learning goals, and methods of assessment; and to base instructional choices on those considerations. Yet schools often forget to apply these same principles when determining the content of the professional learning opportunities they offer their teachers.

The three major goals of professional development are

1. improvements in teachers' knowledge, skills, and attitudes;

2. improvements in teachers' classroom practices; and

3. improvements in students' learning outcomes.

However, schools are often unclear about how effectively their professional learning opportunities accomplish these goals because specific knowledge, skills, and attitudes to be improved are rarely identified in advance, and teacher and student changes resulting from the professional learning are not assessed. In a time of increased expectations, greater accountability and tighter budgets, and heightened importance of effective teacher professional learning, professional development activities must be intentionally and tangibly linked to teacher learning, student learning, and institutional goals.

Content refers to the "what" of professional development and consists of the learning needs of students, and the specific knowledge, skills, and teaching approaches to be acquired by teachers. The Learning Forward standards of Data and Outcomes provide a useful guide for schools and school leaders as they work to determine the content for professional learning. These standards emphasize that there must be "alignment between educator professional learning and its role in student learning" (Learning Forward, 2011, p. 19). School leaders should use a variety of sources and types of data to inform professional development content decisions, should intentionally connect professional development content to desired student outcomes, and should use multiple data sources to assess the extent to which their professional development program is achieving its objectives. This chapter outlines a process educational leaders can use to make content decisions about professional learning activities in their schools.

Identifying Goals

Educators are designers in that an essential part of the profession is the design of curriculum and experiences to promote student learning. Like other design professionals, such as engineers and architects, teachers must carefully consider their audiences. By necessity, professionals in these fields are intently focused on their clients. The effectiveness of their designs corresponds to the extent to which they have accomplished their goals for their clients. Of course, students are our primary clients because the effectiveness of curriculum and instructional planning and delivery is ultimately determined by their achievement.

The most effective instructional designs are "backward." Why are they called backward? Because the most effective instructional designs begin with the end—the specific learning to be acquired by students—and then make curriculum and instructional lesson decisions founded on helping students accomplish the student learning goals that have been set. Not only does backward design call for teachers to set and consider student learning goals before designing instruction, but it also calls for teachers to design ways to best assess student learning prior to designing instruction. Backward design reminds teachers to set student learning goals and create ways to assess the extent to which students meet those goals, *before* proceeding to plan lessons and experiences. The logic of backward design is not new, with Ralph Tyler (1949) outlining it more than 50 years ago, but its use in schools did not become widespread until recently when Grant Wiggins and Jay McTighe (1998) modernized and popularized the concept.

Backward planning is useful for more than determining curriculum goals for students. The process can be adapted and used by principals as they work with teachers to specify the content and goals of their professional development programs. Decisions about professional development content must be intentionally connected to professional development goals that are derived from specific student and teacher learning needs.

Step 1: Identifying Student Needs

What do you want students to know, understand, and be able to do at each grade level and in each academic discipline? What behaviors and attitudes do you want from your students? Answering these questions provides the starting point in creating the goals for your professional development program. It is important to go beyond mandated local, state, and national standards when answering these questions. Principals must engage their faculty in the process of specifying the knowledge, skills, and understandings they want the *students in their building* to gain, and the behaviors and attitudes they want them to exhibit. After determining their standards for student learning, behavior, and attitudes, teachers and school leaders must ask how their students are doing in meeting the standards they have set for their students. Few schools regularly assess the gaps between their standards for students and current student performance, but this is an essential part of determining the appropriate content for teacher professional learning.

The first step in creating the goals of an effective professional development program is to acquire a clear understanding about the gap between where students currently are and where you want them to be. The best way to accomplish this is for teachers to meet in grade-level teams and academic-discipline teams to examine a variety of data about how well students are meeting school standards for academic performance and behavior. The use of multiple data sources leads to a more balanced and comprehensive assessment of student learning needs than is possible through any single source of data. Learning Forward (2011) suggests these data sources:

- Performance on classroom assessments
- Performance on standardized tests
- Collections (such as portfolios) of real student work
- Formal and informal evaluations of real student work
- Descriptive information about student work and work processes (how students accomplish the work)

When grade-level teams and academic-discipline teams use these forms of data, along with their professional expertise, to assess student progress, they can identify areas of student weakness and need.

A clear understanding of student learning needs guides content decisions about teacher professional development, but student data alone are not enough. A thorough understanding of teacher learning needs is also essential to planning effective teacher learning opportunities.

Step 2: Identifying Teacher Needs

Connecting what teachers should know and be able to do to what students should know and be able to do is the focus of step 2. What do your teachers need to know and be able to do to help your students reach the academic and behavioral standards set for them? What new knowledge, understandings, and skills do your teachers need to acquire to effectively address current student needs and weaknesses? It is important that both the principal and faculty are involved in answering these questions. The most frequent complaint I hear from teachers about professional development is that it is a waste of time because it is disconnected from the specific needs and challenges they face in their classroom. When teachers are an integral part of the process of generating the learning goals for teacher professional learning this complaint is eliminated.

The best way to involve faculty in step 2 is to use the same grade-level teams and academic-discipline teams that worked to identify student needs in step 1. They can collaboratively brainstorm the parallel learning that teachers need to experience to address the student needs and weaknesses specified in step 1 and develop learning plans that are submitted to the principal. The principal can then take these plans and make additions, deletions, and revisions to generate a final set of teacher learning needs that will drive decisions about specific activities and strategies selected for the professional development program.

Step 3: Stating Specific Professional Learning Goals

The goals you set for your professional development program should directly connect the knowledge, understandings, and skills teachers need to acquire to the student needs and weaknesses you have identified.

Here are three examples:

1. The academic-discipline teams in a high school have found that students are weak at applying learned concepts and information in their problem solving. They have great difficulty unless the parameters of the problem are similar to something they

have already seen in class. As teachers discussed this student weakness, they realized that they needed to know how to more effectively assist students in applying information to new situations and conditions. A professional development program goal in this case is "Teachers will know and implement skills and approaches that lead to students more effectively applying concepts and information when solving novel problems."

2. Grade-level teams in a middle school have identified reading comprehension as a weakness. Students are having trouble in this area even when teachers have students read assignments in class to make sure the reading actually is being done. The strategies teachers have tried in the past have not resulted in the desired improvements so they have specified this as an area where professional development is needed. A professional development goal in this case is "Teachers will know and implement skills and strategies that result in improved reading comprehension by middle school students."

3. The fourth-grade teachers in an elementary school have identified using and applying math concepts in word problems as a student weakness. Students are able to understand and successfully complete math problems in isolation but are performing poorly when the same math concepts are part of word problems. The teachers have created and tried alternative strategies with little resulting student improvement, and they are really frustrated. A professional development goal in this case is "Teachers will acquire skills and strategies that result in improved student application of math concepts in word problems."

When professional development program goals specifically connect the knowledge and skills teachers need to learn with student needs and weaknesses, they can serve as powerful guideposts for your program. Professional development activities and strategies can be intentionally linked to these goals, and specific evaluations can be designed to assess the extent to which your program goals are being met.

Evaluating Your Professional Development Program

The purpose of professional development is for educators to acquire a body of knowledge and skills to improve the quality of their teaching and, ultimately, to improve student outcomes. With the goals of professional development in mind, evaluating the impact of professional development activities must be at the forefront of planning your professional development program. Evaluation is a way to figure out what is working, what isn't working, and how to adjust things to better accomplish goals.

Is the professional development program or activity achieving its goals? Is it leading to improved instructional practices and enhanced student learning? Is it more effective than what was done in the past? Is it better than another activity you are doing? Is it worth the time and costs? Traditionally, educators have not devoted much attention to addressing these types of evaluation questions (Guskey, 2002). Many consider evaluation a costly, time-consuming process that takes their focus away from the planning, implementation, and follow-up of their professional development activities. Others are unsure how to proceed with a thorough evaluation and therefore neglect this important aspect of their program.

Joellen Killion (2007) defines evaluation as a "systematic, purposeful process of studying, reviewing, and analyzing data gathered from multiple sources in order to make informed decisions about a program" (p. 42). Excellent evaluations do not have to be extraordinarily complicated or time-consuming. They simply involve careful planning and the ability to ask quality questions (Guskey, 2002). Your professional development program involves considerable time and money and should be meaningful. Through evaluation you can gather information you can use to determine whether your program is achieving its goals, and information that can help you improve its quality and effectiveness. Importantly, evaluation also provides valuable data for those interested in knowing about the contribution of professional learning to enhanced student outcomes.

Both formative and summative evaluation should be included in your evaluation process. Formative evaluation occurs during the operation of a program or activity. Its purpose is to provide school leaders with ongoing information about progress toward goals, which can guide decisions about needed program improvements. Flaws can be identified and weaknesses located to make the adjustments required for program success. Summative evaluation occurs at the end of a program or activity. It addresses questions of accountability and provides school leaders and other decision makers with information to inform judgments about the overall merit or worth of the program or activity.

There are important differences between formative and summative evaluation regarding the purposes and audiences for which they are conducted. In formative evaluation, the primary audience is the teachers and school leaders involved in the daily implementation of professional learning activities. Formative evaluation leads to decisions about program modification and improvement, and identifies new learning needs for students and teachers. With summative evaluation, the audience includes teachers and school leaders, but it expands to also include to local, state, and federal decision makers, and the public. Summative evaluation leads to decisions about continuing, modifying, or terminating a program or activity. Professional development researcher and innovator Thomas Guskey (2000) suggests that effective professional development program evaluations involve both formative and summative evaluation and that they consider four important stages or levels of information (see Figure 4.1).

Element 1: Teacher Reactions

The first and most basic element of evaluation focuses on gathering initial teacher reactions about the professional development experience. This is the most common form of professional development program evaluation, largely because it is the easiest type of information to gather and analyze. Teachers are asked if they enjoyed the experience, if time was well spent, if the material was meaningful and understandable, if it was geared to their needs, and if they thought it would be useful in their classrooms. Information on teacher's reactions is usually gathered through questionnaires administered after the professional development activity. Such questionnaires have been criticized for being happiness quotients that tell whether an activity was liked more than whether or not the activity had worth (Guskey, 2002). But measuring teachers' initial satisfaction with a professional learning experience provides important information that can inform program improvements.

For example, both research and common sense tells us that teachers are unlikely to learn what is unpleasant to them, to learn content that they fear they will not be able to master, or to develop skills that they do not feel they will need to use in their classrooms. Like students, teachers learn more readily when they like what they are doing and feel a personal connection to what they are learning. No excellent program evaluation should consist only of gathering teacher reactions, but it would be foolish to ignore this often criticized aspect of evaluation. Gathering teachers' reactions can definitely help you improve your professional development program design and delivery in valid ways.

Element 2: Teacher Learning

In addition to enjoying the experience, finding the material meaningful, and feeling it was geared to their needs, we also want teachers to learn something from the experience. To get an accurate picture of teacher learning, multiple assessment strategies must be used (Easton, 2008). Questionnaires can be employed, asking teachers to describe the essential components of mastery learning and give examples of how these might be applied in their classrooms. Oral personal reflections or teacher portfolios can also be used to document teacher learning.

To provide more direct evidence that teachers have acquired specific knowledge and skills and understood them accurately, additional assessment methods should used. One way to do this is a simulation or demonstration, in which a teacher teaches a lesson involving the targeted knowledge and/or skills to a group of colleagues. A variety of classroom conflicts can be integrated into the demonstration, requiring the teacher to diagnose different situations and determine appropriate courses of action. While some information can be gathered during or immediately following a professional development activity, the most valuable indicators of successful learning should be determined in advance. The teachers and principal assessing the demonstration or simulation should have a rubric or detailed checklist to focus their observations on the knowledge and skills to be acquired. Information gathered about teacher learning is extremely valuable in making decisions about how to improve the content, format, and organization of the professional development program.

Element 3: Teacher Use of New Knowledge and Skills

Element 3 evaluation asks to what extent the new knowledge and skills learned by teachers actually make a difference in their professional practice (Guskey, 2002). This information cannot be gathered until teachers have time to reflect on new knowledge, practice new skills, and develop new lessons that incorporate what they have learned. Furthermore, because adjusting classroom practice is typically a gradual and uneven process it is important to assess improvements in teacher practice at different time intervals.

The most accurate element 3 evaluation information comes from direct observations of teachers in the classroom, done live or by reviewing video recordings. Observations are an extremely important evaluation method, as they allow for authentic assessment of teachers' actual classroom instruction. Checklists or rubrics should be developed in advance to keep observations focused on the effective application of specific knowledge and skills. Information from the observations should be carefully reviewed with teachers to promote their continued progress toward mastery of the targeted knowledge and skills. Element 3 evaluation not only can be used to assess the success of the current professional development program, but it also is invaluable in adjusting future programs and activities to facilitate more consistent teacher application of learned knowledge and skills.

Element 4: Student Learning

Element 4 addresses the bottom line of how a professional development program influences student learning. Particular student outcomes depend, of course, on the specific student learning goals of your professional development program. Measures of student learning typically include traditional cognitive indicators of performance such as grades and standardized test scores. However, to accurately assess the extent to which student learning goals have been met it is important to include additional measures of student learning.

Student portfolios, which typically involve different types of evidence of student learning, are an excellent supplement to grades and test scores. They are generally more subjective, but they also permit students to demonstrate their learning differently than traditional paper-and-pencil tests. In addition, they provide a way to track subtle nuances in student learning over time. An even more subjective measure of student learning is for teachers to assess student work processes and attitudes over time. If your school's student learning goals address the difficult-to-measure areas of critical thinking and problem solving, subjective measures for assessing student learning can be useful in documenting changes in how students think and approach problems. Finally, student questionnaires and interviews can be used to gather information about student work processes, their confidence in specific areas, and their engagement with particular topics.

In addition to assessing the progress toward specific student learning goals, element 4 evaluation measures can also be used to make sure no unwanted or unintended student outcomes have resulted from professional development activities. For example, an elementary school I visited focused their professional development efforts on activities to help teachers develop instructional methods geared toward helping students apply mathematical concepts. In gathering element 4 information, they found significant gains in students' ability to apply mathematical concepts to novel situations.

Figure 4.1 Teacher Professional Development Program Evaluation

Evidence Type	Questions Asked	Method of Gathering Evidence	What Is Assessed?	The Purpose of the Evidence
1. Teacher Reactions	• Did it address their needs? • Did it make sense? • Can they use it? • Was it engaging?	• Questionnaires or interviews after the activity	• Teacher perceptions and satisfaction • The extent to which teachers feel the time was well spent	• To improve the design and implementation of future activities
2. Teacher Learning	• Did teacher knowledge, understanding, and skills improve in the targeted areas as a result of the activity?	• Written tests • Interviews • Simulations • Observation of teacher demonstrations • Written teacher reflections • Teacher portfolios	• Enhanced knowledge, understanding, and instructional skills of teachers	• To improve program or activity content, implementation, and follow-up
3. Teacher Use of New Learning	• Did teachers effectively integrate the new knowledge and skills into their classroom instructional practices?	• Interviews with teachers and administrators • Teacher written reflections • Observations of teachers • Videos of teachers	• The extent to which teachers are effectively applying what they learned	• To identify and improve how teachers use program and activity content
4. Student Learning	• Did it enhance student achievement? • Did it enhance student confidence?	• Questionnaires • Student grades • Standardized test scores • Interviews with students	• Student learning	• To assess overall impact of the program • To improve program and activity design, implementation and follow-up

Source: Adapted from Guskey (2002).

Unfortunately, over the same period they found small decreases in their students' writing skills. This unintended outcome may have occurred because they sacrificed some instructional time for writing to devote more time for students to work on applying math concepts. By combining multiple measures of student learning, element 4 information about the overall impact of your professional development program on student learning can guide improvements in program design, implementation, and follow-up.

Excellent Evaluations Focus on Evidence, Not Proof

Many positive things are done in teacher professional development, but many ineffective, wasteful things are done as well. It is important for educators to know the difference between the two, and evaluation provides the mechanism for making that distinction. Regrettably, most professional development programs are rarely evaluated beyond element 1, if they are evaluated at all. This needs to change, because all levels of evaluation are important. The information gathered at each level of evaluation offers key indications about the extent to which the goals of your professional development program are being achieved. Good evaluations involve all levels and provide useful and reliable information that can help you engage in an ongoing process of making your teacher professional learning activities more effective.

However, basing your professional development program evaluation on these four elements does not mean you will be able prove that it enhances teacher knowledge, skills, and practice, and improves student learning (Guskey, 2002). Professional development programs are implemented in real-world settings and involve many variables. The relationship between professional development and teacher and student learning is far too complex to allow definitive reporting on causal inferences. Isolating the effects of a single program or activity under these conditions is almost impossible. While you cannot prove anything, you can collect good evidence about whether or not your professional development program has contributed to positive change in teacher knowledge and skills and to improvements in student learning. If you carefully specify your goals up front you can search for good evidence about whether or not you have achieved your goals, and most evaluation concerns and challenges will fall into place.

Summary

This chapter outlined a process school leaders can use to develop the goals of their professional development program and discussed an approach for designing a system to evaluate their success in meeting those goals. School leaders often fall into the planning trap of making plans in terms of the activities they want to do, instead of what they want their students to know, understand, and be able to do. In planning your professional development program it is important to plan "backward," beginning where you want to end up and then working back. So before deciding on the specific activities of a professional development program, school leaders must work with their faculty to determine the goals of their program. Professional development program goals should be based on the learning needs of students, which can be identified by grade-level teacher teams and academic-discipline teacher teams collaboratively examining a variety of different types of data. Then, the same teacher teams can work with the principal to specify the knowledge, skills, and teaching approaches teachers need to acquire to address these student learning needs. Finally, school leaders need to work with their faculty to establish a clear protocol for evaluating whether or not the goals of their program are achieved. Four different types of information should be collected that can be used as evidence about whether or not your professional development program achieved its goals: (1) teacher reactions, (2) teacher learning, (3) teacher application of new knowledge and skills, and (4) student learning.

Context—the ongoing process of creating and sustaining an environment to support teacher professional growth—was the focus of Chapter 3 and content—the process of the specifying the goals of professional development activities and how to assess them—was the focus of this chapter. We are now ready to consider the set of experiences that will enable teachers to acquire the knowledge and skills needed to address student weaknesses. Process—the "how" of professional development—is the topic of Chapter 5. Process involves the different types of professional development activities, and the way those activities are planned, organized, implemented, and followed up.

5

Process

Selecting Specific
Activities and Strategies

The unique learning needs of your students and your faculty must be at the forefront when selecting specific professional development activities and strategies.

—Victoria Bernhardt

Picture a school that has, over time, established an environment supportive of professional learning. The environment contributes to increased teacher and student learning; teachers and school leaders know they can always improve their practice, a signal that they are a true professional learning community. A clear vision guides the efforts of teachers and school leaders, and they maintain an unwavering focus on student growth and learning as well as an enthusiasm for collaborating. Teachers open their classrooms to colleagues, ask questions of each other when they face challenges, and share successful ideas and approaches. The school has created a *context* in which all school staff can learn.

Embedded in this context, the adults in this school regularly examine data from a variety of sources to understand the gap between where students currently are and where they want them to be, and to specify the new knowledge, understandings, and skills teachers need to acquire to effectively address current student needs and weaknesses. The school knows the *content* of its professional development program's goals.

Because the school has established a context for adult learning and is clear about the content needs of their professional development program, its members start to address *process*—how they will learn. For example, as part of their collaborative discussions about the gap between where their students are and where they want them to be, high school science teachers at the school have identified "analyzing and interpreting scientific data" as a student weakness. They want to learn how to better help their students understand at a deep level how to make accurate, appropriate interpretations and conclusions from scientific data, whether the data are reported in the form of charts and graphs or exclusively in words. With assistance from their principal and professional development director, the science teachers will conduct research to learn about powerful strategies for professional learning and consider a variety of processes to help them achieve their goals.

One possibility involves the science teachers creating personal learning networks, enabling them to connect with teachers from around the globe. To create personal learning networks, teachers use digital tools such as blogs, Nings, and social networking to connect with educators outside their school to learn how they have successfully helped students with similar learning goals. Another possibility involves the teachers working together to develop, teach, and revise new lessons in a process called lesson study. Lesson study provides multiple opportunities for teachers to work together on their practice and observe one another's teaching. A third possibility is the Critical Friends strategy. This approach involves teachers meeting several times each month to study a specific teaching approach, deepen their knowledge, and talk in depth about student work. As the group members continue to research strategies, they also discuss using teacher rounds, peer coaching, mentoring, and action research. All of these strategies have been used successfully in a variety of schools. Which should they select to help them achieve their goals?

This chapter focuses on selecting and implementing the processes—professional development strategies—to help teachers learn. The strategies themselves are discussed in detail in later chapters of this book. This chapter is intended to help school leaders determine which strategies will best fit their unique context and will lead to teachers learning the specific content to enhance student learning.

The Learning Forward standards of Learning Designs and Implementation provide a useful guide for schools and school leaders as they work to select and implement strategies and activities that will promote teacher professional learning. This chapter examines each of these standards and the roles they play in selecting and applying the best processes for your particular context and content.

Learning Designs

There are many effective professional development strategies and designs to choose from, and all of them involve active teacher engagement, modeling, reflection, application, feedback, and ongoing support. Some strategies focus on individual learning while other forms focus on team-based learning. Most strategies are implemented in face-to-face settings, but technology is rapidly extending professional learning opportunities to online and hybrid settings as well. All designs seek to embed teacher learning into the workday, but some extend learning opportunities beyond the school day. Some are highly structured, while others are more fluid to allow for adjustments in the learning process. With so many options available, it can be confusing for the school leader to decide which strategy, or group of strategies, he or she will use in their school. When choosing designs for professional learning, school leaders should involve many people in the selection process and should focus on connecting particular professional learning strategies with their unique school context and the goals that have been established for their professional development program.

Who Should Be Involved?

The simple and obvious answer is that everyone should be involved. It is critical when choosing professional learning processes or designs to involve those who will be engaged in the designs and who will be affected by the outcomes. For teachers to be engaged in and committed to their professional learning they need to know about the strategies available to them and play a role in selecting them. When teachers are given a significant voice and choice in selecting and shaping professional learning strategies and activities, they find professional development more meaningful, are more committed to the success of professional development, and are more likely to seek out authentic applications of their learning (Penuel et al., 2007).

All the strategies I present in Chapters 6 through 13 work well with classroom teachers, but some (lesson study, Critical Friends, and teacher rounds) involve primarily group work while others (personal learning networks, peer coaching, mentoring, and action research) blend individual and group work. Some require the direct involvement of school leaders while others are characterized by greater teacher independence. Whatever the professional learning strategy or activity, principals and professional development directors should at least be supportive of them, even when their direct involvement is not necessary. Lesson study, Critical Friends, and personal learning networks, for example, do not require direct principal participation but still require his or her support.

Connecting Learning Goals With Specific Strategies

While the entire faculty should be involved in a professional development program, this does not mean that everyone should be learning through the same strategy. One size definitely does not fit all when selecting the strategies for a professional development program (Darling-Hammond, 2010). One of the most frequent complaints I hear from teachers about traditional professional learning is that the entire faculty experiences exactly the same content and strategies. For a professional development program to be effective, it is essential to work with faculty to get teachers involved in activities that fit their particular learning needs. Some professional learning strategies are more conducive to certain teacher learning needs than are others, and some strategies fit with certain school contexts better than do others. All effective professional learning strategies help teachers move beyond surface comprehension of a new idea or instructional skill to a deeper, more complete understanding of its purposes, essential features, and connection to other ideas and approaches. To achieve the ultimate goal of improved student learning, effective professional learning strategies provide multiple opportunities for teachers to practice new learning with ongoing feedback and coaching so the learning can become integrated into their instructional repertoire.

The following questions can serve as guides as you and your faculty consider the best strategies for your specific school culture and your unique teacher learning needs (Easton, 2008):

- Which strategies are particularly good in establishing a professional learning community?
- Which strategies are useful for collecting school data?

- Which strategies are most focused on student work and student work processes?
- Which strategies most emphasize pedagogy?
- Which strategies are best for seeking solutions to specific problems?
- Which strategies are most effective for providing feedback on actual classroom teaching?

Table 5.1 provides a summary of the answers to these questions for each of the professional strategies discussed in later chapters of this book (action research, Critical Friends, lesson study, teacher rounds, mentoring, online professional development, peer coaching, and personal learning networks). Once several strategies have been identified that seem to be a good fit for your specific school culture and your unique teacher learning needs, I suggest that you engage your faculty in reviewing the chapters on the strategies to be sure that they are the best for your situation. This will also increase the commitment of your faculty to the specific strategies that are chosen.

Implementation

The overarching goals for teacher professional development are improvements in teacher instructional practices and increases in student learning outcomes. Improvements in teacher and student learning involve a process that occurs over time and requires support for professional development design implementation to embed the new learning into practices. As school leaders work to choose professional learning strategies that fit their school context and are connected to their professional development goals, they must also consider several issues related to the implementation of the strategies they have selected.

Attend to the Change Process

To implement an effective teacher professional development program, school leaders must realize that change takes time and that some teacher resistance is a normal, natural part of the implementation process. Rather than complaining about this resistance, it is more productive for school leaders to seek to understand it, acknowledge it, and be clear about what they will need to do decrease it over time. When school leaders keep the focus of professional development on

Table 5.1 The Purposes and Rationales for Eight Powerful Professional Development Strategies

PD STRATEGY	PURPOSE AND RATIONALE						
	Good for Gathering Multiple Types of School Data	*Very Helpful in Creating a PLC*	*Emphasizes Pedagogy and Teaching*	*Particularly Focused on Student Work and Student Learning*	*Useful for Problem Solving*	*A Concrete Product Result*	*Provides Feedback to Teachers on Classroom Practices*
Action Research	X	X	X	X	X	X	
Critical Friends		X	X	X	X		X
Lesson Study	X	X	X	X	X	X	X
Teacher Rounds		X	X	X	X		X
Mentoring			X		X		X
Online PD			X		X		
Peer Coaching			X		X		X
Personal Learning Network			X		X		

Source: Adapted from Easton (2008).

student learning, involve teachers in the design and content of professional learning activities, provide ongoing support for teachers as they learn new professional development strategies, help teachers experience early success with new strategies, and provide time for teachers to collaboratively engage in professional learning activities, resistance will be minimal. Further, school leaders build faculty support for implementation by frequently reiterating professional development goals, communicating and celebrating incremental successes, and honestly discussing the complexities and challenges of significant change. Finally, school leaders would be wise to heed the words of Dennis Sparks (1997) when he advises, "Perhaps the most important thing to remember as a school leader facing teacher resistance is that you must model and embody the attitudes and behaviors you seek from your faculty" (p. 23).

The Issue of Time

A common complaint I hear from teachers is that there never seems to be enough time available to engage in meaningful, effective professional learning. Episodic or occasional professional learning does not lead to improved educator practice or enhanced student learning because it does not include ongoing support or opportunities for extended learning. Many studies confirm that instructional change requires that significant time be devoted to professional learning activities, including both the span of time over which the activity is spread and the number of hours spent in the activity (Darling-Hammond et al., 2009). Teacher learning and instructional improvement require significant time commitments to allow for deep discussion of course content, student misconceptions, instructional strategies, and assessment strategies. In addition, teachers need time to try out new practices in the classroom and receive feedback on their teaching. As you select strategies for your needs and context, carefully consider the time demanded by the strategy relative to the time currently used for professional learning (see Table 5.2). If the requirements of the strategy exceed current time availability, you must work with your faculty to find the time needed to fit the strategy.

An effective approach is to build time for professional learning into the regular school day schedule, which is termed "job-embedded professional learning." In Japan and Sweden, two countries noted for both their high student achievement and effective teacher professional learning, time for teacher professional learning is built into the regular teacher workday. As noted educational researcher

Table 5.2 Time Commitments Required by Eight Powerful Professional Development Strategies

PD STRATEGY	Meeting Length		HOW OFTEN — Meeting Frequency			
	Each meeting is 1–2 hours	*Each meeting is an hour or less*	*Daily*	*Weekly*	*Monthly*	*3–4 times each year*
Action Research		X			X	
Critical Friends	X				X	
Lesson Study	X				X	
Teacher Rounds		X			X	
Mentoring		X		X		
Online PD	X					X
Peer Coaching		X		X		
Personal Learning Network		X	X			

Source: Adapted from Easton (2008).

and consultant Sally Zepeda (2008) has emphasized, "The schedule of the day must be restructured to provide teachers with focused opportunities to engage in the type of work called for by research on effective professional development" (p. 29).

So, specifically, how can time be reallocated to provide opportunities for this job-embedded teacher learning? First, schools can adjust teacher roles so they have time to act as mentors or peer coaches. Second, schedules can be designed to provide grade-level teams and department teams with common planning time to engage in lesson study, Critical Friends, or one of the other collaborative learning strategies. Third, rotating teams of substitutes can be hired each month to provide teachers opportunities to engage in collaborative professional learning approaches. Fourth, early dismissal days can be scheduled each month, where teachers can engage in professional learning. A fifth approach is to provide stipends for work outside the school day and/or over the summer. Finally, some faculty meeting time can be used for teacher professional learning groups to meet. By providing and protecting the time needed for meaningful professional learning, school leaders demonstrate in a powerful way their commitment to the ongoing learning of their teachers.

The Issue of Cost

Many strategies discussed in this book require few resources outside of the school (see Figure 5.3). But all of the designs do have time costs associated with them—for example, the time that teachers devote to meeting with colleagues, designing new lessons, and observing one another's classrooms. The time required by some strategies requires spending money for substitute teachers or stipends. The money spent on any of these strategies, though, is likely to be less than the cost of hiring consultants and speakers for traditional professional development approaches. In a time of shrinking educational budgets, the strategies discussed in this book will in many cases result in reduced spending on teacher professional development. However, more important than whether or not your spending on professional development is reduced is the extent to which the money you do spend results in improved instructional practices and better student outcomes. The strategies in this book can help you make sure that the money and other resources invested into professional development results in increased learning by all of the adults in your school—and that the improved teacher instructional practices result in enhanced student engagement and improved student learning.

Table 5.3 Resources Needed for Eight Powerful Professional Development Strategies

PD STRATEGY	Link With Other Strategies		Outside Expertise Required			Cost		
	Yes	No	Yes	Temporary	No	Low	Medium	High
Action Research	X				X	X		
Critical Friends	X			X		X		
Lesson Study	X				X	X		
Teacher Rounds	X				X	X		
Mentoring	X				X	X		
Online PD	X				X	X		
Peer Coaching	X				X	X		
Personal Learning Network	X			X		X		

RESOURCES NEEDED

Source: Adapted from Easton (2008).

Summary

In the last three chapters I have emphasized that the school leader must attend to the critical lenses of context, content, and process to create and sustain an effective teacher professional learning program. Context—establishing the environment or culture for professional learning—was examined in Chapter 3. Content—establishing the goals of professional development activities and how to assess them—was the focus of Chapter 4. Process—the "how" of professional development—was the topic of this chapter. Process involves the types of professional development activities, and the way those activities are planned, organized, implemented, and followed up. This chapter described an approach for selecting your professional development strategies and activities. Of primary importance is carefully selecting strategies that best fit your particular school context and your specific student and teacher learning goals. Whatever strategies are chosen, it is important to involve the faculty in the process of selecting the most appropriate strategies for your context and content, and it is essential that you dedicate sufficient time, preferably during the school day, for teachers to engage in your chosen activities.

The overall purpose of Chapters 1 through 5 was to provide the foundational knowledge practitioners need to design, implement, evaluate, and sustain effective professional learning in schools. With this foundational knowledge in place, we are now ready to discuss eight powerful professional development strategies in detail: lesson study, Critical Friends, teacher rounds, action research, peer coaching, mentoring, online professional development, and personal learning networks. Some designs may seem more formidable than others, particularly if your school is in the early stages of becoming a learning community. However, none of us can wait to engage in the strategies presented in this book. Our students will be more engaged—and will learn more—when we create and sustain a context supportive of adult learning, when we intentionally focus the content of professional development on student needs, and when we carefully choose strategies that help teachers address those needs.

6

Lesson Study

Lesson study provides a collaborative process for teachers to make sense of educational goals and standards and bring them to life in the classroom.

—Catherine Lewis

As part of their collaborative discussions about the gap between where their students are and where they want them to be, a group of high school science teachers have identified "analyzing and interpreting scientific data" as one of their student weaknesses. The science teachers want to learn how to better help their students understand at a deep level how to make accurate, appropriate interpretations and conclusions from scientific data, particularly when the data are reported in the form of charts and graphs.

The six teachers in the department are gathered around the table where they have met weekly over the past month. During this time they have collaboratively analyzed and interpreted different types of scientific data to deepen their understanding and make sure they are all on the same page about what they want their students to be able to do. They have contacted the National Science Teachers Association (NSTA) about research-based best practices for teaching data analysis and interpretation, they have consulted with science teachers from other schools, and they have shared their successful and unsuccessful teaching approaches with one another.

Today they begin discussing the essential components of their first lesson design. "I don't think our students really understand what science is all about and how it is different from religion and other nonscientific areas," says Brad. Debbie agrees and adds, "Yes, I agree that our students do not have a good understanding of the characteristics of science, and it seems important to begin there." "OK, then perhaps our focus should be on helping them understand that science is a way of knowing about the world, and helping them understand the fundamental principles guiding that way of knowing," contributes David. "Yes, we can begin by having them attempt to describe their understanding of how science differs from nonscience, because this would reveal their essential misconceptions and provide a real target for our instruction," says Teresa. "That's a great place to start," says James. "The way I see it is the larger unit of study would focus on developing data analysis and data interpretation understandings and skills, and our research lesson could focus on building the foundational understanding of science needed for later lessons in the unit." Whitney, the head of the department, summarizes, "Okay, let's focus on designing a lesson to really help students understand the essential characteristics of science as a way of knowing about the natural world, and this can be part of the unit on data analysis and interpretation."

Over the next month the lesson study group members complete the planning of their first research lesson; observe one member of the group teach the lesson to his or her class; reflect on what they learned about data analysis, their teaching, and student learning through this process; makes revisions to their lesson; and share what they have learned about teaching and student learning with other teachers in their school. The research lesson is an important part of the process, but it is not the only important product. The lesson serves as an organizer that teachers use as they engage in the essential work of lesson study: studying best-practice teaching materials, discussing content and instruction with colleagues, collaboratively reflecting on their practice, investigating student learning, and applying all that they learn to their classroom practices. The purpose of lesson study is to improve instruction by generating professional knowledge, not by developing exemplary lessons. The power of lesson study is that it promotes discussions about teaching and learning that lead to deeper understanding of content, better understanding of how students think and learn, and improvement of instructional practices.

A Cycle of Instructional Improvement

Lesson study originated in Japan. The concept behind lesson study is simple yet powerful: To improve teaching and learning in schools you must get teachers together to study the processes of teaching and learning, and then have them devise ways to improve teaching and learning. Lesson study is a cycle of instructional improvement. A group of teachers is formed, and its members work together as follows (Wilburg & Brown, 2007):

- The group collaboratively plans a lesson addressing student learning goals.
- One member teaches the lesson to their class while the others observe and gather evidence on student learning and student work processes.
- The group discusses the evidence gathered during the lesson, using it to improve the lesson, the unit, and overall instruction.
- A second group member teaches the revised lesson to another class while others observe to gather additional evidence and improve the lesson again.
- The group writes up a summary of the entire cycle, with a focus on what has been learned about teaching and student learning.

Through this cycle, which is repeated multiple times for each teacher group in a given school year, teachers acquire a clear view of their strengths and weaknesses and gain valuable information they can use to enhance their teaching skills (see Figure 6.1). For example, teachers engaged in lesson study improve their knowledge of academic content, pedagogy, and student thinking, and build relationships with knowledgeable colleagues.

While lesson study originated in Japan, its use as a form of teacher professional development in schools in the United States has grown steadily since James W. Stigler and James Hiebert's *The Teaching Gap* (1999) detailed its role in Japanese student achievement. There is no single right way to do lesson study; the key to successful implementation of this strategy is to remain true to the core elements described in the following while adapting it to your own needs and circumstances.

The Lesson Study Philosophy

From its beginnings in the 1960s, lesson study has focused on the core of what schools are all about: the interactions between teacher and students in the classroom. Lesson study recognizes that teaching is a highly complex endeavor that can only be mastered by giving teachers plenty of opportunities to come together to share ideas and think deeply about the work they do in the classroom. This practice "is in stark contrast to American classrooms where each teacher plans and teaches in almost complete isolation" (Lewis, 2002, p. 9). Lesson study requires "deep thought, inquiry, and collaboration with a collective focus on teaching rather than teachers" (Stepanek, Appel, Leong, Magan, & Mitchell, 2007, p. 2). It is based on the belief that observing somebody's teaching, combined with trying similar lessons on your own, is the best way to progress as a teacher (Fernandez & Yoshida, 2004).

As teachers observe colleagues teaching actual classroom lessons, they gather data on what facilitates and impedes student learning, share the data to create an understanding of the learning of the entire class, and use the information to improve their teaching. The goal is not just to improve the lesson under study, but also to improve their instruction in a more general sense. The real power of lesson study is not product, but process (Lewis & Tsuchida, 1998). It leads teachers to examine their own practice in depth in the context of student learning, connects them with their students and their professional community, and motivates them to continuously improve.

Lesson Study Steps

Lesson study is a simple concept. To improve classroom teaching, it makes sense to have teachers collaboratively plan, observe, and discuss lessons. However, many excellent and simple strategies fail when educators implement surface features of the strategy without understanding and attending to the core elements of the strategy. The steps discussed in this chapter—forming and focusing the group, planning the lesson, observing the lesson, discussing the lesson, revising the lesson, and sharing reflections on the lesson—are useful only when they result in opportunities for teachers to learn about content, pedagogy, and students.

Step 1: Forming and Focusing the Group

The typical size of a lesson study group is between four and six teachers. Depending on your particular professional development program goals and your unique context, groups can be composed of teachers from the same grade level or teachers from the same content area. Lesson study teams are characterized by egalitarian discussion and shared responsibility, and are focused on improving student learning. Lesson study requires significant trust and commitment from teachers so a context supportive of adult learning must be in place for it to be effective.

Establishing group norms will be the lesson study team's first collective effort. These group norms will provide a set of shared expectations for how the team members will interact and how they will support each other's learning. The following guiding questions can be used by lesson study teams as they work to identify group norms (Chokshi & Fernandez, 2004):

- What are our expectations for how we will work together?
- What conditions will contribute to our learning?
- What conditions will interfere with our learning?
- What conditions will create and sustain a sense of belonging and support?
- How will we resolve our differences and disagreements?

After determining group norms, the lesson study team selects a student learning goal to guide their work. A lesson study group will be most effective if it focuses on one specific goal connected to its specific grade level or content area (Lewis & Perry, 2006). As illustrated in the vignette with the science teachers at the beginning of this chapter, lesson study goals emerge as team members discuss gaps between standards they have for student learning and what their students currently know, understand, and can do. Figure 6.2 provides a handout to facilitate this discussion.

Once the group has been formed, group norms have been established, and the learning goal to be addressed has been chosen, the group decides on a time commitment and schedule for each lesson cycle. Weekly common meeting times of one to two hours, either during the day or after school, should be scheduled for lesson study to result in the intended teacher and student learning.

Step 2: Collaboratively Planning the Research Lesson

Planning a research lesson is quite different from the lesson planning done by most teachers. Research lesson planning is highly collaborative and detailed. Teachers draw upon past experiences,

Figure 6.1 Lesson Study Features and Results

Features of Lesson Study

1. Investigation
  a. Consider goals for student learning and teacher learning
  b. Study the content area and pedagogy: key concepts, existing lessons and curricula, research-based best practices

2. Planning
  a. Select and develop research lesson
  b. Simulate lesson in order to anticipate student responses
  c. Write lesson plan, including goals for student learning, anticipated student thinking, data to be collected, rationale for lesson design, connection to goals

3. Research Lesson
  a. Conduct research lesson
  b. Observe lesson and collect data

4. Reflection
  a. Share and discuss data from research lesson
  b. Group members discuss implications for lesson redesign, for teaching-learning more broadly, and for understanding of students and academic content
  c. Summarize in writing what was learned from cycle
  d. Revise and reteach the lesson

Resulting Changes

1. Teacher Knowledge
  a. Content
  b. Pedagogy
  c. Student thinking and how to gather evidence about it
  d. Goals for student learning and how they connect to daily instruction

2. Learning Community Development
  a. Motivation to improve instruction and buy-in to lesson study process
  b. Belief that improvement is needed and is possible
  c. Development of identity as a professional who keeps learning
  d. Development of collaborative working relationships with colleagues
  e. Sense of accountability to colleagues to provide high-quality instruction

3. Teaching-Learning Resources
  a. Tasks that reveal student thinking
  b. Data collection methods that capture key elements of student learning and instruction
  c. Tools that support productive exchange of ideas among teachers
  d. Lesson plans that promote student learning
  e. Written reflections on what the group learned in developing the lesson

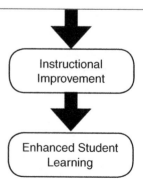

Instructional Improvement

Enhanced Student Learning

Source: Adapted from Fernandez and Yoshida (2004) and Lewis and Perry (2006).

Figure 6.2 Choosing a Lesson Study Goal

Think about your students:

Standards/Benchmarks for Student Learning: The Ideal

What do you want students to know, understand, and be able to do at the end of the course/grade?

Current Student Performance: The Actual

What do your students know and understand, and what can they do at the end of the course/grade?

Student Learning Needs: The Gap Between the Ideal and the Actual

Compare the actual and ideal and determine what gaps are most important to narrow.

The Lesson Study Group Goal

After comparing ideal and actual student learning, select a specific goal to guide your lesson study work.

Source: Adapted from Chokshi and Fernandez (2004) and Lewis (2002).

observations of current students, resource books, and research-based best practices as they discuss how to best design their lesson. The end product of this step is a detailed document that specifies the design of the research lesson. (See Figure 6.3 for a template that can be used as a framework for developing a detailed research lesson plan document.) The detailed research lesson document serves three purposes: It guides the teaching of the research lesson, specifies how data will be collected by observers, and guides reflective discussion after the teaching of the lesson (Perry & Lewis, 2008).

As reflected in the discussion among teachers earlier in this chapter, the planning process begins with the group collaboratively studying the content or concept to be taught and researching successful approaches for teaching the target content or concept. The goal is for group members to deepen their understanding of the target content or concept and identify research-based and practitioner-based successful teaching approaches that they may want to include in their research lesson (Lewis, Perry, & Hurd, 2004).

As they plan, the group members consider the entire unit of study into which their research lesson falls. They document a short introductory section describing the number of lessons in the unit, the major learning goals for each lesson, and where the research lesson falls within the unit. Their purpose is to put the research lesson into a larger context of student learning, both for the members of the group as they plan the lesson and for other teachers who will read the complete research lesson plan document at the conclusion of their lesson study cycle. For example, the research lesson our science teachers are developing centers on helping students understand the core characteristics of science, and this lesson is part of a larger unit on data analysis and interpretation. In the introductory section of the research lesson plan document they will outline how their research lesson will fall early in a unit designed to help students develop these skills, and they will specify the learning goals for both the research lesson and the entire unit.

The next section of the research lesson plan document is quite extensive and is the core of the research lesson. Called "Progression of the Lesson," it describes the lesson in great detail and is typically divided into four areas (Fernandez & Chokshi, 2002; Lewis, 2002). The first explains the learning activities (content and teaching methods are specified) of the lesson, the key questions the teacher will pose at different points in the lesson, and the amount of time allocated for each activity. Questions are carefully worded to promote student thinking related to the core learning goals of the research

Figure 6.3   Template for Detailed Lesson Study Lesson Plan Document

Date:

Grade:

Subject:

Instructor:

Lesson Study Team:

I. Unit Information

   A. Unit Name

   B. Unit Objectives

   C. Instructional Sequence for the Unit

   D. Why Was This Unit Chosen for Lesson Study?

II. Lesson Information

   A. Name of the Study Lesson

   B. Student Learning Goals for the Lesson

   C. How Is the Lesson Related to the Unit Objectives?

   D. Progression of the Lesson

Specific steps of the lesson: Learning activities, key questions and time allocation	Expected student reactions and responses	Teacher responses to student reactions/things for teacher to remember	Data collection plan to assess lesson goals

Source: Adapted from Fernandez and Yoshida (2004) and Lewis (2002).

lesson and larger unit. For example, one of the key questions the science teacher group has chosen to get their students thinking about the core features of science is, "What are five characteristics of science as an academic discipline that are not found in other disciplines?"

The second area lists specific ideas, reactions, and answers the group expects from students during the lesson. One way to produce this section is for the lesson study group teachers to try the activities they intend to present to students. This forces the group to explore the material in greater depth and helps them anticipate potential student reactions. Thinking about things from the student's point of view is a big shift for many teachers, and it is challenging to generate potential student solutions in advance.

The third area lists potential ways teachers can respond to the variety of expected student reactions. For example, what comments will the teacher make or what questions will the teacher ask when students react in a certain way? How will the teacher connect student responses to the ideas he or she wants them to think about during the lesson? This third area also often lists points for the teacher to remember, such as reminders about why a task was included in the lesson or what the teachers are working toward. Areas 2 and 3 of the "Progression of the Lesson" are important because thinking about potential student answers and strategies, and the best way to respond to them, deepens teachers' understanding of how students best learn specific material and leads them to adjust their instruction accordingly.

The fourth area of the "Progression of the Lesson" details how the student learning goals will be evaluated and outlines a specific data collection plan for group members to follow as they observe the teaching of the lesson. Key questions to ask and answer in preparing this area of the lesson plan include

- How will we know if students have learned what we want them to learn?
- What evidence do we need to gather to be confident students have met the student learning goals?
- What specific data will be collected by each observing group member?

Data collected during the research lesson permits group members to collaboratively reflect on the extent to which student learning did or did not progress and how each component of the lesson supported or impeded student learning.

Step 3: Teaching and Observing the Research Lesson

The third step in the cycle is for one of the teachers to teach the lesson to one of his or her classes. The other teachers in the group make arrangements to be there as observers. They bring copies of the research lesson plan document to guide them as they collect detailed data on student learning, motivation, and behavior. While research lessons are also videotaped to aid in later reflection and discussion, it is essential that team members observe the lesson in person so they can accurately capture student reactions during the lesson (Wiburg & Brown, 2007). Since multiple teachers observe the lesson, it is important for them to distribute themselves around the classroom in order to see the lesson from different vantage points and gather as much information as possible.

In addition to the lesson study group members, others (for example, the principal or a teacher from another lesson study group) may observe the lesson. The additional observers also receive copies of the research lesson plan document and are invited to make comments on the document as they observe the lesson. Both group and nongroup observers refrain from interacting with students during the lesson. The observers are there to collect data and act as extra sets of eyes, not extra sets of hands. As lesson study researcher Catherine Lewis (2002) emphasizes, "when observers help students, it's difficult to draw inferences about how well the lesson worked" (p. 68).

Step 4: Discussing the Research Lesson

After the class, the group meets to reflect on the lesson. It is important to meet soon (after school on the day of the lesson is ideal) so the experience is fresh for everyone. From the outset of the meeting, it is important to emphasize that the research lesson belongs to the group, not the teacher who taught it (Fernandez, 2003). The purpose of the post-lesson reflection is not to evaluate the teacher who taught the lesson but rather to share collected data, reflect on what was learned about student thinking, and begin discussing how to improve the lesson (Chokshi & Fernandez, 2004).

Learning how to have an honest and productive discussion about a lesson that a colleague has taught is challenging, but it is made easier when the lesson study group adheres to protocol for exchanging feedback. The purpose of a discussion protocol is to minimize the anxiety and potential for hurt feelings that such feedback can provoke (Lewis & Perry, 2006). Such protocol, however, is not intended to make the feedback less critical or reflective; rather, it is meant to make the process more efficient and productive. The teacher who taught the research lesson speaks first to give impressions about what went well, what did not go well, and what was surprising. The group then turns its attention to discussing the data collected by the observers during the lesson. Group members talk about the data and what it tells them about student thinking and learning. After each teacher has presented and reflected on his or her data, the group members summarize student thinking and learning in the lesson and may begin to discuss potential revisions to their lesson and broader implications of what they have learned for their instruction. More typical, though, is that the step 4 reflection meeting centers exclusively on data from the research lesson and discussions regarding specific revisions and broader implications come at a later time.

Step 5: Revising and Reteaching the Lesson

Next, the group takes what it has learned and discusses needed revisions to the research lesson. Discussion focuses on why specific revisions should be made and how the revisions will move students closer to the learning goals for the lesson and unit of study. The following questions can help guide this discussion (Fernandez & Yoshida, 2004; Lewis, 2002):

- What unanticipated student responses and reactions occurred?
- To what extent were the goals of the lesson achieved?
- Which instructional decisions might have contributed to students meeting specific learning goals?
- What learning goals of the lesson were not achieved?
- Which aspects of the lesson should be reconsidered and revised?

The purpose of this step is to improve the research lesson and reflect on what has been learned. The revision process leads to an updated version of the research lesson plan document, including any changes to the data collection protocol.

At this point, a second member of the group teaches the revised lesson to his or her students while the other group members again come to observe the lesson. A different teacher teaches the revised lesson because varying the teacher and students provides a greater variety of experiences and data to learn from and allows more teachers to be observed by their colleagues.

Step 6: Discussing the Revised Lesson and Summarizing the Learning

The group members meet again to reflect on their observations from the teaching of the revised lesson. As before, the discussion centers on sharing data, observations, and suggestions. One group member takes detailed notes at each meeting, particularly when teachers are reflecting on what they have learned about student thinking, student learning, and their own instruction (Fernandez, 2003). Doing this ensures that a good record of the process will be available for teachers when they turn to writing the report of their work.

At the conclusion of the cycle, the group reviews the detailed notes from the process and reflects on what they have learned about content and concepts, student thinking and learning, and classroom practice. Reflection at this point "helps team members extract knowledge from their experiences, frame questions about the assumptions that influence their teaching, and form new hypotheses (Stepanek et al., 2007, p. 128). It is helpful for the team to consider both what went well and what changes need to be made to improve the next cycle. If teams do not reflect on their lesson study practice, they are in danger of going through the motions of lesson study without reaching the potential for deep learning and instructional improvements.

Team members share what they have learned in a written report that includes both the original and revised research lesson plan documents. These reports serve three purposes (Lewis & Perry, 2006). First, they are a way for the lesson study group to summarize for themselves what they have learned about content, students, and instruction, and to pose additional questions for future research lessons. Our group of science teachers, for example, can use the written report of its research lesson as the foundation for designing a second research lesson to promote its overall goal of enhancing student understanding and skill in the area of scientific data analysis and interpretation. Second, these teachers provide a mechanism for sharing the research lesson and the group's learning with other teachers at their school. This sharing contributes to an overall school context supportive of adult learning, ensures that teachers throughout the school can learn from one another's research lessons, and builds over time a shared knowledge base at the school about effective instruction.

The final purpose of these reports is they provide a mechanism for sharing the group's learning with educators outside their school. In Japan, schools compile their research lesson reports into publications called Research Bulletins that constitute a major form of educational research (Fernandez, 2003). In fact, these Research Bulletins outnumber publications by university education professors in Japan, and lesson study conducted by actual classroom teachers is considered the most valid form of educational research. Together, these Research Bulletins are an important source of professional knowledge and ideas that teachers can draw upon to continue their learning.

The Essential Elements of Lesson Study

Educators new to lesson study often focus on the surface features of the strategy: planning, teaching, observing, and revising classroom lessons. But lesson study is not meant to be a rigid process focused on the perfecting of one lesson. Japanese teachers adapt the approach to their needs and circumstances, and American educators should follow their lead as they bring lesson study to their schools. There are several essential elements at the core of any lesson study adaptation if it is to result in improvements in teacher learning, teacher instruction, and student learning (Fernandez & Chokshi, 2002; Lewis, 2002; Lewis & Perry, 2006).

Adult Learning Context

Lesson study is driven by a context supportive of adult learning. More specifically, collaborative teacher work focused on improving instruction is at the heart of lesson study. In lesson study, teachers come together to reflect on teaching, share their ideas, and pool their collective experience. Through collective work teachers expand their instructional repertoire and build collegial relationships to support ongoing learning. Lesson study is a way to break the isolation that makes it difficult for U.S. teachers to learn from each other and develop a joint body of professional knowledge. Developing such collegial relationships takes time, and the lesson study group will need to navigate through two unproductive tendencies: (1) overly polite talk, where teachers avoid conflict and criticism, and (2) entrenchment, where individuals dig in their heals to protect their own views and practices. The group should take a self-critical stance and consistently remind one another that the ultimate goal is to improve student learning.

Content Knowledge Focus

As the lesson study group discusses how to plan, observe, and revise their lesson, they focus on improving their knowledge about academic content. The teachers themselves come to a deeper understanding of the content of their discipline and how to effectively teach that content to their students (called pedagogical content knowledge). Lesson study is a powerful strategy for helping teachers identify gaps in their own knowledge and skills and for providing the setting, motivation, and support to close those gaps. Through drawing upon content resources, researching best practices, and discussing subject matter with colleagues, group members develop new insights about academic content and how to help students improve their understanding of the content.

Student Learning Focus

Teachers engaged in lesson study move from thinking, "What will I cover in this lesson?" to "What do I want my students to learn from this lesson?" In lesson study, the ultimate focus of collaborative teacher work is to improve student understanding, knowledge, and skill in specific areas. When teachers and school leaders observe teachers in lesson study, they focus primarily on gathering evidence about student thinking, engagement, and learning. Importantly, observers gather evidence only about teacher behaviors when they are linked to student thinking and learning. While observers of teachers in lesson study focus on gathering information about student learning, teacher observation in U.S. schools is typically focused on teacher behaviors. For example, teacher behavior checklists assess teacher effectiveness through items like "teacher uses specific praise" and "teacher concludes with a summary of the lesson." As *The Teaching Gap* authors Stigler and Hiebert (1999) emphasize, when observation involves checklists that keep the focus on teacher behavior, and quality teaching is defined by specific actions of teachers, attention is diverted from the more important goal of student learning. Successful teaching becomes defined by specific teacher actions rather than improvements in student learning. Lesson study, when implemented appropriately, avoids this trap and keeps the focus squarely on student learning and growth.

In-Person Observation

Replacing observing live lessons with video recording is tempting because it avoids the need to find substitutes for the teachers observing the lesson and it allows for repeated viewing of the lesson. While video recording does have a place in lesson study, it should not replace the viewing of live lessons. Many important things can be noticed when the teacher is actually in the classroom rather than watching the recorded lesson. When watching a lesson in person, teachers can better see student engagement, student frustration, moments of sudden student understanding, and progression of student thinking. It is impossible to identify a "good lesson" without in-person observation because a single lesson plan can result in very different actual lessons, depending on the students, the teacher, and the subtle interactions between them. The essential nuances and subtle indicators of student thinking and learning are best captured "live."

Administrative Support and Participation

In the traditional model of professional development, the principal selects strategies and their content and monitors teachers to ensure they attend the required activities and follow the prescribed procedures. In lesson study the relationship between the principal and teachers becomes more reciprocal and interactive to encourage teachers to guide and take ownership of their professional learning. Involving teachers in setting student learning goals, and in the process selecting lesson study as a strategy, sets the stage for a reciprocal principal–faculty relationship in which they work together to improve teaching and learning in the school. Another action principals can take is to work as members of a lesson study team, communicating in a powerful way that they are committed to collaborating with the faculty and to continuing their own professional learning from and with the teachers.

In addition to facilitating the participation of faculty in lesson study, and participating themselves in some way, principals need to provide the support and resources needed for lesson study to succeed. Chief among these is time. Regardless of your creativity in scheduling group meetings, time will seem like a scarce commodity. After carving out dedicated time for lesson study during the day and/or after school, several things can make these meetings as efficient and productive as possible (Lewis & Tsuchida, 1998). First, emphasize that some of the research work on content and instructional best practices can be done individually outside the regular group meetings. Meeting time can be reserved for sharing what has been learned and how it is related to the established student learning goals. Second, have the two teachers teaching the lessons write the initial drafts of the lessons together outside of the regular meeting. The group meeting can then be targeted to discussing and sharing ideas about the evolving drafts.

Challenges to Engaging in Lesson Study: Misconceptions to Avoid

It is important for school leaders and lesson study teams to be aware of common misconceptions that can interfere with the potential benefits of lesson study (Chokshi & Fernandez, 2004). Through addressing these misconceptions in this section, I hope to help lesson study practitioners better understand the purpose of lesson study activities and keep their focus on the intellectual process of lesson study rather than the isolated products of lesson study work.

- **Misconception 1: Lesson study means creating never-seen-before lessons.** When lesson study teams draw up a detailed lesson plan as part of the lesson study process, the ideas for the lesson may be adapted from a variety of sources. Parts of the lesson may be revised from a textbook, modified from other lessons, or generated from the ideas of other educators. In any case, the driving force for the lesson should not be originality alone, but the fact that it provides a vantage point for teachers to develop an instructional plan to address specific student learning needs.
- **Misconception 2: There will be no benefit from just a handful of lesson study lessons.** It is impractical to bring the level of meticulous planning required by lesson study to every lesson a teacher teaches. However, the benefits of intensive work on a small number of lessons can be quite far-reaching. As team members engage in the process of lesson study, teachers begin to carry an informal "lesson study mentality" into their daily classroom practice (for example, paying greater attention to anticipating student reactions). Teachers engaged in lesson study also develop and apply effective instructional practices that they extract from the collaborative examination of practice. They may, for example, pose different types of questions to stimulate and direct student thinking. Finally, the experience of engaging in lesson study can create in teachers a disposition toward continual improvement of their teaching.
- **Misconception 3: Lesson study is about perfecting a single lesson.** It can be tempting for lesson study teams to work to perfect lessons, but they must remember that the reason for conducting lesson study is to improve their practice to enhance student learning. The purpose of revising and reteaching a lesson is for teachers to reflect on what they learned from

developing and implementing the lesson, what it taught them about helping students achieve the learning goals they set for the lesson, and what it taught them about how to improve their practice.

Summary

Lesson study is a professional development strategy that originated in Japan. The lesson study method of professional learning involves small groups of grade-level or content-area teachers collaboratively reflecting on content, instructional practice, and student learning. Through a cyclical process of collaborative lesson planning, lesson observation, examination of student learning, lesson revision, and the sharing of what the group learns with colleagues from separate groups, lesson study is an ideal strategy for building and sustaining a professional learning community, improving instructional practice, and addressing student learning needs. The features and benefits of lesson study are summarized in Figure 6.1. More specifically, teachers engaged in lesson study stand to gain the following:

- Consider student learning goals for a grade-level, content area unit of study and an individual lesson. Doing this helps teachers target their professional learning and classroom instruction to specific agreed-upon goals for student learning. Teacher thinking moves from concerns about what they will cover in a lesson to focusing on what they want students to get out of a lesson.
- Study and learn about best practices for teaching their grade level and/or content area. Teachers engaged in lesson study examine lessons that represent the best wisdom of researchers, and other teachers, and have an opportunity to discuss and adapt what they learn to their context and needs. Importantly, much of what teachers learn during lesson study also helps them improve their instruction in areas beyond the particular lesson and subject matter.
- Deepen their subject knowledge and pedagogical content knowledge. As Catherine Lewis (2002) emphasizes, "American educators assume you always learn content before you plan lessons while Japanese educators think you best learn content by actually planning lessons" (p. 17). As teachers discuss content with colleagues they deepen their understanding of it, and

through the process of designing a lesson and observing student reactions to it, they learn important lessons about student difficulties and how to best help students overcome those challenges. Further, they discover gaps in their own knowledge and are able to work to acquire the content knowledge to fill those gaps.

- Strengthen collaborative relationships with colleagues. As educational researcher Richard Elmore (2002) says, "isolation is the enemy of professional growth and learning" (p. 25). Yet few American teachers have regular opportunities to work with colleagues on the improvement of classroom instruction. The discussions during lesson study not only lead to improved teacher learning, teacher instruction, and student learning for the specific research lesson. They also sustain an overall context supportive of adult learning, which leads to numerous more informal discussions about teaching and student learning that yield additional dividends of improved instruction and student learning.

- Strengthen motivation to continuously improve as a professional. As teachers work together to gather data and improve lessons, they come to see problems of practice as challenges to be shared, researched, and solved. Lesson study enhances teachers' sense of efficacy and professionalism. As one American teacher told me about her lesson study experience, "lesson study encourages teachers to act like other professionals, to always be examining problems of practice and help one another solve them so we can all be better at what we do."

- Develop their ability to see their instruction through the eyes of their students. During lesson study, visiting teachers carefully observe students to gather evidence about student motivation, engagement, misconceptions, aha moments, and anything else to help them better understand student thinking and learning. This attention to student thinking and learning tends to transform teacher instruction long term, causing them to consistently consider their students more carefully and thoughtfully as they design and deliver lessons.

Lesson study requires considerable effort, but the investment of time and energy is well worth it as the process strengthens a learning community, enhances teacher collaboration, and professionalizes teaching. It can lead both to improved classroom instruction and to greater student achievement.

7

Critical Friends

Participating in a Critical Friends Group helps educators improve their teaching by studying together and giving and receiving feedback on day-to-day practices.

—Deborah Bambino

For several years Pamela, a social studies teacher, has met after school one or two times each month with seven middle school colleagues. The teachers come from different grades and disciplines—two English teachers, one art teacher, one science teacher, two math teachers, and another social studies teacher. Pamela remembers being skeptical that the new Critical Friends strategy they were trying would be any better than the usual professional development speakers and workshops, and she wondered how social studies and math teachers could possibly work together professionally in a meaningful way. Now, after two years of collaborating, she appreciates how all of them have grown through this group.

Today it is Pamela's turn to bring her work to the group. She has been working on ways to get her eighth-grade students to analyze the events, people, and themes in history more thoughtfully and more deeply—with few good results. After meeting with Mitchell, who was scheduled to take his turn as group facilitator, she chose the assignment protocol over several other options to guide the group's discussion.

Mitchell begins the meeting with the usual 10 minutes for connections, a time when each person can, if he or she chooses, briefly share something that will help everyone transition from the school day to the work of the group. Mitchell then shifts the conversation to an article the group agreed to read for this meeting. "Which of the author's suggestions for developing critical-thinking skills in middle school students really hit home with you?" he asks. Each group member ponders and writes quietly for a few minutes, and then Mitchell leads them through a structured discussion about the article. Mitchell ends the discussion after 30 minutes, saying, "It's time to move on, but please remember to communicate with the group as you try some of the things suggested in the article."

Mitchell then turns to Karen, one of the math teachers. "Karen, can you give us a quick update on how things have gone since our last meeting? We discussed your desire to get your students to look for multiple solutions to problems. What did you end up trying with them and how has it gone?" The group created this update section to help members follow up on intentions stated during each meeting. "Getting the students working in groups of three has really helped, because they are able to share different problem-solving strategies with each other," Karen says. "I think what you said," adds Mitchell, "applies to the entire group, because regardless of the discipline we all want students to develop multiple strategies for solving problems."

Most of the remaining meeting time is devoted to Pamela's presentation. Mitchell frames it, saying, "Pamela, you indicated that you wanted to use the assignment protocol to discuss an assignment you have developed, so let's jump right into it." He briefly reviews the steps of the protocol and then turns things over to Pamela. "I've been really frustrated that my students are superficial in their analysis of the events, people, and themes in history we have been reading about and discussing. I want them to go deeper, and I have been working on an assignment to push them in that direction. I'd like you to examine my assignment and tell me if it is clear and if you think it will help them go beneath the surface of things," she says. At this point Mitchell asks the group for clarifying questions. "Have they done something similar to this before?" How long will they have to complete the task?" "What background information do they have on the topic?" "Do they have any experience assessing sources outside their texts?"

The clarifying questions continue for several minutes, then Mitchell asks the group to begin the assignment as if they were Pamela's students. After 15 minutes Mitchell says, "Let's discuss

Pamela's assignment while Pamela steps back from the group and just listens and takes notes." Mitchell turns to the group and adds, "Remember that we want to look at what we think works, as well as what we think Pamela can improve." The group members examine the assignment carefully, pointing out its strengths, its weaknesses, and the extent to which they think it will accomplish Pamela's goals for student learning. After 20 minutes, Mitchell says, "our time for feedback is up so let's invite Pamela back in and hear what she thinks about our comments."

Pamela thanks the group for the comments as she hold up her notes. "I agree that I need to do a better job of modeling for my students the types of thinking that I want from them," begins Pamela. "And I also need to make sure my students have enough background knowledge to dig deeply into historical events the way I want them to," adds Pamela. She continues, generally agreeing with the group members' responses. She thanks them for their feedback and indicates she will report on her progress at the next meeting.

After Pamela concludes her comments, Wilson, the process observer, gives the group feedback about their work at the meeting. "We are definitely getting better at clarifying questions, and our feedback to the presenter seems to primarily be focused on how to improve instructional practices to enhance student learning." Wilson comments, though, that the group cut off one another's comments on several occasions and reminds everyone to remember to let people finish their thoughts at the next meeting. Mitchell then concludes the meeting by thanking the members for their participation and reminding the group about the facilitator and presenter for the next meeting.

The Origins of Critical Friends

Seeking alternatives to ineffective traditional methods of professional development, members of the Annenberg Institute for School Reform gathered in 1994 to design a new approach to teacher professional learning (Curry, 2008). They wanted to develop a professional development approach involving teacher collaboration and focused on helping teachers improve their instructional practices. The approach they created was the Critical Friends strategy (Bambino, 2002). As the preceding vignette suggests, Critical Friends Groups (CFGs) have diverse memberships characterized by interdisciplinary and multi-role group composition, are teacher driven, focus on classroom practice and student learning, are highly collaborative, and rely on structured conversation guides called protocols. The CFG approach "asks participants to draw on one another's skills and ideas, as well as on knowledge bases outside the school, to expand repertoires in ways specifically tailored to their own environment" (Curry, 2008, p. 735). From their inception, CFGs have been intended to (Dunne & Nave, 2000)

- support the creation and maintenance of a professional learning community;
- build a foundation for sustained professional learning based on a spirit of inquiry;
- help teachers develop strong collaborative relationships focused on improving instruction and student achievement;
- help teachers raise questions about whether their classrooms and assignments are accessible to all students, are culturally responsive, and reflect high expectations for all students;
- help teachers support one another in developing new and better ways to address student learning needs; and
- provide a setting and context for teachers to better understand their work, their colleagues, and their ideas, beliefs, and assumptions about teaching and learning.

A CFG is composed of six to eight teachers who meet once or twice each month, with meetings lasting about two hours (Hollins & McIntyre, 2004). They are found in lower, middle, and upper schools. In elementary schools, groups usually consist of teachers from the same grade, while in middle schools and high schools group members often teach different subjects and different grades. Meetings involve structured discussions centered on outside readings and the challenges of the members' work, and are intended to deepen professional knowledge and skill. The group collectively discusses instructional methods, works to build a shared knowledge base, and examines in great depth how to improve specific aspects of student learning.

Members of CFGs rotate carrying out certain roles that increase the efficiency and productivity of the process (see Figure 7.1). In addition to the facilitator, CFGs have a presenter (the person presenting an idea, assignment, assessment strategy, or instructional approach to be refined through a protocol), a note taker, and a process observer who attends to group dynamics and reports his or her observations at the end of each meeting. Other group members act as discussants, engaging in focused conversations about the work the presenter brings to the group.

Structured discussion guides, called protocols, are used in group meetings to direct discussions about readings, guide examinations of classroom practices and student work, and promote the exchange of ideas on a particular question or issue (see Figure 7.2). They keep the group focused, deepen discussions, and help the group work efficiently. Protocols are often resisted, but as a method to discuss important professional challenges and issues they help to keep conversations respectful and targeted so that CFGs remain safe places for colleagues to discuss their teaching and how to improve it (Quate, 2008). Finally, protocols help educators learn how to carefully confront issues and challenges with colleagues rather than talking around or avoiding difficult conversations.

Figure 7.1   Group Member Roles in a CFG

Facilitator	Presenter	Process Observer	Discussants
• Plans the protocol and focusing question with the presenter • Makes sure the protocol is followed during the meeting • Keeps track of time during the meeting • Monitors meeting conversations and ensures that all group members participate • Keeps attention focused on the question the presenter brings to the meeting	• Presents an idea or piece of work that raises a challenging question or professional problem of practice • Plans the protocol and focusing question with the facilitator • Takes notes on the discussants' comments • Responds to the discussants' comments • Reports at future meetings about actions taken	• Notes the dynamics of the group and describes how the group works together • Notes interruptions, domination, and depth of discussions • Notes body language during the meeting • Observes how the protocol was followed and how time was distributed • Reports observations to the group	• Discuss the outside reading and presenter question. • Follow the protocol and group norms • Provide positive and negative feedback, and question feedback • Invite all group members to participate • Welcome opposing points of view

Source: Adapted from Key (2006) and Quate (2008).

Figure 7.2 Critical Friends' Protocols and Their Uses

Type of Protocol	Protocol Uses
Challenging Issues	To explore options for addressing a professional problem of practice
Collaborative Assessment	To describe work without judgment
Consultancy	To examine work connected to a presenter's question about a concrete dilemma
Chalk Talk	To comment on a specific issue or question, or the ideas of others; is done in complete silence
Data-Driven Dialogue	Build understanding of views, beliefs, and assumptions about school and student data
Ghost Visit	To identify sources and types of evidence to use in assessing student learning
Text-Based Seminar	Expanding the understanding of a piece of reading
Tuning	To refine classroom practice by examining a piece of teacher or student work
Assignment	To provide nonjudgmental feedback on a newly developed assignment

Source: Zepeda (2007) and Quate (2008).

The Philosophy of CFGs

Isolation blocks improvement, and this has been particularly true in American schools where teachers have historically worked alone. Indeed, teachers rarely attend to what their colleagues do in their classrooms let alone collaborate monthly to examine artifacts of classroom practice. When teachers do meet, they often converge in departmental configurations or in grade-level groups organized to accomplish work-related tasks, rather than in inquiry-oriented collectives comprising staff members teaching different subjects and grades.

The Critical Friends approach is based on the conviction that classroom practice must be at the center of teacher professional learning and that strong collaborative teacher relationships need to replace teacher isolation as the norm in schools (Jametz, 2002). The developers of the strategy believe that schools cannot be intellectually engaging places for students unless their teachers also are actively engaged in collaborative learning, thinking, reading, and discussing (Curry, 2008). CFGs depart from traditional "one-shot" professional development by emphasizing that teachers grow professionally when they consistently study best practices together and give one another feedback on their classroom practices. Because honest, direct feedback can be a rare commodity in schools, the Critical Friends strategy emphasizes that CFGs need to be nonthreatening, trusting contexts where feedback can be given and received (Dunne & Honts, 1998).

Days set aside for professional learning are typically scheduled sporadically throughout the school year and are often disconnected from the daily challenges facing teachers. And even when information is relevant, processes are rarely in place to help teachers integrate new ideas into their classroom practices. Even desiring to make instructional improvements, teachers typically drift back to habitual ways of teaching. Critical Friends Groups are intended to break this pattern. Through focused collaboration, CFGs give teachers new perspectives on instruction and student learning, broaden their range of instructional approaches, and cause them to more carefully consider daily instructional decisions (Bambino, 2002). Unlike traditional professional development, CFGs provide teachers with the ongoing support, guidance, and feedback they need to learn more effective teaching practices. Finally, building strong collaborative professional relationships energizes teachers to continue learning and leads them to enjoy their work more fully, both of which can lead to improved classroom instruction.

Critical Friends Steps

The term *critical friends* often leads to misunderstanding, because it combines two words that seem to have almost opposite meanings. Many people equate critique with judgment, and when someone offers criticism they prepare themselves for negative comments. However, in the context of a CFG the word *critical* means *essential* or *urgent* as in the term *critical care*. A critical friend in a CFG is a trusted colleague who provides honest, supportive feedback, poses insightful questions, and works to help all group members improve their instruction (Bambino, 2002). Teacher collaboration is crucial, so when a CFG is formed norms for how to appropriately give and receive feedback are discussed to ensure that group members feel safe and comfortable.

Like lesson study, the idea behind the Critical Friends strategy is a simple one. The premise of the approach is that to improve classroom instruction and student learning, teachers must have ongoing opportunities to learn from and with one another. Critical Friends can and should be adapted to your specific student and teacher learning needs and your school context. However, certain elements are necessary if the strategy is to have an impact on school culture, classroom instruction, and student achievement.

Forming the Group

Depending on your professional development program goals and your unique context, CFGs can be composed of teachers from the same grade level or teachers from the same content area, but it is more common for them to be composed of teachers from different grades and academic disciplines. The rationale behind this is the belief that teachers expand their perspectives and instructional practices best when collaborating with colleagues who bring a variety of ideas, views, and methods to the group. If teachers meet only with teachers from their grade level or content area, the group will have a more narrow range of perspectives and methods and will have less influence on expanding the thinking, knowledge, and practices of group members (Curry, 2008).

Each CFG must have someone who has been trained in the correct implementation of the Critical Friends meeting protocols. This can be done with little difficulty or time by contacting the National School Reform Faculty, a national organization dedicated to supporting collaborative teacher professional learning. Other than making sure a protocol-trained teacher is in each group, there is enormous variety in how CFGs are formed. Whatever method you choose, be sure to include teachers in the process of forming the groups. This will enhance teacher buy-in and help the CFGs start on a positive note. As with all highly collaborative professional development strategies, the Critical Friends approach requires great trust and commitment from teachers, so a context supportive of adult learning must be in place for it to be effective.

In lesson study, the research group typically focuses on one specific student learning goal each year connected to their grade level or content area. CFGs, on the other hand, usually focus on multiple student learning goals in a given year. Each member selects a student learning goal from those identified by the faculty using the steps outlined in Chapter 3, and members take turns bringing their selected student need before the group at scheduled meetings (Silva, 2005).

The teacher bringing his or her students' need to the group is called the presenter, and the group helps him or her develop practices to address specific student needs. In this way, all group members obtain feedback connected to their student needs and instructional practices, and give feedback to all other group members.

Once the group has been formed, the first meeting will involve discussing and setting group norms (see Figure 7.3 for a handout to facilitate this process), deciding on a meeting schedule, and beginning the process of learning the meeting protocols from their trained group member. All CFGs meet at least once each month for two hours, but CFGs will be more effective if they meet for two hours twice each month. CFGs typically meet at school at the end of the school day, but it is not uncommon for them to schedule evening meetings at the homes of group members on a rotating basis. Once the group has been formed, the protocols taught, and the meeting schedule set, the group is ready to begin preparing for the first meeting.

For CFGs to be effective, group members must take turns carrying out specific roles for group meetings (Key, 2006; Supovitz, 2002):

- The *facilitator* distributes the agenda for the meeting and any discussion articles for the meeting, and works with the selected presenter to prepare for the meeting. The facilitator reviews the overall process and specific protocols at the outset of the meeting. During the meeting, the facilitator monitors time, draws all group members into the conversation, and helps to keep the discussion focused on the discussion article and the presenter's topic. Finally, at the conclusion of the meeting, he or she leads a brief summary of the meeting and reminds everyone of his or her roles for the following meeting.

- The *presenter* prepares an issue or topic for the group that is connected in some way to a professional dilemma and a selected student learning need in his or her classes. The presenter may want feedback on a new assignment, may seek ideas related to a classroom dilemma, or may want to explore how to best implement a new teaching approach. Unlike other collaborative teacher work described in this book, the presenter does not participate in the group discussion. He or she sits outside the group listening and taking notes, and then later responds to the feedback of the group.

- The *process observer* attends to group dynamics such as focus, domination, passivity, body language, and interruptions, and reports his or her observations at the end of the meeting. Having a process observer helps group members attend to the

Figure 7.3   A Process for Establishing Group Norms in CFGs

We are going to focus on setting some norms that will help our CFG work more effectively. By setting these norms we are accepting ownership for how we work as a group.

1. Think of behaviors that lead to effective collaborative group functioning

2. Examine the example norms listed below for ideas.

3. As a group, discuss the question, What norms might make our work together more effective and productive?

4. If you pose a norm, tell the group why the norm is important

5. Choose someone to record the group discussion.

6. After 10 minutes, stop and look for common themes to refine the list.

7. Determine which five norms will be most beneficial to our group work

The facilitator will reproduce this list and bring it to each CFG meeting.

Potential Group Norms

- Begin on time.
- End on time.
- Attend all meetings.
- Respect questions.
- Monitor your speaking time.
- Follow the meeting protocol
- Do assignments prior to meetings.
- Hold yourself personally accountable.
- Do not use argumentative language.
- Respect the group.
- Listen attentively.
- Attend to goals and objectives.
- Listen respectfully.
- Discuss issues, not people.
- Examine ideas; do not criticize people.
- Show respect for views of others.
- Don't interrupt while others are speaking.
- Assume positive intentions.
- Avoid use of cell phone and checking personal emails.

It's important to remember this is a starting point. The list may be revised after you have applied these as you work with your CFG. The list may also change as you work with other teachers in your school. We will develop our own list of norms for our CFG and revisit them in each session.

Source: Adapted from Curry (2008) and Quate (2008).

fact that respectful, active participation by all group members is needed for the group to function effectively.

- *Discussants* address the topic brought by the presenter and provide feedback that is cool (critical), warm (positive), and hard (questioning). All feedback should be given in a supportive manner, and discussants should also provide specific practical suggestions for making improvements.

Meeting Preparation

CFG meetings are highly structured and all group members need to be well prepared for them to be productive. Meeting preparation involves all of the following (Curry, 2008; Nave, 2000; Quate, 2008):

- The facilitator distributes the meeting agenda and articles for discussion at least one week before the meeting and secures a location for the meeting. Often, the facilitator will include a list of questions to promote thinking and reflection as group members read the articles. It is, of course, important that all group members read the chosen articles.
- The facilitator meets with the presenter to discuss the issue or work to be presented. They reflect on why the presenter wants to bring the particular work or issue to the group and how it is connected to specific student learning needs. Finally, they create an overarching question that best captures what the presenter hopes to gain from the discussion.
- The facilitator and the presenter select the protocol they feel will be most likely to lead to the results sought by the presenter. The founders of the Critical Friends strategy designed the protocols to remove the barriers that keep teachers from observing and providing useful feedback on one another's work. As educational researcher Marnie Curry (2008) emphasizes, "protocols are so valuable because they give CFG members permission to ask challenging questions, critique the practice of their peers, and offer explicit instructional advice" (p. 764). Each of the protocols has a specific purpose (see Figure 7.2). Some are intended to explore potential solutions to a problem or dilemma while others are targeted for examining student work. Some produce specific advice while others are meant to expand thinking on a particular issue. See Figures 7.4 and 7.5 for outlines of two frequently used protocols, the assignment protocol and the consultancy protocol.

The Meeting

Variations are common, but productive CFG meetings include five core steps (Hollins & McIntyre, 2004; Quate, 2008; Zepeda, 2007).

The Transition

Teachers come to CFG meetings after facing the challenges and frustrations of teaching all day, so it is important to give them an opportunity to switch gears before jumping right into the work of the meeting. A transition period of 10 to 15 minutes opens each meeting and is a way for members to ease from the pace of their teaching day to the topics they will be exploring in the meeting. The transition period, called *connections* by CFG researchers (Bambino, 2002), is intended to give group members time to reflect upon an issue, a thought, a story, or a question they are bringing into the meeting and then to connect it to the work of the meeting. The transition period is not meant to be a discussion, and the facilitator must encourage group members to keep their reflections short and concise. The rules for the transition period are simple: Speak if you want to, don't speak if you don't want to, and speak only once until everyone has had a chance to speak.

Discussing the Reading

The reading to be discussed is typically an article or a chapter from a book that addresses a dilemma or issue of importance to the group. For example, the middle school CFG described at the beginning of this chapter might read an article by Larry Lewin on teacher questioning strategies that could help them explore how to get their students to read in a deeper, more probing manner. An additional example comes from a CFG in a high school I visited, which decided to focus on portfolio assessments and discussed chapters from books written by Sue Clark Wortham and Clare Kilbane. One of the members then designed a portfolio assessment framework for their class that was discussed at the next meeting. I have even seen some CFGs substitute video clips for readings. Whether it is an article, a section of a book, or a video clip, the essential thing is that it stimulates members of the group to think about and discuss an important professional issue. The facilitator works to draw everyone into the reading or video discussion and keeps the length of this step between 30 and 45 minutes.

The Update

Regardless of the field, ongoing practice with feedback is an essential part of making improvements. The designers of the Critical Friends strategy recognized that one of the key problems with traditional professional development is the lack of follow-up opportunities for teachers. The update section of the meeting builds follow up into the CFG process. During the update, the presenter from the previous meeting reports on his or her progress in addressing the issue or question brought to the group at the last meeting (Curry, 2008). This update holds group members responsible for carrying through with their intentions, ensures that each member will receive ongoing feedback, and helps group members gain important professional insights from the work of their colleagues.

The Presenter and the Protocol

The facilitator begins this section of the meeting by reviewing group norms, reviewing the steps of the chosen protocol, and briefly describing the presenter's topic or issue. The presenter then describes the specific student learning goals he or she is concerned about, how he or she is working to address these needs, and poses the guiding question to frame the conversation.

The next step in most protocols (see Figures 7.4 and 7.5) is for the group to pose questions aimed at clarifying and better understanding the presenter's question and context. The facilitator makes sure the discussants avoid advice or suggestions as there will be opportunities for both later in the meeting. Clarifying questions are followed by probing questions, which challenge the presenter's thinking, encourage the presenter to question assumptions, and encourage the presenter to consider alternative perspectives.

The third, and longest, step of the protocol centers on group members discussing the presenter's goals, context, and guiding question. The presenter moves to a seat away from the group to listen and take notes, but not participate in the group discussion. This is meant to get the presenter reflecting on the comments of the group rather than his or her own responses. The facilitator keeps the conversation focused so the presenter's needs are met, encourages multiple perspectives to be voiced, and reminds group members to avoid speaking directly to the presenter. After approximately 30 minutes, the presenter rejoins the group. The presenter shares his or her notes with the group and asks questions of the members to better understand their perspectives and to acquire what is needed to address the question.

Debriefing

It is important that the group summarizes and reflects on the ideas and insights of the meeting. This is the time when group members can comment on their own professional learning, the learning of other group members, and the development of the group as a learning community. The facilitator encourages members to connect the meeting's discussions to their classroom practice and the learning needs of their students. The presenter follows with thoughts about how he or she intends to follow up on the ideas and suggestions from the group. The presenter will send out a more detailed follow-up plan to the group for feedback in the week after the meeting. The process observer shares his or her observations of the dynamics of the group during the meeting. If significant problems are noted, the group sets aside time at the beginning of the next meeting to address them. Finally, the facilitator concludes the meeting and reminds everyone who the presenter, facilitator, and process observer will be for the next gathering.

Between Meetings

For the Critical Friends strategy to be effective, group members should continue the work of improving their practice between meetings. In successful CFGs, group members observe one another teaching, meet in groups of two or three to examine student work, and have ongoing informal conversations connected to the unique student learning needs of each group member (Dufour, Eaker, & Many, 2006). For example, a high school CFG I know has mapped out a schedule for visiting one another's classes. They all receive feedback on their instructional practice and gain insights from observing the teaching of all the group members. In another CFG, group members meet weekly over lunch and rotate sharing ideas for alternative types of assessments. These meetings have resulted in all group members expanding their assessment repertoires. In both cases their weekly ongoing learning conversations have contributed to a stronger learning community, both within the group and the entire school, and have led to more interdisciplinary instruction in the classroom. As Marnie Curry (2008) states, "when CFGs continue their collaborative work between meetings, a true sense of mutual responsibility for the learning of the students in the building emerges, and teacher relationships move beyond polite congeniality to professional collaboration" (p. 758).

The Essential Elements of Critical Friends

Principals and teachers new to the Critical Friends strategy tend to focus on the surface features of the practice (specified group member

Figure 7.4   Steps in the Consultancy Protocol

The Consultancy Protocol

Purpose: To explore potential solutions to a professional dilemma

Steps

1. The facilitator reviews the steps of the protocol. The presenter describes their dilemma and then poses a focus question for the group. (10 minutes)

2. Clarifying questions are posed by the discussants (the other group members). Clarifying questions are for the benefit of the discussants since these questions are geared toward helping discussants better understand the presenter's dilemma and its context. (5 minutes)

3. The discussants ask the presenter specific questions. These questions are primarily for the benefit of the discussants. They ask the presenter "why" and are open-ended. Questions should be worded to help the presenter clarify and expand their thinking about the problem of practice that has been raised. The purpose is for the presenter to analyze and learn more about the issue they have brought to the group. The presenter responds to the discussants' questions, but the group does not discuss the responses of the presenter. (10 minutes)

4. The group discusses the dilemma brought by the presenter. What are potential solutions? What steps should be taken? What additional information is needed? The presenter moves outside the group, listens to the group discussion, and silently takes notes. (15 minutes)

5. The presenter moves back to the group and responds to the points raised in the discussion. The group remains silent. (5–10 minutes)

6. There is open discussion about the question or issue and potential strategies for the presenter to implement. (10–15 minutes)

7. The facilitator and process observer debrief the process. (5–10 minutes)

Source: Adapted from Quate (2008) and Zepeda (2007).

roles and structured meeting protocols), and they initially may view this approach as excessively rigid. However, as with all of the strategies discussed in this book, you must adapt it to your school's needs and context if it is to be effective. You may find that your CFGs want to add something to the meetings or shorten some aspects of them, but certain essential elements need to remain at the core of any Critical Friends adaptation if it is to result in improvements in teacher learning, teacher instruction, and student learning (Dufour, 2004).

Figure 7.5   Steps in the Assignment Protocol

The Assignment Protocol

Purpose: To obtain feedback on a new lesson

Steps

1. The facilitator reviews group norms and the steps of the protocol. The presenter describes the lesson, explains the student learning goals for the lesson, and poses a question to the group. (10 minutes)

2. Clarifying questions are posed by the discussants (the other group members). Clarifying questions are for the benefit of the discussants since these questions are geared toward helping discussants better understand the presenter's assignment and its context. (5 minutes)

3. The group (including the presenter) works through the assignment as if they were students. (10–15 minutes)

4. The presenter moves outside the group, listens to the group discussion, and silently takes notes.

5. The group discusses the assignment. What are the strengths and weaknesses of the assignment? What will students know, understand, and be able to do at the end of the assignment? What types of student thinking are needed to complete the assignment? Factual recall? Application of knowledge? Analysis of facts or issues? Synthesis of knowledge? How does the assignment connect to students' existing skills and knowledge? What questions does the assignment generate? What specific steps can be taken to improve the assignment? (20 minutes)

6. The presenter moves back to the group and responds to the points raised in the discussion. The group remains silent. There is then an open discussion about the assignment and potential strategies for the presenter to implement to improve it. Discussants also discuss insights the assignment has provoked for their own instructional practices. (10–15 minutes)

7. The facilitator and process observer debrief the process. (5–10 minutes)

Source: Adapted from Quate (2008) and Zepeda (2007).

Commitment From the Top

Guiding teachers to take ownership of their professional learning is one of the most challenging and important tasks faced by a principal. This can't be forced, so wise principals learn to lead from the side and involve teachers in the process of identifying student learning needs, specifying instructional needs, and selecting a particular professional development strategy (Nave, 2000). If the Critical Friends strategy is selected with faculty input, teachers are more likely to commit to the strategy and get something out of it.

Once Critical Friends is chosen, the principal needs to do all he or she can to support the CFGs by encouraging meetings, providing needed training, securing necessary resources, and carving out time for group meetings. "It is clear that ongoing, tangible administrative support is essential for the creation and maintenance of effective CFGs" (Dunne & Nave, 2000, p. 34). A principal who models inquiry and articulates the connections between CFG work and the mission of the school facilitates the development of effective CFGs. Another way the principal can communicate commitment to and support of Critical Friends is to work as a member of a CFG. This says in a powerful way that the principal is committed to continuing his or her own professional learning from and with his or her faculty. Furthermore, it helps the principal better understand the CFG and more effectively support the work of other CFGs in the school.

Training and Resources

Having witnessed schools trying to implement the Critical Friends strategy without training some of their faculty members in the CFG protocols, I strongly suggest that you don't skip this step. Protocols are critical to CFG work because they allow teachers to really analyze and critique teacher and student work without hurting feelings. The reason the training is so valuable is that it not only covers the basic elements of the CFG protocols, but it also helps participants better understand how to facilitate groups and engage them in deep conversations about professional practice. Due to teacher norms of isolation, "it is often quite beneficial, and even necessary, to train teachers new to CFGs in how to engage in productive collaborative professional discussions" (Supovitz, 2002, p. 1593).

In addition to providing training for some teachers, principals must attend to providing the resources, needed for CFGs to succeed. Time is the most valuable resource, and, regardless of your creativity, it will seem like a scarce commodity. In addition to setting aside time for CFGs to meet after school several times reach month, it also is important to carve out—and protect—time for CFG subgroups to meet during the school day between meetings. They need to be visiting one another's classes, collectively analyzing student work, and collaboratively reflecting on what they are learning.

Collaborative School Culture

While the Critical Friends strategy can strengthen and sustain an existing professional learning community, it is not likely to be successful if you do not have at least the beginnings of a context supportive of adult learning in place. "In schools with established cultures of collaborative adult professional learning, teachers view CFG work as natural and readily absorb themselves into their CFGs" (Bambino, 2002, p. 27). Trusting, collaborative teacher relationships are crucial in successful CFGs, and without a learning culture teachers will resist participating in CFGs or will work superficially. Even with an established collaborative culture, each CFG will need time to establish its particular group norms and to feel completely comfortable giving and receiving supportive, honest feedback.

Focus on Instructional Practice

The focus of the CFG must remain on group members improving their instructional practice so they are better able to address specific student learning needs. All group readings, meeting presentations, meeting discussions, and subgroup activities between meetings should be geared toward improving the instructional practice of group members and the learning of their students (Dunne & Nave, 2000). The feedback that group members provide to one another should not be focused on the presence or frequency of certain teacher behaviors, but rather on helping one another understand the result of their instructional practices on the thinking and learning of their students. "When groups spend their meeting time focused on the rigorous task of analyzing student work and seeking solutions to professional problems of practice, improvements in teacher knowledge and instructional practices are likely to follow" (Dunne & Honts, 2000, p. 5). The Critical Friends strategy is a powerful way to help teachers identify gaps in their own knowledge and skills, and it provides the setting, motivation, and support to close those gaps. When teachers learn together in CFGs they pool their knowledge, experience, and ideas, and expand their abilities to successfully teach their students.

Benefits of CFGs

There are many benefits associated with implementing the CFG approach to teacher professional learning. Specifically, schools and teachers engaged in CFG work stand to gain the following:

CFGs Foster a Culture
of Community and Collaboration

Through such activities as sharing ideas and student work samples, meeting to discuss problems, working to develop materials, and seeking advice about professional issues and problems, CFG work involves significant collaboration and supports the creation and maintenance of a professional learning community. Further, CFGs foster shared professional commitments and collective responsibility for student learning.

Finally, "participation in CFGs interrupts the norms of teacher isolation, creates collegial ties across departments and grades, promotes greater awareness of the student learning goals of other teachers, and leads to greater curricular coherence" (Curry, 2008, p. 764).

CFGs Enhance Teacher Professionalism

Participation in CFGs supports a teaching identity that is more profession oriented than technician oriented. Group members seek to continually experiment with teaching in order to learn and improve. They exhibit a sense of urgency in figuring out how to best meet the needs of their students. Participation in CFGs leads teachers to regularly have conversations with one another about how to better teach their students. As one CFG teacher said to me, "One of the big differences from our CFG work is that we no longer sit around and whine about things before school or between classes; instead, we behave like real professionals and share instructional ideas about how to improve what we do."

CFGs Influence Teacher Thinking and Practice

Results from multiple case studies demonstrate the changes in teacher knowledge and instructional practices that can result from teacher participation in CFGs (Curry, 2008; Nave, 2000). Teachers participating in CFGs often "shift from focusing on covering the curriculum to addressing student learning needs, more intentionally work to connect curricula, assessment strategies, and pedagogy, and move from teacher-centered to student-centered instructional approaches" (Franzak, 2002, p. 267). Curry (2008) adds that CFG work "heightens teachers' awareness and implementation of pedagogic best practices and helps them acquire a common language of academic rigor, rubrics, and assessment" (p. 758). One science teacher I know summed up the impact of CFG work on teacher practice by saying, "Not only did the group provide curricular support, it helped me extend my knowledge of how kids work, how kids think, and how I can design better learning experiences for them."

Summary

The Critical Friends strategy for teacher professional learning grew out of dissatisfaction with ineffective traditional methods of teacher professional development. The Critical Friends approach embodies all of the research-based characteristics of effective teacher professional learning: an emphasis on pedagogical content knowledge, a focus on student learning, implementation over time, a connection to teacher needs, and ongoing teacher collaboration. Through ongoing collaborative work, both in the full group structured meetings and the more informal subgroup sessions, the Critical Friends strategy is designed to accomplish the following:

- Build and sustain a professional learning community
- Make instructional practice explicit by discussing classroom practices
- Foster collaborative, reflective professional relationships
- Provide a context for teachers to better understand teaching and learning, and their work with students
- Help teachers translate educational theory into effective classroom instruction
- Provide a context for teachers to address student learning needs
- Improve teaching and student learning

At this point you may be wondering if you and your school have the time, energy, and effort required by the Critical Friends strategy. However, the investment of time and energy is well worth it as evidenced by both research reports and anecdotal stories showing that CFGs strengthen learning communities, enhance teacher collaboration, advance teacher's content knowledge, and lead to both improved classroom instruction and greater student achievement. Chapter 8 examines another highly collaborative approach, the teacher rounds strategy, which is patterned to some degree after medical rounds done in teaching hospitals.

8

School Rounds

Rounds is an approach that improves schools and teaching by engaging teachers in an ongoing process of examining and solving problems of practice.

—Elizabeth City

Claire hosted the rounds group earlier today as they visited her environmental science class and is looking forward to the post-rounds debriefing session and the perspectives of her colleagues. As part of a unit on global warming, she has been working on getting her students to more closely examine the sources and validity of ideas and information to consistently ask the questions, "How do we know this is accurate or true?" and "What conclusion is the best fit with the data?" Despite her efforts, she hasn't seen her students make much progress in this area and has been growing increasingly frustrated.

In the pre-rounds meeting, she described the activity she had planned for her class, explained why she chose it, specified the learning goals she has for the unit, and outlined the learning goals she has for her students this year. She asked the group to look for evidence about whether students were moving toward the intended learning targets. As she walked into the room for the debriefing, she was anxious to hear what the group had seen and what suggestions they had for improving student learning.

Claire opened the session asking, "Okay, did students show any inclination to evaluate the sources and validity of ideas and information, and did they challenge conclusions not backed up by good data?" "I saw several students in the group by the clock pause at one point and begin asking one another if they could trust the information given to them, but they did not seem to know how to take the next step," said Emma. "Yes," added Kerry, "that indicated to me that these students understand the need to know whether or not information comes from a reliable, valid source, but they may not understand how to then investigate and evaluate the source." "I agree that most of the students seem to understand the need to assess the reliability and validity of a source, but they are less clear on how to actually go about doing it," added Rena. "Yes, that is where my frustration lies," replied Claire. "I just don't see them understanding how to do this, and I feel like I've tried several different things with them. And because they have trouble actually assessing data and information, they have a tough time assessing the validity of alternative conclusions."

The remaining time in the session is spent discussing ways to help students take the next step and begin to appropriately examine the validity of the information and ideas they encounter. The tone of the discussion is nonjudgmental, and the focus is on how to design activities and learning environments to improve student learning. Claire feels supported to improve her instruction, rather than feeling evaluated. After the debriefing, Claire takes her notes from the session and watches the videotape of the rounds class. She thinks hard about what she sees students doing, what the rounds group has said, and what she has learned about how to adjust her instruction to bring about the desired learning. She prepares a post-rounds reflection and sends it out to the group for feedback.

Claire is doing something most educators have never done: look at classroom instruction in a focused, systematic, purposeful, and collective way. In the coming weeks and months the rounds group will continue to rotate, visiting one another's classrooms and will engage one another in dialogue about student work, student learning, and instructional practice. They are adopting a learning framework familiar to anyone who has watched a medical drama on television: doctors' rounds. In the school version, called teacher rounds, educators emulate the practice of doctors' rounds by visiting classrooms together and then discussing their notes and observations to make better "diagnoses" for improving instructional practices.

A Lesson From Medicine

The medical rounds process is the major way in which physicians develop their knowledge of practice and, equally importantly, the major way in which the profession builds and propagates its norms of practice. The medical rounds model embodies a specific set of ideas about how practitioners work together to solve common problems and to improve their practice. In typical rounds at a teaching hospital, interns and residents visit patients with a teaching physician, and review, discuss, and examine the evidence for particular diagnoses together (Teitel, 2010). After thoroughly analyzing the evidence, the most promising treatments are discussed and one or more are chosen.

Over the past two decades, several adaptations of medical rounds have been created in schools as educators have asked, "Why can't professional learning for teachers be more like how doctors learn in medical schools?" There are differences in what emerging models of rounds emphasize. One model, called teacher rounds, grew from the work of Del Prete (1990, 1997, 2010, 2013) and others at Clark University. Teacher rounds involves a team of teachers focused on improving instructional practices and student outcomes in their classrooms. Teacher rounds is a means for teachers to share knowledge about instructional practices and jointly consider how to best address the problems of practice they face. A second model, called instructional rounds, was developed by Dr. Richard Elmore (2002) and his colleagues at Harvard in the 1990s to better understand the instructional practices of an entire school or school system. In instructional rounds a team of educators visits classrooms to gather evidence about how to better understand and improve a problem of practice a school or district is seeking to solve. While instructional rounds focuses on broad instructional practices in a school or district, teacher rounds "strive to understand teaching and learning in detail and depth, in context, so that participants might better understand and develop their own practice" (Del Prete, 2013, p. 8). The details and descriptions in this chapter are a synthesis of the ideas and methods of both instructional rounds and teacher rounds. This chapter focuses on how the resulting synthesis, called "school rounds," can both improve the instructional practices of individual teachers and build a professional learning community.

A school rounds group is made up of four to six teachers who go through a rounds cycle two to three times each month. These groups are found in elementary, middle, and high schools. In teacher rounds, a teacher hosts a group of visiting colleagues in his or her classroom and engages them in discussion about student learning and instructional practices. School rounds are a way for teachers to share, understand, and reflect on their instruction and the problems of practice they face. Rounds provide teachers with opportunities to focus together on specific learning events before, during, and after they occur and to collectively "diagnose" how to improve outcomes for their students.

School rounds are an ongoing cycle of teacher instructional learning and improvement where groups of teachers work together to do the following (City, Elmore, & Fiarman, 2009; Del Prete, 2013).

- One member of the group (host teacher) plans a lesson to address a "problem of practice," a specific student learning need that has been difficult to meet.
- The host teacher holds a pre-rounds meeting to give the group the learning goals for the lesson and ask for feedback on specific items.
- The group observes the class and collects evidence on student learning for the host teacher.
- The group meets in a post-rounds debriefing session to discuss and reflect on the instruction and student learning from the observed lesson, and suggests how to adjust instruction to improve student outcomes.
- The host teacher watches a video of the lesson, reviews his or her notes from the debriefing session, and prepares a post-rounds reflection summarizing what has been learned about the problem of practice and how he or she plans to design instruction to meet learning goals.

School rounds puts all teachers in a learning mode and emphasizes that they can figure things out by working together to solve the professional challenges they face. The strategy says, "Let's take the evidence we gather, see where we are, and see what we think we need to do to make improvements." School rounds results in observing teachers identifying instructional practices they'll continue to use because they saw other teachers employing them effectively, identifying practices they currently use that they will now reexamine in light of what they observed, and identifying practices they don't currently use but will try because they saw other teachers use them well (Del Prete, 2013). While the concept of rounds is straightforward, many teachers find it difficult in the beginning because the strategy requires individuals to focus on evidence without being judgmental and asks teachers to determine what actually is happening in classrooms before discussing what should be happening.

The Rationale for School Rounds

The education profession has traditionally lacked a mechanism for sharing best practices and building a professional body of knowledge, and the teacher rounds strategy was designed to address this need (Fullan, 2007). School rounds is intended to be a way for educators to develop their knowledge of instructional practice and be a way to build and communicate a knowledge base of instructional best practices. School rounds is designed to place collaborative discussions of instruction at the center of teacher and school improvement efforts. Student outcomes and school culture improve when teachers regularly work together to observe, analyze, discuss, and understand instruction and student learning (City et al., 2009; Del Prete, 2013). The goal is to create a common understanding about what quality instruction is and how to best achieve it in the classroom. Furthermore, like medical rounds, school rounds is a mechanism for replacing ineffective practices with more effective ones.

School rounds is based on the premise that one of the key parts of improving practice is breaking down norms of teacher isolation and replacing them with norms of teacher observation. Several other professional development strategies also emphasize various forms of teacher observation, calling them learning walks, walk-throughs, classroom visitations, and other names. Rounds, however, is quite different from all of the strategies falling under the "walk-through" umbrella (Meirink & Meijer, 2007). Walk-throughs are often cursory, typically involve a small number of observers, and frequently result in simplistic messages about what needs to be fixed. Walk-throughs are frequently connected to teacher evaluation more than teacher learning, and judgments about whether a teacher is "good" or "bad" are made on the basis of checklists that have little to do with the direct experience of teachers in the classroom and the knowledge and skills they need to acquire to enhance student learning. Walk-throughs done in this way are "antithetical to teacher rounds and the principles of effective teacher professional learning" (Fullan, 2009, p. 105).

Unlike typical walk-throughs, school rounds focuses on teaching, not the teachers, and requires group members to develop and practice skills of observation and debriefing. The idea behind rounds is to get teachers working on their practice, to create a common language of instructional improvement, and to subject every teacher's practice to critique, scrutiny, and improvement (Marzano, 2011). As teachers participating in rounds take turns hosting visits and offering and taking criticism, they develop trust in the process and one another, and conversations move from polite congenial ones to direct and honest collegial ones. Greater candor also stems from the rounds' focus on description, rather than judgment, that grounds criticism in comments about observable phenomena in the class, rather than opinions and judgments.

The specific purposes of rounds include the following (Marzano, 2011):

- To promote dialogue among teachers linking theory and practice
- To support teacher efforts to assess student learning and student thinking
- To foster reflective and productive dialogue on instructional practice
- To build and sustain a learning community based on shared practice
- To build and sustain a learning community focused on understanding and improving the teaching-learning process

The Steps in School Rounds

The power of school rounds, like the medical rounds approach upon which it is based, is in the work and discussion that occurs during the process. The goal is to establish a process of continuously creating better learning opportunities and outcomes. This section describes the steps of the teacher rounds process—forming the group, pre-rounds orientation, rounds observation, post-rounds debriefing, post-rounds reflection—and the work that must take place at each step for the strategy to result in improved instructional practices and a stronger learning community (Del Prete, 2013; Sisk-Hilton, 2011).

Forming Rounds Groups

Traditionally it has been more common for medical rounds groups to be composed of physicians in the same specialty area, such as cardiology or neurology, but medical rounds groups involving physicians across specialty areas also occur. Likewise, depending on your professional development program goals and your unique context, school rounds groups can be composed of teachers from the same grade level, teachers from the same content area, or be composed of teachers from different grades and academic disciplines.

Of greater importance is the mix of experience levels within each rounds group. A medical rounds group comprises physicians with varying degrees of experience and expertise, ranging from recent medical school graduates to attending teaching physicians. This group composition helps less experienced physicians expand their knowledge and perspectives and learn the norms of the profession, and pushes more experienced physicians to stay on the cutting edge of research and best practices as they discuss proper treatments with the group. A mix of experience levels is also desirable when forming your school rounds groups to ensure that each group contains a variety of ideas, views, and methods. "Just as in a medical rounds group, a school rounds group with a variety of experience promotes the learning and growth of every member of the group" (City et al., 2009, p. 18).

One aspect where the school rounds approach diverges from the medical rounds model is the concept of an attending physician. In the medical rounds model the attending physician is the recognized leader of the group and typically provides the problems of practice that drive the work of the group. While school rounds groups involve teachers of varying experience and expertise, there is no "attending teacher" in each group, and group members rotate selecting problems of practice to drive the work of the group.

Problems of practice are the focus of the school rounds group (Del Prete, 2013). A problem of practice is a student learning goal that is not being met despite repeated attempts by the teacher. The teacher bringing the problem of practice to the group is called the rounds host. Group members rotate bringing their problems of practice to the group, and they seek diagnoses regarding why previous treatments (instructional approaches) have not worked and offer suggestions about alternative treatments (instructional strategies). In this way, all group members obtain feedback connected to their student needs and instructional practices and give feedback to all other group members.

The school rounds strategy requires great trust and commitment from teachers, so it is essential that a context supportive of adult learning must be in place in the school. Even with a collaborative culture in place, once groups are formed they will need to set expectations and norms to support a culture of trust, problem solving, and continuous improvement. It is particularly important to establish, and frequently revisit, collaborative norms that encourage participants to move beyond the land of nice to a culture of respectful challenge (see Figure 8.1 for suggested collaborative norms for rounds groups). "The ultimate goal of rounds is to solve problems of practice, and thereby improve instruction, but this can only happen if participants regularly engage in dialogue which challenges ineffective teaching approaches" (City et al., 2009, p. 54).

Once norms have been set, the group decides on a schedule. The rounds cycle of pre-rounds orientation, rounds observation, post-rounds debriefing, and post-rounds reflection takes place two to three times each month. The pre-rounds orientation typically is held before school and the post-rounds debriefing is held after school. With norms and a schedule in place, the group is ready to begin the rounds cycle.

Figure 8.1 Norms of Collaboration for School Rounds

1. **Paraphrasing**—Paraphrasing what others have said before putting forth your own view helps members of the group to hear and understand each other as they discuss things.

2. **Pausing**—Pausing before responding or asking a question communicates care and thoughtfulness, allows time for processing and thinking, and contributes to effective dialogue, discussion, and decision making.

3. **Probing**—Using open-ended probes or inquires such as "Please say more . . ." or "Can you tell me more about . . ." or "Then, are you saying . . . ?" increases efficiency and focus of the group's thinking.

4. **Challenging conclusions**—The goal is to come up with better treatments (instructional approaches) for the problems of practice brought to the group so participants must consistently challenge one another's conclusions about effective instruction. For example, you might say, "What evidence suggests that is effective?" or "Why is that approach better than this other approach?"

5. **Putting ideas on the table**—Ideas are the core of meaningful collaboration. Group members must be mindful to own their ideas and specify the intention of their ideas as they put them out for the group to consider them.

6. **Attending to self and others**—Meaningful collaboration and discussion are promoted when each group member monitors what they are saying, how they say it, and how others in the group respond to their words and actions. This includes paying attention to your learning style, and the learning styles of others, when planning for and participating in group meetings. Responding to others in their own language forms is one manifestation of this norm.

7. **Assuming positive intentions**—Assuming that other group members have positive intentions eliminates unintentional rebukes and keeps the dialogue positive and productive. Using positive intentions in your speaking is one example of this norm.

8. **Pursuing a balance between advocacy and inquiry**—Maintaining a balance between advocating for a position and inquiring about one's own and others' positions assists the group in keeping the focus on solving problems of practice.

Source: Adapted from Garmston and Wellman (2009).

Rounds Preparation

The host teacher selects a problem of practice and prepares a one-page rounds sheet for group members, which includes these sections:

The *background* describes the problem of practice, instructional approaches used to address the problem in the past, and the specific approach the host teacher is using in the present lesson. It may also give some perspective on the place of the learning goals and learning activity in the course curriculum, and it will refer to any research that has been used to design the current lesson.

The *focus* specifies the specific learning goals for the lesson/activity. The *rounds questions* list three to five queries focused on student learning in relation to instructional practice to guide the observations of the group members. For example, Claire, the environmental science teacher in the vignette at the beginning of this chapter, asked, "Do students question the validity and reliability of sources during activity one of the lesson?"

The host teacher leads a brief (10–15 minutes) pre-rounds orientation meeting on the morning of the rounds lesson, giving each group member a rounds sheet and explaining the problem of practice, the specific student learning goals of the lesson, and the rounds questions they have constructed to guide the observations of group members. Group members have opportunities to ask questions to make sure they understand all aspects of the rounds sheet.

The Rounds Lesson

Group members sit around the periphery of the classroom for focused observation based on the student learning goals and rounds questions from the orientation meeting. Group members must learn to be nonjudgmental and to remember that their job is to collect meaningful evidence directly related to the work of teaching and learning. Unlike lesson study, observers may speak with students at appropriate times to gain insight about what students are doing and thinking (Marzano, 2011). It is important for observers to focus on what students are actually doing, not what the teacher has asked them to do. Just as a physician consults with their patients to obtain evidence regarding the success of a treatment, educators should more frequently speak with students to gather evidence about the success of an instructional approach (Egodawatte & McDougall, 2010). For example, an observer of Claire's environmental science class may say to a student, "I heard you say that you need to know if the information is valid, and I'm wondering how you are going go about making that determination." It is important to understand how students engage with an activity or a lesson to get an accurate picture of its success or failure.

The Debriefing

The purpose of the post-rounds debriefing is to examine and discuss the collected evidence of the group from the rounds lesson and reach a consensus about what they saw and what they have learned. The debriefing is often a powerful learning experience as one teacher new to rounds makes clear by saying, "I came into the group feeling I was a pretty good judge of good teaching, but as soon as my team members started sharing their observations I realized I had much to learn." There are three steps in the debriefing process (Del Prete, 2013; Marzano, 2011):

1. Group members describe the evidence they gathered. They focus on evidence directly related to the problem of practice of the host teacher, avoid judgmental or editorial comments, and strive to listen and learn as others speak.

2. The group organizes the evidence that has been gathered and collectively asks what it tells them about student learning and student thinking. In the vignette at the beginning of this chapter, the group members saw a pattern emerge from their observations indicating that students were getting stuck at a particular stage of the intended learning process. Once the evidence has been analyzed and a diagnosis has been made, the group can move to a discussion of potential instructional options to improve student outcomes.

3. Proposed courses of action are suggested and discussed to address the stated problem of practice and bring about improved student outcomes.

Taken together, the debriefing steps encourage group members to describe the specific behaviors, structures, and approaches they see that cause, enable, or impede learning. The focus is on improving teaching and learning by developing clarity about what works and what does not work with students in the classroom.

Post-Rounds Reflection

The post-rounds reflection is done by the host teacher to summarize and document what has been learned about instruction and student learning related to the problem of practice. The host teacher reviews a video of the rounds lesson, reads notes from the debriefing session, and reflects on how he or she plans to adjust instruction to bring about better student outcomes. The written reflection is then sent to the other group members for feedback and is revised by the host teacher based on that feedback.

The post-rounds reflection serves several important purposes. First, it is a way for the rounds group to summarize for themselves what they have learned about student thinking, student learning, and instruction, and to pose additional questions for future rounds lessons. (Claire, for example, may want to try the group's suggested instructional adjustment when her next rounds lesson turn comes up.) Second, it provides a mechanism for sharing the group's learning with other teachers at their school. This sharing contributes to a stronger professional learning community, ensures that teachers throughout the school can learn from one another's efforts, and builds over time a shared knowledge base about effective instruction.

The post-rounds reflection centers on the host teacher's problem of practice and how he or she can adjust instruction to solve it, but this stage of the rounds process can also be an occasion for reflecting on teaching and learning in relation to broad questions linked to the behaviors, attitudes, knowledge, and skills teachers want to see in their students (see Figure 8.2 for examples of these broad questions).

Figure 8.2 Broad Learning Questions for the Post-Rounds Reflection

A Learning Community

- What did we learn about how different students work together? In what sense did they cooperate or collaborate? Did all students have an equal chance to participate?
- Did students support one another in learning? Did they encourage one another? Did they work to understand one another? Did they support one another in expanding their thinking?
- Were students actively involved in learning?

Student Thinking Habits

- What questions did students ask that indicate their willingness to inquire and reflect?
- Did students demonstrate openness to alternative ways of thinking and communicating?
- Did students demonstrate an inclination to examine the source and validity of ideas? For example, did they ask, "How do we know that is true?"

(Continued)

(Continued)

- Did students reflect on the significance of what they were learning? Did
- they ask, for example, "Why is it important to learn this?" or "So what?"
- Did students reflect on their own thinking? Did they talk about what they were trying to do or learn and how?
- Did students discuss how they were going about things and whether there might be other possibilities?

Student Language

- What are the patterns of student talk? Are students elaborating on what they are learning and describing things in their own words? What does their language say about what they do and don't understand?
- How does student language reflect an understanding of how knowledge is developed in this specific discipline?

Understanding of Content

- Were students developing their own understanding of content? How do you know?
- To what extent did students develop depth and breadth of understanding? How do you know?
- Did students gain understanding considered essential in this discipline?

Modes of Learning

- What different modes of learning (e.g., kinesthetic, interpersonal, visual) were targeted in the student activity? How did different students respond?

Source: Adapted from Del Prete (2013).

Learning With Rounds

Why have medical rounds been so successful in the professional learning of physicians, and why does the school rounds model hold such promise for the professional growth of educators? Five important learning principles lie at the core of both medical rounds and school rounds (City et al., 2009; Del Prete, 2013), and it is the combination of these principles that explains why rounds is such a powerful teacher professional learning approach.

- *We improve the work by doing the work, reflecting on the work, and critiquing the work.* People learn best by doing, not by reading about how to do something or being told how to do something. Teachers need opportunities to practice new approaches, integrate new ideas, receive feedback, reflect on the work, express feelings and understandings about the work, and critique the work.

Rounds provides these opportunities and helps convert questions about problems of practice into individual and collective learning.

- *Focus on the practice, not the person.* The rounds process is based on the premise that for schools to improve teachers must develop shared best practices and a shared understanding of the relationship between effective instruction and excellent student outcomes. This is best done by separating people from their practices, and by focusing on the teaching instead of the teacher. The focus must be on developing and implementing increasingly more effective instructional practices while discarding practices shown to be ineffective.

- *Learning is both a solitary and group activity.* Rounds is designed to transform isolated, individualized practices into collective practices. The goal is to have individual teachers and entire schools learning at the same time. It is the accumulation of learning across classrooms and schools that improves learning and student performance.

- *Trust is essential for individual and group learning.* Collaborative learning requires a sense of trust so that individuals can freely share their questions and understandings without fear of judgment by colleagues. Rounds leads to a common language for describing and analyzing instructional practice and common norms for collective learning that build trust among educators. Teachers must feel safe enough to break away from the "land of nice," where they are reluctant to give and receive feedback on their instruction.

- *Learning improves individual and group effectiveness.* When teachers develop greater understanding about the cause-and-effect relationship between how teachers teach and how and what students learn, the instruction of the entire school improves. The efficacy of the group depends on collective work and collective understanding. Ideas and best practices must move up through individual teachers to the group level for significant improvements in student learning to occur schoolwide.

Summary

Your goal as a school leader is to improve student learning, so your first challenge is to improve the instructional practices of your teachers. It sounds so simple, but schools have not traditionally been focused on helping teachers enhance their knowledge and instructional practice. If we want to improve instruction, we need to identify the gaps between what we want our students to know and be able to do and what they actually do know and are able to do. Then we must make classroom walls transparent, and get teachers working together to examine the best ways to design instruction so that the identified gaps in student learning can be closed.

If professional development in the form of medical rounds can save lives, why can't we develop a professional learning strategy for teachers that helps to save minds? Is the educational health of our children so much less important than their physical health? Why can't we develop a way to eliminate ineffective teaching practices and replace them with more effective ones? Modeled after medical rounds, the school rounds process was developed in response to these types of questions. School rounds gets small groups of teachers focused on the instructional core—the actual interactions between teachers, students, and content in the classroom. Like lesson study and Critical Friends, the rounds process is a powerful strategy for getting teachers collaborating in meaningful ways about teaching and learning. Teachers examine problems of practice together, design instructional approaches to solve those problems, provide feedback to one another after observing actual classroom instruction, and assess the success/failure of their attempts to improve instruction and student learning. Through this process, teachers collectively come to a better understanding about what quality instruction is and what it looks like, discard ineffective teaching approaches, and build up a shared knowledge about best instructional practices within their group and the entire school. "The rounds focus on classroom instruction anchors professional learning efforts and provides an essential source of data to inform educators whether their instructional improvement efforts are actually influencing student learning" (Fullan, 2009, p. 111).

The last three chapters have focused on three strategies with much in common. Lesson study, Critical Friends, and teacher rounds all involve small groups of teachers collaboratively examining problems of practice, and designing and testing new instructional approaches. All three can be used to help build and sustain professional learning communities and foster the ongoing growth and development of teachers in your school. The strategies discussed in the next three chapters (action research, mentoring, and peer coaching) may be used by themselves but are often used in combination with one or more of the other strategies discussed in this book. Action research, mentoring, and peer coaching may be done in small groups, but more commonly they involve pairs of teachers working together on very specific aspects of professional practice. As each is discussed, be thinking about the best mix of approaches for your needs and context.

9

Action Research

Educators advance their instruction and enhance student learning when they examine and assess their own work as researchers and then adjust their teaching based on the results.

—Ernest Stringer

In their school's professional development goal-setting process, Rhoda and the two other kindergarten teachers identified developing literacy skills as a student learning need. Helping children expand their vocabularies is an important part of achieving this goal, and the three teachers have grown increasingly frustrated with this task over the past year. Their collective question—"How can we better help our students expand their vocabularies?"—leads the group to investigate best practices in this area.

"I would like to implement the Picture Word Inductive Model (PWIM) to see if it will help them improve their vocabulary learning," Rhoda says. "I'm skeptical about that approach because I think it may be too demanding for our students," says Anne. "I also have my doubts," Debbie adds, "but the research I've done indicates this approach has been successful in many schools, so I say let's test it out." The kindergarten team develops a plan for testing their chosen approach with their students. "Okay, what types of data do we need to collect to help us evaluate this new approach?" asks Anne. "We definitely need to keep track of the numbers and types of words they learn for several units and compare this to what we have been seeing in the past," says Debbie. "Yes," adds Rhoda, "and I think we also need to video our classes so we can gather information about how the children respond to the new approach." "Great," says Debbie. "Maybe we even should ask our children questions about the new approach to get their perspective."

Over the next month the teachers try the new approach and gather various types of data. They then meet to examine the data, discuss what it means, and make decisions about what modifications in instructional practice, if any, should be made on the basis of the data. "All of our classes showed gains," Rhoda says, "with students achieving a mean gain of 12 sight vocabulary words in unit 4 and a mean gain of 20 sight words in unit 5." "I collected more detailed data in my class on each child's word knowledge before and after unit 5, and on the specific strategies individual students were using," says Anne. "I saw your data, and it not only indicates a gain in the number of words known, but also an expansion in the strategies children are using," Debbie says. Based on their data, the group decides to adopt the PWIM approach to help their students expand their vocabularies. Over the course of the school year the kindergarten team continues to use this process of action research to examine other student learning needs they have identified.

Action research is quite different from typical educational research because those most responsible for and most directly connected to student learning—the teachers—are the ones conducting it (Huang, 2010). Rather than dealing with the theoretical, action research allows practitioners to address those concerns that are closest to them, ones over which they can exhibit some influence and change in a positive direction. The utility and power of action research lies in the idea that teaching and student learning improves when educators use research techniques to carefully and systematically examine their own instructional practices. "The idea of action research is that educational problems and issues are best identified, investigated, and solved where the action is: with teachers at the classroom level. When teachers engage in research activities with their own students, findings can be applied immediately and problems solved more quickly" (Miller & Greenwood, 2003, p. 15).

A Hands-On Approach

I often hear teachers complain that the professional development activities at their school are not relevant to them and the challenges they face. Action research guarantees relevance because the focus is always determined by the teachers themselves. Action research directly addresses the problem of the division between theory and practice. Unlike traditional educational research, action research is carried out by teachers with their students and at their schools on questions they generate about the problems they face in their daily work with students.

Rooted in the work of educational Progressives like John Dewey, action research was first introduced to schools in the 1950s by Stephen Corey, who believed that "researching our own teaching is more likely to change and improve our practices than reading about the theories of somebody else" (Corey, 1953, p. 70). It is now growing in popularity in response to the recognized need for more relevant and practical knowledge in education. Action research is a way for teachers to grow and learn by making use of their own experiences. It is a process in which teachers systematically study and reflect on their work and then make informed changes in their practices (McNiff & Whitehead, 2006). Action research can involve a single teacher investigating an issue in his or her classroom, but more commonly it involves a small group of teachers working on a common problem. Action research is different from the traditional notion of educational research as there is less concern for universality of findings, and more value is placed on the relevance of the findings to teachers and the school. As action research proponent William Borg (1981) emphasizes, "action research involves teachers in solving problems in their own classrooms and has as its primary goal teacher training and improvement rather than acquisition of general educational theoretical knowledge" (p. 53).

Effective action research is *not* a narrow, limited practice but instead uses a range of methodologies to better understand practice and solve specific problems (Ferrance, 2000). It is *not* problem solving in the sense of trying to find out what is wrong, but rather is a quest for knowledge about how to improve. Action research is *not* about doing research on or about students, or finding all available information on a topic looking for the correct answers. It involves teachers working to improve their skills, techniques, and strategies. Action research is *not* about learning why we do certain things, but rather how we can do things better. It is about how we can change our instruction to enhance student learning. The entire process involves evaluating teacher practice to improve instruction in the classroom (Koshy, 2005). There are six important process characteristics of effective action research (Glanz, 2005; Schmuck, 2006; Zepeda, 2007).

1. It is practical and leads to changes in professional practice through the reviewing of current data.

2. It is a participative process in which teachers work together to learn how to solve a real problem in their practice.

3. It empowers teachers to believe they can influence and contribute to the improvement of their instruction and their schools.

4. It is an interpretive process where the perceptions and attitudes of participants are gathered during the inquiry.

5. It is a tentative process that is focused on getting solutions from the diverse views of participants.

6. It is critical, being centered on finding practical improvements for the situation at hand while also seeking to create positive change for the whole school.

Action research is an ongoing process of work and reflection that involves six cyclical steps (Hewitt & Little, 2005; Schmuck, 2006):

1. A concern about how to improve or better understand some aspect of classroom practice leads to specific questions that become the focus of the investigation.

2. A plan is developed about how to answer the research questions.

3. Data are collected to address the research questions.

4. The practitioner examines and reflects on the meaning of the data with colleagues.

5. Decisions and actions are made based on the data and the discussions with colleagues.

6. The results of the investigation are shared with other colleagues in the school.

Through this cycle, which is repeated multiple times for each group in a given school year, teachers gain valuable information to enhance their teaching skills. Action research has the potential to generate genuine and sustained improvements in schools. It gives educators new opportunities to reflect on and assess their teaching; to explore and test new ideas, approaches, and materials; to assess the effectiveness of the new approaches; to share feedback with colleagues; and to make decisions about which new approaches to include in the group's curriculum, instruction, and assessment plans.

Why Choose Action Research?

Action research provides teachers with a professional development experience that is quite different from traditional approaches. Four important themes underlie the utility of action research: empowerment of teachers, collaboration through participation, acquisition of knowledge, and improvement in instructional practice. Action research is useful in schools because of the following (Caro-Bruce, 2008; Fairbanks & LaGrone, 2006; Sagor, 2000):

- Current theories and programs are not the products of practitioners. Action research changes this because teachers, who have the most significant influence on student outcomes, develop it. The conventional research paradigm of education professors formulating the research questions and doing basic research while teachers apply the outcomes is rejected in favor of teachers formulating the questions and acting to bring about change. The premise of action research is that educational problems are best identified and investigated at the classroom level. By integrating research into classroom settings and engaging teachers in research activities, findings can be applied immediately and problems solved more quickly.

- For schools and teaching to improve, those most directly involved (teachers) in impacting student outcomes must be committed to planned changes. Action research has been shown to enhance teacher commitment to improving their instruction (Marzano, 2007). Action research is inherently rewarding because teachers are in control of their professional learning, and are able to tailor everything to address the most significant challenges they face in their daily work with students. Traditional professional development can impede the development of teacher efficacy by treating them as empty receptacles to be filled with knowledge, while action research recognizes that teachers can identify what they need, can examine their own work using research techniques, and can use data to improve their instruction. Teacher commitment is enhanced because their thinking, their questions, and their instruction are placed at the center of professional development.

- Action research recognizes that teachers need time to reflect on their work and test new instructional approaches if they are to improve their teaching and student outcomes. Time for this important work is typically not built into traditional professional development activities. Teachers who regularly reflect on their work with colleagues influence student outcomes because they question their assumptions, test new ideas, look thoughtfully and critically at their own instructional practices, and use data from a variety of sources.

One of the most powerful aspects of action research is that it prods teachers to ask questions about their practice. What is working in my classroom, in my teaching? Who is learning? Who is being left out? How does the curriculum provide opportunities to learn? What things are my students just not getting? Questions such as these can be uncomfortable to ask, and they may produce even more discomforting answers. But unless and until teachers step out of their comfort zones to grapple with the hard questions, teaching and learning won't improve. As educational researcher Sally Zepeda (2007) says, "Action research works because it leads teachers to ask tough questions, collect different types of data, consider instructional alternatives, and weed out ineffective instructional approaches, all in the service of improving student learning" (p. 266).

The Action Research Process

The specific form that action research takes will be dependent on the contextual characteristics of your school and the teachers who engage in the process. However, certain elements are necessary if the strategy is to have an effect on school culture, classroom instruction, and student achievement. Figures 9.1 and 9.2 outline the essential elements of the action research process. The process is intended to result in opportunities for teachers to learn about academic content, instructional best practices, and how students best learn (Miller & Greenwood, 2003).

Individuals or Groups?

A single teacher focusing on a specific issue in his or her classroom can do action research. A teacher may be seeking solutions to problems related to classroom management, or may be investigating how to improve student learning in a specific area. Regardless of the actual type of problem, individual action research may be appropriate and beneficial when no other teachers share the problem *and* the problem can be addressed on an individual basis.

Of course, one of the major drawbacks of individual action research is that the ideas, perspectives, and feedback of colleagues are not part of the process. Because collaboration with colleagues is such an important part of professional growth and learning, group action research is the preferred approach when implementing action research in your school (Brighton & Moon, 2007). Group action research may include as few as two teachers or as many as four or five. A shared

Figure 9.1 The Action Research Cycle

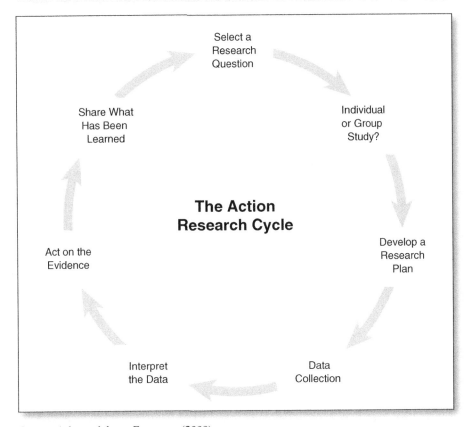

Source: Adapted from Ferrance (2000).

Figure 9.2 Steps in the Action Research Process

Action Research Steps	Processes for Each Step
Step 1: Individual or group?	Decide if problems of practice fit better with individual or group action research
Step 2: Selecting a focus	Formulate a concise, higher-order question focused on a significant problem of practice
Step 3: Developing a plan	Establish a plan (with timeline) to answer the question
Step 4: Collecting data	Gather data needed to answer your question; data should be both qualitative and quantitative
Step 5: Analyzing and interpreting data	Reflect with colleagues on the meaning of the data
Step 6: Taking action	Modify instructional practice based on the meaning of the data
Step 7: Writing and sharing	Summarize what has been learned and share it with colleagues

Source: Adapted from Glanz (2003).

problem of practice is the determining factor in the size of the group. For example, in the story at the beginning of this chapter, three kindergarten teachers came together around a common frustration in helping their students expand their vocabularies. Another example would be four English teachers across grade levels in an upper school coming together to investigate how to improve writing instruction.

Like many of the collaborative approaches discussed in this book, groups may form within a grade level, within a specific academic discipline, or across grade levels and academic disciplines. However, unlike lesson study, Critical Friends, and teacher rounds, action research groups tend to be much more fluid as groups form, disband, and new groups form multiple times in one school year. For example, after the group of three kindergarten teachers completes their study of which instructional approaches enhance vocabulary acquisition, they may find that other problems of practice are best explored with a different combination of colleagues.

As with the size of the group, the key factor determining the composition of the group is each member sharing a problem of practice with the other members. More than with any other strategy discussed in this book, action research group membership will change frequently depending on your school and the unique challenges faced by your teachers (Glanz, 2005). This aspect of action research keeps the focus of the strategy squarely on the primary purpose of professional development: finding ways to improve classroom instruction and student learning.

Selecting a Focus

Many teachers find that the most difficult part of beginning action research is learning how to frame a good question. Good questions emerge from the challenges teachers face in their daily work and from the gaps in student learning, behavior, and motivation that teachers are struggling to address (see Figure 9.3 for a worksheet to help teachers generate action research questions). A teacher may want to examine how to motivate struggling students to become more actively involved in class or to help students understand a specific concept more deeply. Most teachers have more than one question they want to investigate, but it is important to limit each action research study to one question that is meaningful and doable in the parameters of their daily work. In addition, teachers should ask themselves why a particular question interests them, how they might go about answering it, and what the benefit would be of answering it. Finally, the

Figure 9.3   Worksheet for Generating Action Research Topics and Questions

1. One part of my teaching I would really like to improve is . . .

2. I don't understand . . .

3. My students seem to particularly struggle with . . .

4. I wonder what would happen if . . .

5. Something I need/would like to change is . . .

6. An instructional approach I would like to try in my class is . . .

7. I want to learn more about . . .

8. Something that would make a big difference with my students is . . .

9. Something that really frustrates me is . . .

Source: Adapted from Caro-Bruce (2008) and Zepeda (2007).

question should be connected in some way to the student needs identified during the goal-setting process for the school professional development program.

So what makes for a good question? There are several criteria to keep in mind (Brighton & Moon, 2007; Johnson, 2011). First, the question should be a higher-order question that cannot be answered with *yes* or *no*. Second, it should be stated in common language, free of educational jargon. The question should use simple everyday words that are clear to all. Third, questions should be chosen for which the answer is not known in advance. Fourth, questions should focus on practices that influence student achievement, behavior, and/or motivation. Fifth, questions should motivate teachers to take action to find answers for them.

An important guideline in selecting a question is to ask if it is something over which the teacher has control. Is it something of interest and worth the time and effort that will be invested? Often there is a specific problem that is readily identifiable. Or the problem to be studied may come from a feeling of discomfort or frustration in the classroom. For example, a teacher may be using the latest fashionable teaching method, without really knowing or understanding what or how students are learning. Finally, it is important for teachers to remember to keep their question narrowly focused on the specific area where they seek improvement. The broader the focus, the more difficult it is for teachers to know if what they are investigating and learning is making any significant difference.

Creating a Plan

This step encourages teachers to think like researchers so they don't jump to collecting data without carefully considering the types of data they will need to gather to answer their question. In developing their plan, educators should gather information to make sure they have a clear understanding about the issue/area they are investigating. This may include consulting with colleagues (both in their school and from other schools) who wrestle with similar issues and reviewing research-based best practices on the topic of their action research study. Once teachers begin to implement their plan, to actually begin their investigation, their plan will change as new ideas, questions, and understandings emerge. A good plan specifies the steps the teacher will take to answer their question, including a timeline for each step, and details the types of data to be collected to answer their question (Caro-Bruce, 2008). See Figure 9.4 for a worksheet teachers can use as they develop their action research plan.

Figure 9.4   Worksheet for Developing an Action Research Plan

1. Research topic:

2. Research question:

3. Timeline:

Steps to be taken	By what date?	Who is responsible?	Resources needed

4. Data collection:

Data tools and sources	Purpose of the data	When will it be collected?

Source: Adapted from Caro-Bruce (2008).

In developing their plan, teachers should pose and answer the following questions (Stringer, 2007):

- What is it that I want to know and why do I want to know it? How will this knowledge help me improve my instruction and student learning?
- What instructional modification will I test in my study? The modification you are testing is your proposed solution to your problem of practice. The solution will be a new instructional technique, strategy, new environment, or new material that you feel has potential to correct the problem.
- What is the sequence of steps for my study, and what is the timeline for my study?
- Do I need to investigate best practices in this area to inform my study? Who can help me do this?
- What types of data do I need to collect to answer my question, and how will I collect the data?
- Who can help me develop data collection instruments, and who can help me collect my data?

Collecting Data

Many teachers do not have a strong background in data collection and analysis, and may be apprehensive about this step. However, extensive knowledge about data collection is not needed to do action research. Data collection begins by answering several questions: "What do I want to learn?" "What evidence do I need to convince myself I have answered my question?" and "When, where, and how will I collect that evidence?"

It is important to collect both quantitative and qualitative types of data (Caro-Bruce, 2000). Quantitative data are numerical, and examples include surveys, graded student work, report cards, and attendance records. Qualitative data is highly descriptive and non-numerical, and examples include interviews, observation notes, video recordings, and journals. Action researchers collect data from more than one source, at more than a single point in time, to get a balanced view of the issue they are investigating and increase the validity of what they are learning. In fact, teachers doing action research "should collect at least three different forms of data to make sure the results they are getting are real and will stand up to scrutiny" (Schmuck, 2006, p. 97). Teachers should be prodded to select data sources from multiple perspectives to provide them with breadth, to select data sources that go beneath the surface of their question to provide them with depth, and to search for corroborating data sources during their study to confirm what they are learning (Caro-Bruce, 2008).

As teachers collect data during their study, they may revise their data collection strategy. It is important that they repeatedly remind themselves of what they want to learn and why they want to learn it to make sure the data they are collecting are directly connected to those goals. Staying true to their research question leads teachers to implement a data collection process based on curiosity and problem solving. The research journal is the place where teachers can write about what they are doing in their study, what the data are telling them, what they are learning about their question, and tentative thoughts about how they may modify their instruction. A well-organized research journal can be extraordinarily useful when it comes time to analyze and interpret data and to make decisions about what to do based on that data. It provides context for the data and helps the teacher to keep a record of how their thinking has evolved over the course of the study.

Analyzing and Interpreting Data

Data analysis and interpretation is about teachers making sense of their experience with action research. The bottom line in this step is that you are trying to determine whether your proposed solution had an impact on solving your problem of practice. It is a messy and exciting step as teachers work to synthesize what they have learned and bring all of the disparate pieces of evidence together into a concise summary of the investigation. Even when action research has been conducted by an individual teacher, it is important for teachers to collaborate on this step so that important patterns and themes are not missed and potential conclusions can be challenged (McNiff &Whitehead, 2006).

Teachers should follow these steps as they analyze and interpret their data (Anderson, Herr, & Nihlen, 2007):

- *Count and look for patterns.* For your quantitative data, what do the numbers tell you about your question? Do your quantitative data suggest a course of action you can take to solve your problem of practice? If you have been trying a new teaching approach, do the numbers support its effectiveness in improving student learning? In the vignette at the beginning of this chapter, the quantitative data collected by the kindergarten team supported their new teaching approach and suggested how the teachers could move toward solving the problem of practice underlying their action research project. If you also collected qualitative data, ask yourself if any themes, patterns, or big ideas emerge from your observations, interviews, and journal notes. Ask yourself what story is told by your qualitative data. Confidence in your conclusions justifiably grows when both your qualitative and quantitative data suggest a particular course of action to take to solve your problem of practice. On the other hand, when your qualitative and quantitative data point to different conclusions you would be wise to reflect on potential reasons for the disparities with colleagues before you decide on the steps you will take to address your problem of practice.

- *Share the evidence with colleagues.* Whatever your initial conclusions may be, it is important to reflect on them with colleagues. Ask colleagues how they interpret your data and encourage them to challenge your initial conclusions.
- *Examine what different conclusions could be drawn from the data.* Work with colleagues to generate alternative meanings for the data, and ask one another if multiple conclusions are consistent with the evidence gathered.
- *Revisit assumptions about the students and the learning situation.* Work with colleagues to surface and challenge assumptions you may have about your own instruction, and student thinking and learning. Ask yourself if these assumptions have influenced your interpretation of the data in any way.
- *Formulate a trial explanation.* Generate an explanation that you feel is best supported by the evidence you have gathered and state the reasons underlying your conclusions.

Taking Action

The traditional researcher gains insights through research findings and builds associated theories, but the central purpose for teachers engaged in action research is "How will our instruction change now that we have all of this new information?" Action research is a unique form of research because it includes immediate action as an essential component of the process. This can be either by revising your intervention and returning to step 2 to test another intervention or by changing your practice to reflect a successful new technique. The kindergarten team described earlier in this chapter initiated a challenging project not just to learn about a particular instructional approach, but also to solve a problem and bring about change in their classrooms. The kindergarten team members learned that the PWIM approach had a positive impact on their students' learning of vocabulary. As a result of this finding, they will use this approach until they find one that leads to even better student learning. Figure 9.5 presents a worksheet teachers can use to guide them as they consider what action to take as a result of their action research study.

Figure 9.5   Using What Has Been Learned to Take Action

As a result of doing your study and analyzing your data, what actions will you take?

1. What have you learned about your topic/question? What are your conclusions about your question?

2. Are you surprised by what you learned? Did you expect your conclusions?

3. Have your assumptions about teaching and learning changed as a result of your study? In what ways?

4. Who else may be interested in your conclusions? With whom will you share your findings?

5. What new questions have been generated from your data, and what you have learned?

6. What actions will you take based on your data and your conclusions? What outcomes do you expect from taking these actions?

7. What will you investigate in your next action research study? Will it be connected to the topic of this study?

Source: Adapted from Caro-Bruce (2008).

Sharing What Has Been Learned

As in lesson study, writing about the study and sharing what was learned with colleagues pushes teachers to a deeper level of understanding about their problem of practice. It leads them to summarize for themselves what they have learned about content, students, and instruction, and to pose additional questions for future action research projects. Our group of kindergarten teachers, for example, can use the written report of their action research project as the foundation for designing additional projects focused on the development of other important literacy skills. In addition, writing and sharing contribute to an overall school context supportive of adult learning, ensures that teachers throughout the school can learn from one another's action research projects, and builds over time a shared knowledge base at the school about effective instruction.

For some teachers, writing about the study can be a daunting task. It may be helpful to emphasize that they should just focus on telling the story of their study in their reports. Important components and questions in these written reflections include the following (Zeichner, Klehr, & Caro-Bruce, 2000):

- *A description of the problem of practice that inspired the study.* What was your research question, and why was it important to answer this question? What frustration led you to this question? Provide enough background information so that readers can understand why it was important.
- *A description of actions taken to learn about the topic.* What did you learn about best practices related to your problem of practice? What led you to select a specific intervention? For example, our kindergarten team members would explain why they chose the PWIM approach over other strategies.
- *A description of the methods and data sources used in the study.* What was the timeline for the study, and what steps were taken along the way? Why were specific data collection methods chosen? How were they connected to their research question?
- *A description of your data analysis and interpretation.* What patterns and big ideas emerged from the data? What conclusions were supported by the data? How did the data help you answer your research question? What additional questions have been generated by the study?
- *A description of actions you are taking based on the study.* How have you modified your instruction? Are you pursuing another study connected to this one?

Benefits of Action Research

Perhaps the most important challenge facing school leaders today is to find ways to support the ongoing growth and development of their faculties. Action research is a useful strategy because it fosters the growth and learning of teachers by putting them in control of their learning and by making use of their own experiences. Action research starts with the instructional challenges teachers experience on a daily basis and gives them a process for learning how to successfully address these challenges over time. The specific benefits of action research include all of the following (Ferrance, 2000; Schmuck, 2006):

- *Building reflective practitioners.* Opportunities for teachers to carefully and thoughtfully examine their instruction and student learning are regrettably rare in many schools. Action research is about teachers studying their instruction in a structured manner. As teachers identify problems of practice, research best practices, test alternative instructional approaches, gather evidence regarding student learning, and analyze and interpret their data, they develop important habits of reflection about how to improve their instruction to enhance student achievement. These habits of reflection will likely take hold and continue, even when the teachers are not in the midst of an action research study. Action research helps teachers develop a mindset in which they consistently reflect on their instruction and how to improve it.

- *Building a community of learners.* Isolation is the enemy of learning, and yet teacher isolation has been the norm for many years in both our public and independent schools. The action research process brings teachers together to collaboratively examine their practice and how to make it better. "As the process of action research becomes part of the school culture, we see increased sharing and collaboration across departments, disciplines, and grade levels" (Hendricks, 2008, p. 123). Teachers discuss their own teaching styles and strategies and learn about the approaches and ideas of colleagues. They also work with colleagues to identify best practices related to the problem of practice that is the focus of their study. Through this work with colleagues, they not only improve their content knowledge and instructional practices but also develop collegial relationships and a learning mindset that help transform the school into a true learning community. In schools where action research is the norm, multiple action research studies occur simultaneously, and no one feels obligated to pursue another's priority—yet the faculty knows that all the work will ultimately be shared and will therefore contribute to the learning of the whole school.

- *Fostering greater professionalism and improved instruction.* When teachers begin conducting action research, their school begins to take on the feel of the workplaces of other professionals. The wisdom and knowledge that informs practice begins to flow from those doing the work. Even more importantly, when teachers collaborate around problems of practice, the multiple perspectives that emerge and contribute to the discussions tend to lead to better professional decisions. When the combined time, energy, knowledge, and creativity of a group of teachers are focused on a common problem of practice, significant improvements in classroom practice and student learning are almost inevitable.

Summary

Many teachers argue that the problem with educational theory is that it ignores practice. Theory is often tied to large-scale research projects designed and conducted by educational researchers, with little or no teacher input, and often with little relevance to the daily challenges teachers face. Of course, formal research occupies an important place in the field of education, but it can be difficult to translate its findings into new instructional practices. Action research bridges this gap to connect educational research directly to the challenges teachers experience. It allows teachers to pursue critical inquiry to activate changes in their instructional practices, on their own terms.

Action research is not problem solving in the sense of trying to figure out what is wrong, but rather it is a search for knowledge about how to improve in a specific area. It is about empowering teachers by engaging them in a collaborative process focused on improving their skills, techniques, and strategies. It is about figuring out how to do things better so teachers can modify instruction to positively impact students. Action research is a powerful professional development strategy because it is directly connected to the needs of teachers and students, involves teachers in the process of reflecting on how and why specific instructional decisions are made, promotes the development of strong collegial relationships, and furthers the development of a professional learning community.

10

Mentoring

A Japanese proverb says that one day with a good mentor is worth one thousand days of diligent study. With a good mentor, teachers are supported, encouraged and inspired as they grow in their profession.

—Carol Bartell

During a recent visit to a school, I asked a group of teachers to describe the professional development support they experienced during their early years in the profession. Marla, a 15-year veteran, volunteered first. "During my first several years as a teacher, I was just trying to survive," she said. "All of the professional development involved workshops done as an entire faculty, and it never seemed to address what I was going through." "Yes," added Dan. "There was no collaborative work at all, and professional development was disconnected from what I and other teachers really needed. I received the preps veteran teachers didn't want, and it was just a sink or swim experience."Amy, with 20 years of experience, was next. "Looking back, it was just a blur, a real day-to-day survival sort of thing for me. I felt all alone and spent nights and weekends trying to keep my head above water. I questioned on a daily basis whether teaching was the right thing for me."

Steven, a 10-year veteran, had been nodding his head with increasing conviction as the others spoke, and joined in at this point.

"Everything I'm hearing sounds very familiar. My early years were also very tough, and I don't think I would have made it through were it not for a colleague reaching out to me." Steven told a story about how Robert, a veteran teacher in his department, noticed his struggles and offered to meet with him weekly to discuss how to successfully navigate through his challenges. Steven concluded his story by emphasizing what this mentoring relationship had meant to him. "I met with Robert every Thursday after school for the rest of my first year and much of my second year. I talked about my frustrations, and he offered encouragement and specific advice. I could see improvements in my classroom and really began to feel that I was becoming competent as a teacher. If it weren't for Robert I'm sure I would have left teaching after that first year."

Steven was fortunate to find a mentor to help him learn and grow during his early years in the teaching profession. Strategies aimed at supporting the professional growth of beginning teachers are an important, but often neglected, aspect of school professional development programs. Imagine a recent medical school or law school graduate being given the most difficult patients or clients with little direction from more expert and experienced colleagues. Even when not disastrous, the results would be less than ideal. Yet too often we have done something similar in our schools, and both the development of talented young teachers and the learning of their students have suffered as result. Mentoring strategies offer a way to reverse this practice. "A mentor helps teachers make sense of the realities that they face in teaching, learn their significance, and use what they have learned to improve their teaching skills" (Pitton, 2006, p. 7). Ideally, mentoring helps to ensure that new teachers have access to the accumulated instructional knowledge and expertise of their colleagues in ways that contribute to student success.

The Power of Relationships

Mentoring as a form of professional development for beginning teachers emerged in the 1980s, and it has begun to grow in popularity in recent years as more and more schools have begun to recognize its power in attracting, retaining, and developing beginning teachers (Wechsler, Caspary, Humphrey, & Matsko, 2010). Mentoring can be an important lifeline for beginning teachers, helping them to manage the frustration, uncertainty, and steep learning curve that are part of being a new teacher. Even the most well-prepared beginning teacher needs individualized assistance during their first several years of professional practice. Pam Robbins (1999) describes mentoring as "an intentional, confidential process through which an experienced teacher provides a new teacher with information, support, resources, feedback, and guidance to help the newcomer develop and refine his or her skills and knowledge" (p. 38). Specific ways mentors help include (Gratch, 1998; Robbins, 2008) the following:

- Co-planning or co-teaching lessons
- Working to help the mentee effectively address instructional, curricular, student, or parent challenges
- Modeling professional behavior and conduct
- Modeling effective instructional approaches
- Having mentees observe mentors' thinking as they create, teach, and evaluate lessons
- Observing the classroom practices of mentees and providing feedback
- Investigating instructional best practices together
- Connecting mentees with veteran colleagues who have important methods or information to share
- Bringing other mentor/mentee pairs together in a larger group to share challenges and effective strategies

Mentoring also promotes the professional growth and development of the mentor teachers, giving them an opportunity to leave their mark on their school by transferring their knowledge, experience, and skill to newcomers. As James Stigler and James Hiebert lament in *The Teaching Gap* (1999), U.S. schools historically have not done a good job of helping to build the knowledge base of the teaching profession. When teachers retire or move on to another school, too often their library of knowledge leaves with them. Mentoring helps teachers and schools to save some of the tried-and-true lessons and instructional strategies that in the past would have left the school. Furthermore, mentoring can help mentor teachers improve their work with students as they reflect on their own practices in preparation for conversations with their mentees.

Why Mentoring Matters

Suppose you are an avid hiker and you want to become a mountain climber. You have all of the equipment—and abundant energy and enthusiasm—but you have never climbed anything more than small hills. There are two ways to begin your quest (Wilson & Daviss, 1996).

One way is to take a practice climb with a person who has substantial experience and the skill to share it. With this method you are likely to avoid dangerous obstacles, learn how to navigate significant challenges, and gain confidence that you can take further steps toward reaching your goal. The other way is to be dropped off at the bottom of a large mountain and told to climb to the summit or quit. With this approach you are likely to get frustrated or even injured, and to fall short of reaching your goal. Moreover, you're likely to avoid similar challenges in the future.

Too often beginning teachers are left alone at the base of a tall mountain and expected to figure out how to successfully climb to the top. In essence, "teaching is the only profession that requires beginners to do the same work as experienced veterans" (Gratch, 1998, p. 14). Traditionally, beginning teachers face the following challenges (Veenman, 1984):

- Taking on a full teaching load, often with preps other teachers do not want
- Learning unfamiliar routines, policies, and procedures
- Understanding the school curriculum and expected instructional strategies/approaches
- Motivating students
- Dealing with problems of individual students
- Establishing classroom management structure and procedures in their classes
- Managing extracurricular assignments on top of everything else

Over a third of new teachers leave the profession within several years, citing lack of support and assistance as a key reason (Darling-Hammond, 2003). Mentoring provides two types of important support to attract and keep beginning teachers in the profession: psychological support and instructional support.

Mentors provide psychological support to meet the immediate emotional and personal needs of beginning teachers (Baranik, Roling, & Eby, 2010). Psychological support protects the new teacher from isolation and provides him or her with suggestions about how to balance the demands of students, parents, and school administrators. Mentors providing psychological support listen, offer advice to manage the inevitable stress, and assure beginning teachers that their experiences are normal. Mentors also provide instruction-related support to help new teachers understand the school's culture, policies, and procedures, and help them improve their instructional practices and classroom management methods. Mentoring works because it pairs new teachers with professional, nonjudgmental, experienced colleagues who offer support where and when it is most needed.

In addition to providing psychological support and instructional support, effective mentoring programs also focus on *development*. Development involves building a personal understanding of pedagogy—the art and science of teaching and learning—that allows a teacher to continually refine and adjust his or her practice in order to consistently and effectively help students master content and skills (Harrison, Dymoke, & Pell, 2006). Mentoring for development centers on helping novices begin to craft a professional identity through their difficulties with and explorations of students and subject matter.

Essential Steps in Building a Mentoring Program

An effective mentor-mentee relationship involves trust, risk taking, collaboration, reflection, and learning, and it will not flourish without the support of the entire school community. Like the other professional development strategies discussed in this book, the success of your mentoring program for beginning teachers will be greatly influenced by the extent to which your school has a culture supportive of adult learning. Once you have, or are in the process of establishing, a professional learning culture, it is important to carefully consider how to build your new mentoring program. The details will, of course, vary from school to school, but the steps outlined next (Robbins, 2008; Zachary, 2011) will help guide you in building the foundation for an effective mentoring program for new teachers. (See Figure 10.1 for important questions to ask and answer as you move through these steps.)

Step 1: Creating a Vision

How do we define mentoring, and what outcomes do we hope to achieve through a mentoring program? Schools with successful mentoring programs wrestle with and answer these questions up front. While the entire faculty should have input into how these questions are answered, the process can begin with the principal and department heads drafting a statement and then sending it to the faculty for their review. A school I worked with in Virginia defined a mentor as "a master teacher who helps beginning teachers make sense of the realities they face in teaching, and who supports, guides, and coaches new teachers to improve their instructional practices." They continued their statement by describing the purpose of mentoring as "a mechanism to ensure that new teachers have access to the wealth of knowledge, experience, and expertise of their colleagues in ways that result in positive student outcomes." Being clear from the start about what a mentor is and the outcomes you expect from a mentoring program will help you keep the program focused as you work through the other essential steps in getting it off the ground (Portner, 2005).

Step 2: Competencies and Responsibilities

What qualities and skills must a teacher have to be a prospective mentor, and what will he or she be expected to do? Answering this question early will make your mentor selection process much easier later on. Educational researcher Lois Zachary (2000) states that "the best mentors exhibit a passion for teaching, exercise diplomacy and empathy in collegial relationships, and model a devotion to the profession" (p. 17). Surveys of schools with successful mentoring programs (Gareis & Nussbaum-Beach, 2008; National Education Association, 1999) have found that the qualities, skills, and responsibilities of effective mentors fall into four areas (see Figure 10.2). First, the attitude and character of the prospective mentor are important. The teacher must be enthusiastic about being a mentor, be willing to receive some training on mentoring skills, and be respected by colleagues as a true professional. Second,

Figure 10.1   Questions to Ask and Answer in Building the Foundation for an Effective Mentoring Program

1. How do we define mentoring, and what do we hope to achieve through a mentoring program?
2. What qualities and skills must a teacher have to be a prospective mentor, and what will he or she be expected to do?
3. Who is involved in answering questions 1 and 2?
4. Will mentors teach the same grade level or discipline as the mentee, or both?
5. Which teachers will receive mentoring? Only first-time teachers out of college or also teachers new to the school? Teachers changing grade levels or course assignments?
6. How will mentors be chosen?
7. How often will mentors and mentees meet, and how will time be found for these meetings?
8. How, when, and by whom will training for mentors occur?
9. Will mentors receive stipends, reductions in teaching assignments, or both?
10. What policies and practices are barriers to effective mentoring and how will these barriers be overcome?

Source: Adapted from Robbins (1999) and Robbins (2008).

while the mentor does not have to be a master teacher, he or she should possess a high degree of professional competence and experience. The mentor should have excellent content and pedagogical knowledge, be abreast of best practices in their area, feel comfortable being observed by colleagues, and be viewed by colleagues as an outstanding teacher. Third, the mentor should possess excellent communication skills. For example, he or she needs to be able to offer feedback in positive, productive ways; to ask questions that promote reflection and critical thinking; and to listen attentively. Fourth, the mentor must exhibit superior interpersonal skills. He or she should be approachable, able to earn the trust of others, patient, and able to work with people from a variety of backgrounds and cultures.

Figure 10.2   Qualities of Effective Mentors

Personal Qualities

- Is a role model for other teachers
- Demonstrates a commitment to lifelong learning
- Is reflective and learns from mistakes
- Enjoys sharing ideas and information with colleagues
- Is flexible and open-minded
- Believes mentoring improves teaching
- Willing to receive training on mentoring
- Enjoys new challenges and solving problems

Communication Skills

- Excellent listening skills
- Poses questions that promote reflection and critical thinking
- Offers feedback in positive, productive ways
- Maintains confidentiality
- Conveys enthusiasm and passion for teaching and learning
- Clearly explains effective instructional approaches

Qualities of Effective Mentors

Interpersonal Skills

- Able to build and maintain trusting professional relationships
- Is approachable
- Works well with people from a variety of cultures and backgrounds
- Is sensitive to the school political climate
- Is patient
- Able to express care for the mentee's emotional and professional needs

Professional Ability and Experience

- Regarded by colleagues as a superior teacher
- Excellent content and pedagogical knowledge
- Excellent classroom management skills
- Comfortable being observed by colleagues
- Confident in his/her instructional skills
- Understands school policies and procedures
- Works to stay up with best practices in their area
- Collaborates well with colleagues
- Enjoys new challenges and solving problems

Source: Adapted from National Education Association (1999).

Step 3: A Structure for Mentoring

The traditional model matches a single mentor with a single mentee. Ideally, the mentor teaches the same grade level and/or subject as the mentee, ensuring that the mentor has personal experience with the instructional and classroom management challenges the mentee is facing (Pitton, 2006). It is also useful if the mentor is located near the mentee in the building to facilitate both formal and informal conversations. While the traditional model is still the most common structure for mentoring programs, schools increasingly are choosing to adopt a model that matches the mentee with multiple mentors in a "mentoring mosaic" (Gareis & Nussbaum-Beach, 2008). In this structure, different mentors offer guidance in a variety of specific areas, such as grade-level or content-area expertise, technology use, classroom management, and school policies.

The benefits of this model include opportunities for new teachers to get expertise in a variety of areas and to observe teachers with different instructional approaches—the very things that beginning teachers often say they need most. Furthermore, this new model eliminates what is often a daunting task: finding a quality mentor who teaches the same grade level or content area as the mentee and is located nearby in the school. Ultimately, you need to choose the model that will provide beginning teachers the guidance, coaching, and support they need to survive and thrive in your school.

Step 4: Finding the Time

Perhaps the most common reason that fledgling mentoring programs do not succeed is the failure to allocate sufficient time for mentors and mentees to meet. The typical teacher's day includes little time without direct teaching or supervisory responsibilities, and "open" periods tend to be filled with lesson planning, grading, and conferring with grade-level or department colleagues about shared responsibilities. Beginning teachers and their mentors must carve out additional time for mentoring work, or they must find a way to borrow time from already scheduled school activities. "Multiple studies confirm that weekly time for mentoring must be found for it to have the intended benefits for both the mentor and mentee" (Feiman-Nemser, 1999, p. 4). Questions that should be answered in finding the time for effective mentoring include (Pitton, 2006) the following:

- Where will the time come from for scheduling mentoring activities? Will it come from existing planning and preparation periods? Will mentoring time be scheduled before school, after school, or at lunch? Will any mentoring work be scheduled over the summer?

- What types of logistical issues must be solved in finding time for mentoring? Will class scheduling have to be adjusted? Will teacher room assignments need to be considered?
- Are there costs associated with allocating time for mentoring activities? Will mentors be compensated for their time? Will substitutes be needed? If there are costs, how will they be funded?

Whatever methods and structures you employ, mentors and their mentees should have opportunities for both formal meetings and informal conversations. Ideally, the mentor and mentee meet formally each week to discuss pre-arranged topics and challenges, and engage almost daily in informal conversations before school, between classes, over lunch, or after school. The combination of planned meetings and short informal conversations allows the mentor to explore important areas in some depth while also supporting and coaching the new teacher with his or her day-to-day challenges.

Step 5: The Mentor Selection Process

The goal here is to design a process that identifies and selects prospective mentors with the qualities and skills specified in step 2 (see Figure 10.2). A committee, consisting of the principal, one other school leader, and one respected veteran teacher, invites teachers nominated by their colleagues to apply. The demands of mentoring and the desire to have your very best candidates apply highlight the importance of incentives, particularly in the early stages of your mentoring program (Ormond, 2008). A reduced or modified course load is often more effective in attracting candidates than monetary stipends (and a reduced or a modified course load is also advisable for mentees).

The application process should have some meat to it, both to communicate that you and the school are serious about quality mentoring and to allow you to select candidates who possess the qualities you seek. The process may include the following (Robbins, 2008; Scherer, 1999):

- A written application that includes one recommendation from a colleague, and requires teachers to respond in writing to questions about the skills and knowledge connected to being an effective mentor

- Recognized teaching excellence from the members of the committee
- A formal interview during which the applicant responds to questions and critiques a video of a beginning teacher at work in the classroom. Candidates should be asked to describe the instructional strategies and student learning on display and offer detailed suggestions for how to improve the quality of the teaching and classroom management in the class. In addition, the applicant should be asked how they would have a conversation about teaching with the teacher in the video.

Conducting a formal interview in this way can give the committee important insights into the applicant's instructional knowledge and skill, their communication skills, and their interpersonal skills. After all, it is important that they are not only an excellent teacher, but it can also clearly and carefully articulate that craft knowledge.

Step 6: Determining Training Methods

It is essential to provide training and ongoing support for your mentors. Both are crucial in helping your program get started on a positive note. Training lasting anywhere from two to five days is commonly conducted over the summer, and can be provided by college education faculty or teachers from other schools with successful mentoring programs. Training topics should include the following (Pitton, 2006; Robbins, 2008; Zachary, 2011):

- Mentoring roles and responsibilities
- Establishing collaborative relationships based on trust and confidentiality
- Facilitation, conflict resolution, and problem-solving skills
- Critiquing and providing constructive criticism
- Role-playing mentor–mentee situations
- Observation tools
- Listening skills
- Lesson planning
- Common challenges for beginning teachers

Effective training includes "explanations of key concepts, modeling, practice, feedback on practice and follow-up activities so participants can be prepared to apply new skills in their schools" (Robbins, 1999, p. 16). While the initial training provides the foundation for new mentors to begin their work with their mentees, schools with effective mentoring programs also provide ongoing support for their mentors by carving out time for mentors in the school to meet with each other to discuss mentoring strategies, share their challenges and successes, and plan additional ways to assist their mentees. As one new mentor told me, "I really needed someone to mentor me as I was working to be an effective mentor, and the weekly meetings with experienced mentors in my school helped me grow and provide helpful support to my mentee."

The Work of Mentoring

Once you have built the foundation for your mentoring program, it is time to get down to the actual work of mentors interacting with beginning teachers. Creating and maintaining an effective mentoring program ultimately rests on strong mentor–mentee relationships characterized by respect and trust. As in any relationship, trust and respect will take time to develop. Mentors should take care to use effective communication skills from the beginning of the mentoring experience to ensure their mentees' comfort. They also should make trust and confidentiality the foundation of their mentor–mentee relationships. Figure 10.3 presents some questions mentors can use to help them begin to connect with their mentee in their initial meetings. In addition, mentors can build strong mentor–mentee learning relationships by attending to the following (Bartell, 2005):

- *Engage in active listening.* Really listen to what a mentee is saying without judgment. Sometimes, instead of truly listening, the mentor may be thinking about his or her response, or something else entirely. The mentor must work to calm these thoughts and remain fully engaged in the task of listening. Mentors can communicate they are listening by reflecting back what the mentee is saying (for example, "So, you feel you need some strategies to get students speaking more in class discussions."). This helps the mentor check whether he or she understands the mentee, and helps the mentee feel understood by the mentor. Finally, mentors must be mindful that nonverbal cues (making eye contact and nodding the head) are extremely important in communicating that they are listening to their mentee.
- *Practice self-disclosure.* The mentor can share appropriate personal feelings, opinions, and experiences to increase the intimacy of communication and encourage the mentee to open up (for example, "I understand your difficult situation. I have experienced something similar and remember being very frustrated. I hope I can help you move forward from here.").

- *Admit what you don't know.* The mentor should not expect or pretend to have all the answers. Honest admissions about where knowledge begins and ends can go a long way to building rapport and trust (for example, "I don't have much experience with that, so let's brainstorm possible solutions in that area.").

- *Stress commitment, follow-through, and honest communication.* Commitment, demonstrated by a willingness to go the extra mile, communicates care and professionalism. In addition, few things build trust and respect more rapidly than mentors doing what they say they will do. Finally, honest, direct communication builds trust. The mentor must truthfully acknowledge and discuss areas of mentee weakness. This should always be done in a constructive, positive manner and should always be done privately.

- *Take time to learn about the mentee's culture.* This can include unique foods and holidays, and culturally appropriate ways to greet and interact with mentees. Taking the time to learn about and understand a different culture communicates respect in a powerful way.

- *Ask for and receive feedback from the mentee.* This communicates respect and appreciation for his or her knowledge, ideas, and experience. Of course, it is important that the mentor work to apply constructive feedback to improve the mentoring relationship.

- *Maintain confidentiality.* This is an essential component of the mentor–mentee relationship. Without appropriate confidentiality, mentors will find that it is difficult, if not impossible, to build trust and establish rapport with their mentees. To maintain confidentiality with their mentees, mentors need to be sensitive to when and where to have conversations with and provide feedback to their mentees. Confidentiality is especially important when the mentor–mentee pairing does not match traditional cultural hierarchies. For example, ensuring confidentiality is especially critical when the mentor and mentee are not of the same gender, the mentor is younger than the mentee, or the mentor is of a different ethnic group than the mentee.

The Beginning of the Year

Successful mentors seek to help their mentees expand their repertoires of skills, strategies, and knowledge useful in different teaching situations and settings. However, it is important for mentors to recognize that beginning teachers learn and progress in stages (Gareis & Nussbaum-Beach, 2008; Robbins, 2008). The mentor should be careful not to overwhelm the mentee with excessive advice and information at the

Figure 10.3   Questions to Help Mentors Connect With Mentees

1. Why did you want to become a teacher? Who or what inspired you?

2. What are your biggest hopes for this year? What are your biggest fears?

3. What are your strengths as a teacher? What are your weaknesses?

4. What is the ideal classroom, and how you would go about building such an environment?

5. How can I best support you this year? What kinds of feedback do you prefer?

6. Tell me some things about you that will help me facilitate our working relationship.

7. What would you like to know about me?

Source: Adapted from Robbins (2008) and Zachary (2000).

beginning of the year. What new teachers need most at this time is support, encouragement, and assistance with logistical details such as where things are located, school rules, policies and procedures and how to set up grade books with the computer software. The mentor should check in frequently with the mentee during the first several weeks of the school year to address questions, problem solve, and build the trust and rapport that will fuel growth and learning throughout the year.

In the weeks that follow, mentors will struggle with how to best further the growth and learning of their mentees. A skillful mentor works with a mentee to determine what level and type of assistance to provide and when to provide it. One common question I hear from mentors is how to introduce their mentees to the culture of their schools, particularly those aspects that are negative. A veteran mentor I know described his struggle this way: "Like many schools, we have some teachers who are real complainers, who just suck up positive energy wherever they go. These teachers constantly whine about the students, the administrators, and even their colleagues. Their negativism is toxic, and I have seen them do significant harm to the attitudes of young teachers." Mentors are responsible for supporting new teachers and helping them to grow and develop in their profession, so they must work to direct their mentees away from negative influences and toward more positive colleagues in the school.

Another dilemma is how to give advice and suggestions without being perceived as pushy and without making the mentee overly dependent. The goal is for the mentee to improve his or her instructional and classroom management skills, while also growing more confident and independent. Mentors may not only want to offer unsolicited assistance, but also may worry how they will be perceived by their mentees if they never offer advice on their own. A mentor I know came up with what I believe is an elegant solution to this dilemma. "I came to the conclusion that I had several choices. First, I could initiate things and share my thoughts and resources with my mentee, invite my mentee into my classroom, visit their classroom, and reflect together on the experiences. The other option would be to encourage my mentee to ask for help when they need it, and then pull back and wait for them to ask."

The mentor chose the first option, and I strongly believe the choice was a wise one. Beginning teachers are isolated from their peers for a majority of their day, and they are expected to take on the same responsibilities as longtime veterans. In addition, they may refrain from asking for help for fear of appearing incompetent. Mentors should not wait until there is a crisis, but rather should reach out to their mentees. As noted educational consultant Pam Robbins (2003) emphasizes, "you don't foster the growth and learning of new teachers by giving them a mentor to call when they are in trouble so you'd better decide to be proactive" (p. 2).

Disillusionment, Frustration, and Rejuvenation

At some point during the first semester, most beginning teachers report feeling overwhelmed. Preparing for classes, grading papers, meeting with parents, and managing extracurricular responsibilities leave them feeling exhausted and disillusioned. Beginning teachers are busy and stressed; they're struggling just to survive. They can begin to doubt their competence, and their self-esteem and morale decline, yet they may not ask for much assistance. Mentors can offer extra support and encouragement during this stage. For example, mentors can make a big difference by offering to co-plan lessons, inviting mentees to watch them teach, problem solving with them, or just listening as they vent (Robbins, 2008).

One mentee shared how her mentor helped her work through this difficult time. "She stopped by every day and said we would make it through together. She role-played with me, helped me develop practical solutions to my most pressing challenges, and the fact she always used the plural 'we' made a huge difference. And she made me laugh, something I had not done in weeks." While ups and downs will remain common, once the disillusionment stage has been successfully navigated the mentoring relationship can shift gears from survival mode to one characterized by greater focus on improving specific instructional practices and classroom management skills, and greater attention to ongoing professional learning connected to the assessed learning needs of students. The mentor and mentee can begin to reflect on and celebrate real improvements in classroom practice—and this leads to corresponding feelings of competence and esteem. "I began to think, 'Maybe I can do this,'" said one new teacher, "and that really fueled my commitment and desire to continue to work on improving my work with my students."

Reflecting and Planning

As the year draws to a close, it is important for the mentor to reflect with their mentee on the progress that has been made and the challenges that lie ahead (Ormond, 2008; Robbins, 2008). A beginning teacher once told me that this process was depressing, exciting, and inspiring all at the same time. "I thought about all of the mistakes I had made and it was depressing, but then I thought about all I had learned and how much better I would do the next year. I ended that first year feeling really excited about what I would do with my classes the following year, and really grateful for having such a committed mentor." It is also important for the mentor-mentee pair to assess areas of strength and weakness for the mentor so that he or she can continue to develop and grow in that role. A veteran mentor emphasized the importance of reciprocal year-end feedback, saying, "As important as it is for me to give my mentee direct, honest feedback, it is equally important that he or she communicates to me how I helped them and how I didn't help so I can make improvements and adjustments from year to year."

In addition to the important mentor–mentee reflections, many schools hold formal ceremonies for the mentor–mentee pairs to gather to celebrate successes, recognize the hard work of all involved in the program, and reflect on how to improve it going forward (Evertson & Smithey, 2000). As one veteran mentor told me, this end of the year gathering has both a function and symbolic importance. "It is an important time to take stock of the program and how we can improve the work we do, but it also models for our mentees the importance of always reflecting on your practice, always asking for and welcoming feedback, and always looking for ways to improve what we do so our students can learn all they can learn."

The Role of the Principal

The success of a mentoring program depends on strong and active support from the principal. Of course, principals directly influence the quality of the program because they are involved in the mentor application and selection process. They also impact the quality of the program in other, less direct ways (Rowley, 2000):

- Assume the role of the "lead mentor" by attending mentor training, scheduling periodic brief check-ins with the entire group of mentors, and by adopting an attitude that says "We will support our mentors to make this program successful."
- Provide time for mentoring. Principals communicate, in a not so subtle way, whether or not a program is a priority by their allocation of time for it.
- Show support publicly, frequently, and symbolically. Just as mentors provide consistent, ongoing support of their mentees, the principal should pump a constant supply of energy and support into the program, particularly in the start-up phase. "Our principal always kept the mission of the mentoring program in front of us," one mentor told me, "and this, combined with her visible support, really got our program off to a good start."

- Make sure mentors and mentees have reasonable class assignments, and shelter mentees from additional assignments during the first year. As with allocating time for mentoring, adjusting teacher responsibilities communicates that mentoring is a priority.
- Recognize the efforts of mentors and mentees privately and publicly. One of the most significant motivators is feeling that your efforts are appreciated. Mentoring, for both the mentor and the mentee, requires commitment, time, and energy, and appreciation from the principal provides fuel to keep it going.
- Be available to problem solve. When the principal gets directly involved in helping to solve problems, he or she communicates, "This is important and we need to find a way to make it work."

Essential Elements

Mentoring policies, practices, activities, and structures will vary based on your school's context and mission. However, successful mentoring programs attend to these essential elements (Bartell, 2005; Robbins, 2008; Zachary, 2011):

- *Develop a clear vision of what mentoring is and what it can achieve for the school.* It is time-consuming to do this but being clear from the beginning about what a mentor is and what you hope to gain from a mentoring program creates ownership and commitment. A clear vision clarifies the roles and expectations of mentors and mentees and can be used by the division head to keep all involved moving toward the same goals.
- *Put incentives in place to attract and retain mentors.* These can include stipends or adjusted course loads, but they should also be professional and emotional. Principals should help mentors feel appreciated and should communicate that mentoring work is important to the school. Mentors in effective programs see mentoring as professional learning for themselves, not just for their mentees. They are invested in the growth of the mentee and their students, and get emotional rewards from positive mentee feedback.
- *Develop skills to support mentoring.* Ongoing training and support for mentors is crucial to the success of any mentoring program. Essential skills include, but are not limited to, communication skills, conflict resolution skills, problem-solving strategies, learning how to have difficult conversations, observation strategies and methods, and active listening.

- *Allocate resources.* Mentoring programs are unlikely to succeed if time is not available during the school day at least once each week for the mentor and mentee to meet. It is also helpful if time is periodically available for the mentee to observe their mentor or other teachers in action in their classrooms. Other essential resources include materials, emotional support, and money. Materials such as articles, videos, and books can support the work of mentors and mentees in their meetings. Emotional support in the form of active nonjudgmental listening, compassion, and encouragement should be provided by the principal and the mentors. Finally, consider the cost of time and materials when designing the mentoring program.
- *Create a clear plan of action.* Effective mentoring programs have plans that answer the questions posed in Figure 10.1. They also undergo formative and summative evaluations to assure program quality and ongoing improvement. The mentoring committee, with faculty input, develops the plan of action and evaluation.

Summary

Thankfully, it is no longer acceptable to drop new teachers off at the bottom of Mount Everest and expect them to climb to the top. Giving new teachers a full course load and extracurricular responsibilities with no structured support system in place impedes the growth and development of the teacher, increases the likelihood they will leave the profession, and negatively affects the students in their classes. Schools that provide mentoring programs communicate that beginning teachers are valued, that their growth and learning will be supported, and that the school wants them to stay in the profession. Mentoring works because it offers the new teacher an experienced, nonjudgmental professional to help them understand the culture and procedures of the school, guide them in developing strategies to successfully address their challenges, and work with them to improve their classroom practices. Teacher quality is the most important factor in student learning, and mentoring helps new teachers make that difference in the lives of their students. Educational researcher Linda Darling-Hammond (2003) says it best: "In every school it is important for new teachers to begin with models of excellence who have gone before them. And it is not only a matter of lesson plans, instructional approaches, and classroom management, although all of those are important. It is also a matter of being drawn into the profession of teaching by mentors, of realizing its challenges and rewards, and committing fully to helping students succeed" (p. 11).

11

Peer Coaching

Peer coaching is a process through which two or more colleagues work together to reflect on current practices; expand, refine, and build new skills; share ideas; teach one another; conduct classroom research; and solve problems of practice.

—Pam Robbins

Kristen was beginning to implement cooperative learning methods in her fourth-grade classroom. One of her challenges with the method was finding a way to engage quiet students so that they would not feel overwhelmed by more vocal, dominant personalities. Her goal was for each student to contribute to the group, and she knew that she had to teach her students the group skills and social skills needed for cooperative learning. She also knew that it takes time for students to develop these skills. Unfortunately, what sounded great in theory just was not materializing in her classroom. There was bickering at team tables, students were not engaged in projects, and dominant students were frequently taking control of groups. Kristen went to her peer coach to express her frustrations and ask for help. "I want all my students involved productively in the groups, but things are just degenerating," she said. "I feel like I have taught them the social skills and group skills they need, but I just don't see them being used in their groups."

Susan, her peer coach, responded, "Well, what do you think about me getting into your class some this week to give you another set of eyes, to give you another perspective, and perhaps we could also video your class some so we can observe your cooperative groups together." "That sounds great—particularly your suggestion about reviewing the video together," Kristen said. Susan observed Kristen's class twice, and then sat down with her to review a video of the fourth-grade cooperative learning groups. Kristen was frustrated, and a little embarrassed, by what she heard from Susan and what she saw on the video. "Wow," said Kristen, "I may have thought I did a good job teaching them the skills they need to work productively in a group, but all the evidence says that the groups just aren't working."

"You may need to review some of the skills," advised Susan. "But there could be other reasons why your cooperative groups are not leading to the result you want. You may want to revisit your group project plans to make sure students not only have individual tasks but must also truly collaborate to accomplish something." "Maybe I need to redesign what I'm asking them to do to get them collaborating more effectively," Kristen said. "One other thought I had is that you may want to develop some type of reminder for the students to use the skills you have taught them," Susan suggested.

After brainstorming possible ways to do this, Kristen offered the following approach. "To remind the quieter students of how to be involved in the groups, I could tape cards to their desks with sentence starts like 'I think that . . .,' 'My view is . . .,' or 'I need . . .'" "I really think that will help," said Susan. "Maybe you also can do something for the students who have been dominating the groups to remind them to get others involved. The sentence starts for those students might be something like 'What do you think . . .' or 'Do you have something you want to add . . .'"

Kristen returned to her classroom with renewed energy, optimism, and ideas. She met with Susan several weeks later to view a video of her cooperative groups, and they agreed that student engagement, behavior, and learning had improved significantly. The approaches they had developed together had helped both the quiet and vocal students work well in the groups. At other times during the year Kristen helped Susan with an instructional dilemma she was having. Together, they helped one another address problems as they emerged so they could develop more effective instructional practices and improve the learning of their students.

Harnessing Peer-to-Peer Wisdom

While mentoring typically targets beginning teachers, peer coaching is about mutual consultation between teachers of the same status.

Unlike instructional coaching, where the coach does coaching full time and is often hired by the school from an outside organization, peer coaching is a professional development strategy involving teachers within a school working together to improve their teaching (Gottesman, 2000). "Peer coaching has nothing to do with evaluation and is not intended to be a remedial activity or strategy to 'fix' teachers" (Robbins, 1997, p. 3). Peer coaching provides opportunities for teachers to support and learn from each other and to engage in practical discussions and conversations about instructional best practices and their students' learning.

In peer coaching, teachers take turns assuming the role of coach. The teacher who asks a coach for assistance, referred to as "the inviting teacher," guides the process. In the preceding story, Susan assumed the coaching role when Kristen came and asked for her assistance in solving her instructional dilemma about cooperative learning groups. At another time Kristen may serve as the coach to help Susan solve one of her instructional dilemmas. Peer coaching most commonly involves pairs of teachers from the same grade level or content area. However, some schools have successfully modified the strategy so that groups of three or four teachers coach one another, while other schools conduct peer coaching across grade levels or content areas.

In the world of sports, coaching is well understood. The coach helps athletes hone and develop their skills. The coach uses expertise, communication skills, listening skills, and problem-solving skills to help people move closer to their goals. As a strategy for teacher professional learning, coaching involves the same concepts and skills (McNeil & Klink, 2008). As in the sports world, a peer coach seeks to take a teacher from where they are to where they want to be. In the vignette at the beginning of the chapter, Susan worked to help Kristen solve her problem of practice. That story illustrates an important advantage of peer coaching: It is learner driven and can be tailored to the specific needs of teachers. To borrow a phrase from Thomas Friedman in *The World Is Flat*, peer coaching is just-in-time professional development, addressing important teacher needs as they emerge.

Peer coaching can take three general forms (see Figure 11.1), and because it is a complex activity, it often involves a mix of all three (Lipton & Wellman, 2001). The first form, directive coaching, is what comes to mind for most people when they hear the word *coach*. Directive coaching happens when one teacher asks another teacher to give specific assistance and instruction in how to do something. In directive coaching, one teacher guides the other teacher by actively teaching him or her various skills and strategies to achieve success.

When you seek help on how to operate an interactive whiteboard, you are seeking directive coaching; when you seek help on how to design a rubric, you are seeking directive coaching. Directive coaching works best when (Barbknecht, 2001; McNeil & Klink, 2004)

- the coach has expertise in the area being addressed;
- the coach can articulate the instructions so they can be understood;
- the teacher asking for coaching is motivated to improve and wants the instructions;
- the teacher asking for help has enough knowledge, skills, and experience to translate the instructions into improvements in the targeted area; and
- the teacher and coach are searching for a quick solution to a need.

The second form, collaborative coaching, happens when a teacher and coach work together to analyze a problem and generate alternative

Figure 11.1   Comparing the Three Types of Peer Coaching

Directive coaching works best when . . .	Collaborative coaching works best when . . .	Nondirective coaching works best when . . .
1. The coach has expertise in the area being addressed. 2. The coach can clearly communicate instructions and ideas. 3. The teacher asking for coaching is sincerely interested and wants the assistance. 4. The teacher asking for coaching has enough knowledge, skills, and experience to use the instructions to improve instructional practices. 5. The teacher and coach are searching for a quick solution to an existing problem of practice.	1. There is a very high level of trust among the teachers. 2. The coach and the teacher seeking assistance both have enough knowledge and skill to solve the problem. 3. Both teachers agree on the characteristics of the problem and the outcome they desire. 4. Both teachers agree to explore multiple ways to solve the problem.	1. There is a very high level of trust among the teachers. 2. The process is based on the needs of the teacher with the instructional dilemma. 3. The coaching teacher focuses on the desired needs of the other teacher. 4. The teacher bringing the dilemma allows his or her underlying assumptions to be discussed and challenged. 5. The coaching teacher has the expertise and confidence to address the teacher's dilemma.

Source: Adapted from Lipton and Wellman (2001) and McNeil and Klink (2004).

approaches for solving it. It is an appreciative approach that recognizes and encourages the talents and expertise of each teacher. It also appreciates that each teacher has the potential to be creative, resourceful, and develop customized outcomes specific to him or her and their situation and circumstance. Kristen and Susan were engaged in collaborative coaching as they sought solutions to Kristen's problem of practice. Collaborative coaching works well when (Heider, 2005; McNeil & Klink, 2004)

- there is a high level of trust among the teachers;
- questions, opinions, speculations, or suggestions are offered by the coaching teacher in a manner that conveys genuine respect, interest, and appreciation for the other teacher's expertise;
- the coach and the teacher seeking assistance both have enough knowledge and skill to solve the problem;
- both teachers agree on the nature of the problem to be solved and the solution they are seeking; and
- both teachers agree to consider alternative ways to solve the problem.

The final form of peer coaching is nondirective coaching, which is similar in some ways to collaborative coaching. Like collaborative coaching, nondirective coaching involves teachers agreeing on the desired result and working together to explore potential solutions. However, in nondirective coaching the coaching teacher works to help the other teacher confront and understand the assumptions that may have contributed to the current problem. For example, if Kristen believes that some students can't work in cooperative groups, then all of the brainstorming and problem solving in the world may not help her make cooperative groups more effective as a learning method. The great benefit of nondirective coaching is that the teacher uncovers approaches and solutions they would never have discovered on their own, yet will take full ownership of the solutions, thus feeling a sense of empowerment to make needed changes.

For nondirective coaching to work, the teacher acting as coach must use a variety of approaches to bring the other teacher's thinking processes to the surface. The following conditions must be in place (McNeil & Klink, 2004; Robbins, 1997):

- There is a deep level of trust among the teachers.
- The process is based on the needs of the teacher with the instructional dilemma.
- The coaching teacher focuses on the desired outcomes of the other teacher.

- The teacher bringing the problem allows his or her underlying assumptions to be discussed and challenged.
- The coaching teacher has the expertise and confidence to address the other teacher's need.
- The teacher bringing the problem generates potential solutions.

Peer coaching seeks to help teachers find solutions to their instructional problems so that student learning challenges can be addressed quickly and effectively. Schools with successful peer coaching programs report that teachers benefit both from being coached and doing the coaching. When being coached, teachers get assistance, which helps them improve their classroom instruction; when coaching, teachers not only improve their own instruction by helping the other teacher solve their problem; they also learn from being exposed to an increased number of students of varying ages, abilities, and learning styles.

The Rationale for Peer Coaching

When Cliff announced his retirement after teaching high school English for 37 years, his colleagues honored him with a party. At this gathering, they reflected on how he had touched their lives, and the lives of his students. "Whenever I had a student who needed help structuring an essay, I sent them to Cliff and their writing improved immediately," said one teacher. Another teacher nodded and added, "Yes, I did the same thing and had the same results." At this point a third teacher jumped in and asked, "How did he help all of these students; what is it that he did?" The teachers looked at one another and realized that they had worked with Cliff for years but did not know what made him so successful in helping his students learn.

The story about Cliff is an all too common one in our schools. It wasn't a case where Cliff didn't want to share but rather that his school had no mechanisms in place for teachers to share best practices with one another and assist one another with professional dilemmas. Peer coaching is an effective professional development strategy because it addresses the deficiencies of traditional methods of teacher professional learning and provides an avenue for productive professional collaboration. In peer coaching, teachers work together "to reflect on current practices; expand, refine, and build new skills; share ideas; teach one another concepts and skills; conduct classroom research; and solve professional dilemmas" (Robbins, 1997, p. 2). Six benefits of peer coaching provide a powerful rationale for engaging in this approach (Robbins, 1997):

1. *Peer coaching helps to break patterns of teacher isolation.* A long-standing tradition of isolation permeates the teaching profession. Both physical characteristics (separate one-room school houses repeated down a long corridor) and cultural norms impose barriers to sharing effective instructional practices. Peer coaching can break this isolation and give teachers opportunities to tap the teaching knowledge of colleagues. When teachers work together in peer coaching to discuss, analyze, and refine classroom practices, new norms of collaboration can be established.

2. *Peer coaching helps teachers solve problems of practice.* As I have emphasized throughout this book, one of the primary reasons traditional professional development methods are ineffective is that they are disconnected from student and teacher needs. Peer coaching is just-in-time learning that is effective because it is immediately useful and relevant for teachers in solving problems of practice and addressing the needs of their students. Peer coaching provides a venue for teachers to explore, with a trusted colleague, those challenges that are most significant in their day-to-day work with students. It gives them an opportunity to examine why problems exist and explore a variety of potential ways to solve them.

3. *Peer coaching helps teachers work smarter.* Teachers often spend hours on their own planning, grading, and documenting, and any improvements in instructional practices are often the result of trial and error. This is not a very effective or efficient way to meet workplace demands while growing in the profession. When teachers work together in peer coaching they "learn from one another and share tasks, and this helps in dealing with the multitude of demands on the teacher's role and saves time too" (Robbins, 1997, p. 12). Further, the collaborative sharing and reflecting of peer coaching assists teachers in learning from one another rather than by errors alone.

4. *Peer coaching helps teachers transfer newly learned skills to the classroom.* Another significant deficiency of traditional professional development approaches is a lack of follow-up. The peer coaching strategy addresses this problem by providing a way to follow up on the topics, skills, and approaches presented at workshops and conferences and apply them in a very practical way to the daily work of teachers. As noted researcher Thomas Guskey (2000) emphasizes, "When teachers experience

the successful implementation of an instructional approach rather than just hearing about it, their learning will stick and their classroom practices and beliefs will be changed for the better" (p. 8).

5. *Peer coaching puts teachers in charge of their professional learning.* Peer coaching allows teachers to direct their professional learning and tailor activities for their unique needs. Peer coaching is consistent with the well-established principle that adults learn best by doing. Rather than sitting and listening to someone talk about an approach, in peer coaching teachers select approaches to fit their needs and use them in their class-rooms. It leads teachers to apply what they learn directly to their work and then make additional adjustments if the approach is not resulting in the desired outcome.

6. *Peer coaching provides time for teacher reflection.* Teachers face many demands in and out of the classroom on a daily basis. The rapid pace of the typical work day means that teachers rarely have time to reflect on what is working, what is not working, and how they can do things better. Teachers need opportunities to reflect to gain insights about their teaching and to alter what they are doing to better meet student needs. Peer coaching provides the time to collaboratively reflect on professional dilemmas and how to solve them.

Essential Steps of the Peer Coaching Process

The success of peer coaching depends on the environment of the school. Teachers must be comfortable collaborating with colleagues, with shar-ing what has traditionally been private. For example, teachers must feel comfortable sharing learning goals, teaching strategies, classroom mate-rials, pacing, questions posed to students, frustrations and concerns about student learning and behavior, assessment strategies, and student results. This type of powerful teacher collaboration builds trust, leads to greater willingness to innovate and take risks, to learn from mistakes, and share successful strategies and approaches with colleagues.

Once a context supportive of adult learning has been established, the process of conducting an effective peer coaching program can be broken down into six key steps (see Figure 11.2): get things started, identify a need and specify an outcome, understand the current real-ity, explore assumptions, create and test alternative solutions, and monitor progress (McNeil & Klink, 2008; Zwart, Wubbels, Bolhuis, & Bergen, 2008).

Figure 11.2   The Peer Coaching Process

STEP 1

Get things started. Group membership is set and time is scheduled for groups to meet.

STEP 2

Need and specify an outcome. The inviting teacher brings an instructional need, and the peer coaching pair works together to specify the desired outcome.

STEP 3

Understand the current reality. The peer coaching group works to understand the gap between the current reality and the desired outcome.

STEP 4

Explore thinking processes. The coach works with the inviting teacher to test assumptions that may be interfering with the teacher being able to help his or her students reach the desired outcome.

STEP 5

Generate and test alternative solutions. The coach works with the inviting teacher to explore and then select an action to achieve the desired outcome.

STEP 6

Monitor progress. The peer coaching pair must decide how they are going to assess the approach they have selected. Ideally, at least three forms of evidence should be used in monitoring the progress toward achieving the desired outcome.

Source: Adapted from McNeil and Klink (2004).

Step 1: Get Things Started

The two most significant issues to consider when beginning a peer coaching program are time and selecting peer coaching partners. Even with an established professional learning community, time should be set aside for some initial training with the peer coaching teams. Whether your trainer is from a local university or from a school with an established peer coaching program, he or she will focus on helping your peer coaching teams practice important communication skills and will assist them in understanding the essential steps of peer coaching. Peer coaching teams must also have time to meet and observe one another's classes.

Selecting group membership can be a sensitive matter, whether your peer coaches work in pairs or groups of three or four. Some programs employ self-selection, whereas others favor a more structured approach. Most programs have teachers from the same grade level or content area work together, but others mix it up across grade levels and content areas. Whichever method you employ, trust among peers is an essential component.

The importance of trust in peer coaching is illustrated by the experiences of a school I visited several years ago. During my visit I learned that their peer coaching pairs often consisted of teachers from different grade levels or content areas. When I asked why they had made this decision the head of school said, "We tried mandating that teachers from the same grade level or content area work with each other, and it was not working as we wanted. We asked our teachers how we could improve things and they came up with the idea of self-selecting across grade levels and content areas. That change made a big difference, and I'm convinced it was because comfort and trust is such a vital part of the whole peer coaching concept."

Step 2: Identify a Need and Specify an Outcome

Once coaching pairs or groups have been formed and trained, the work of peer coaching can begin. Because the purpose of peer coaching is to help teachers develop practical ways to improve their classroom instruction, the process begins with one teacher bringing a current instructional need to the other teacher who will act as the coach. For example, David, an upper-school science teacher I know, was having trouble getting his students to correctly identify sources with misleading and unreliable information. He brought this instructional need to his peer coach and asked for help with the problem. However, identifying an instructional need is only part of step 2. After a need has been determined, the teacher and coach work to specify the desired result, what the result will look like, and what types of evidence will indicate the desired result has been realized.

After discussing it with his coach, David decided that the desired result was students being able to independently, and correctly, assess the validity and reliability of data and conclusions in popular and scientific print and video media. Evidence that they were able to do this, they decided, would come from two sources: student performance on assignments designed by David to specifically assess these skills and the sources students selected to support arguments and conclusions on their lab reports and research proposals. Once an instructional need has been determined and a desired result has been specified, the peer coaching pair is ready to move to the next step of the process.

Step 3: Understand the Current Reality

In this step, the peer coaching pair explores and analyzes current student achievement in the area of interest, and discusses actions that have already been taken to improve student performance. The pair also works to identify assumptions about teaching, students, and learning that may be related to the instructional need the presenting teacher is experiencing. Questions that help get this conversation started include the following (Qualters, 2009):

- What does student performance in the area of interest look like right now, and in what specific ways does it need to improve to achieve your desired result?
- What have you done in the past to help students reach your desired result?
- Have any had some degree of success? Which ones, and why have they been somewhat successful?
- Which ones have not worked at all, and why do you think they have not worked?
- What obstacles are keeping you from being more successful in this area?

The goal in discussing these questions is for the pair to be clear about the gap between the current reality and the desired result and for the pair to understand what has already been tried so they don't repeat things that have not worked.

The pair can then move to perhaps the most difficult aspect of peer coaching: unearthing deeply held beliefs and assumptions of the presenting teacher about teaching, students, learning, and schools that may influence getting to the desired result. Due to traditional methods of teacher professional learning, and the conflict-averse nature of most schools, such assumptions and beliefs have historically not been discussed in schools. However, in many cases underlying beliefs and assumptions need to be identified to remove barriers to achieving the desired result. The teacher acting as coach can help to surface assumptions and beliefs by carefully crafting questions about the presenting teacher's instructional need. For example, David's coach posed the following questions:

- What is the primary reason that your students have not been able to achieve your desired result? Why have your previous methods not been successful? Does it have more to do with your instructional approaches or your students?
- Do students have the foundational skills and knowledge to achieve your desired result? How do you know?
- Are the resources available to achieve the desired result?
- Why is it important that your students be able to achieve your desired result?

Once the current reality is understood and the underlying assumptions have been surfaced, the next stage of the process can begin.

Step 4: Explore Assumptions

Once underlying beliefs and assumptions surface, it is useful to confront them by asking whether they are based on fact or opinion. Our beliefs and assumptions about students, teaching, and schools are connected to the mental models we create to make sense of the world. At times, changing instructional practices necessitate modifying mental models and the beliefs and assumptions emerging from them. For people to adjust their mental models, they must be confronted with evidence that their mental model does not fit current reality (Allen & Leblanc, 2004). Confronting mental models and assumptions is difficult because the common responses are "X is an established principle," or "We all know that X is important." The coach must ask, "Who is *we*?' and "Upon what knowledge and facts are that principle based?"

It is normal and natural for teachers to assume that what brought them success in the past will bring them success now and that what was once an accepted principle of quality teaching and learning will remain so (McNeil & Klink, 2008). For example, one of the beliefs underlying David's instruction is that students should be able to perform a new skill once they have memorized the steps involved in it. This assumption has worked well for David in the past with basic lab procedures, and in helping students understand the steps involved in conducting an experiment. However, it may not be the best approach when helping students critically evaluate the validity and reliability of scientific information. Memorizing specific steps may not be enough for them to understand the nuances of what makes data valid and reliable. Multiple opportunities for practice with feedback from David may be more appropriate to accomplish the desired result.

The goal in step 4 is for the coach to work with the presenting teacher to test assumptions that may be interfering with the teacher being able to help his or her students reach the desired student learning goal. Once this is done, the peer coaching pair can begin to consider alternative actions to reach the goal.

Step 5: Create and Test Alternative Solutions

In step 5, the coaching teacher works with the presenting teacher to explore alternative instructional approaches. The coach poses questions to get the presenting teacher to reflect on prior approaches and why they have not been successful. The goal is to help the presenting teacher begin to see actions that he or she has not tried that hold promise for bringing about the desired result. For example, David's coach asks the following questions: "Why have your past approaches been unsuccessful?" "What other options have you considered but not tried in the past?" and "Have you researched best practices in this area to see what other teachers do?"

These questions led to a rich discussion in which David identified likely reasons for past approaches not working and began to formulate an action plan to address his problem of practice. David concluded that he has been expecting students to master this complex skill too quickly, and has been relying on methods not suited to this learning goal. David and his coach developed a new approach in which the desired student outcome becomes one of the overarching goals of his course, rather than a discrete part of a unit, and where his instructional approach centers on giving students multiple opportunities to practice the desired skill with corresponding feedback from him.

It may be that the alternative actions identified in this step will require the presenting teacher to develop new skills. For example, David may not be comfortable developing and guiding authentic opportunities for his students to practice assessing the validity and reliability of scientific data. If the coach has experience and expertise in the area, he or she can work with the presenting teacher to develop the needed skill. Otherwise, the coach must work with the presenting teacher to identify another source, inside or outside his or her school, to provide help in developing the skill. Of course, once a plan has been developed and the required skills have been practiced, it is time for the presenting teacher to test the new approach with students to see if it results in the desire student outcome.

Step 6: Monitor Progress

Ultimately, effective peer coaching is focused on student learning. Therefore, the peer coaching pair must decide how they are going to assess the approach they have selected. Ideally, at least three forms of evidence should be used in monitoring the progress of students toward achieving the desired outcome (Hampton & Rhodes, 2004). First, the presenting teacher should keep a journal of his or her experiences with the new instructional strategy, reflecting on student performance and the challenges the new approach brings. Second, student artifacts can be collected and discussed with the coaching teacher to determine if students are moving closer to the desired goal. Third, the coaching teacher can observe the presenting teacher in action to gather evidence about student thinking and performance connected to the desired student outcome. As evidence is collected, the peer coaching pair can meet to discuss progress toward student learning goals and can make adjustments in their plan as they are needed.

David began implementing his new approach at the beginning of the first semester, and he discussed progress with his peer coach each month for the entire school year. Numerous adjustments were made along the way as they sought to fine tune their approach to foster better student outcomes.

Essential Elements

Peer coaching is a flexible professional development strategy, with the actual process differing greatly from one coaching group to another. Some steps will happen in a brief meeting while others may involve conversations over the course of a year. While the peer coaching path is often crooked, the following elements are characteristic of successful peer coaching programs:

- *Make time available.* Time must be made available during the school day at least once each week for the peer coaching group to meet. It is also helpful if time is periodically available for the coaching teacher to observe the presenting teacher in action in the classroom.
- *Provide training to teachers.* Training must be provided to teachers before beginning a peer coaching program to help them develop an understanding of the peer coaching process

and practice the skills they will need as a peer coach. Essential skills include communication skills, conflict resolution skills, problem-solving strategies, how to have difficult conversations, observation strategies and methods, and active listening.

- *Build a trusting, collaborative school culture.* Effective peer coaching requires close examination of teaching practices, and this will not happen without a high level of trust between teachers in each peer coaching group. There must be a sense in the school that people care about one another and are willing to help one another.

- *Foster an unwavering focus on improving instructional practices.* Effective peer coaching is always focused on addressing current teacher instructional needs so that student learning can be improved.

- *Do not connect to teacher evaluation.* Peer coaching relationships are characterized by equality and have nothing to do with teacher evaluation. The focus is on teaching and student learning, not the teacher. The coach's role is to ask questions and help the inviting teacher reflect, analyze, and plan. After a new approach has been tried, the coach does not evaluate but rather helps the inviting teacher to understand the results and what may be adjusted to improve future results.

- *Provide administrative support.* Once peer coaching has been chosen, the principal needs to do all he or she can to support peer collaboration by encouraging meetings, providing needed training, securing necessary resources, and carving out sufficient time for group meetings. "It is clear that ongoing, visible, tangible principal support are essential for the creation and maintenance of effective peer coaching programs" (Heider, 2005, p. 7). A principal who models inquiry and articulates the connections between peer coaching work and the mission of the school facilitates the development of effective peer coaching work. Another significant way the principal can communicate commitment to and support of peer coaching is to periodically work as a member of a peer coaching pair or group. This says in a powerful way that the principal is committed to continuing his or her own professional learning from and with his or her faculty. Furthermore, it helps the principal better understand peer coaching and more effectively support the work of the peer coaching in the school.

Summary

While conferences, teacher sabbaticals, workshops, and speakers may enhance teacher knowledge in various areas, the true test of a professional development approach is the extent to which it leads to improved classroom instruction and enhanced student learning. Effective professional development is more practical than theoretical and leads to teachers successfully addressing the most significant instructional challenges they face in their classrooms. The peer coaching strategy bridges the gap between educational theory and the day-to-day realities teachers face in their classrooms.

Peer coaching works because it is specifically focused on helping teachers improve their classroom instruction by providing them with opportunities to share instructional strategies, observe and be observed by colleagues, collaboratively brainstorm and test alternative teaching methods, and monitor the progress of their efforts. Further, peer coaching helps teachers investigate underlying assumptions about teaching, students, and learning that may be connected to current professional dilemmas they are facing. David, the science teacher discussed throughout this chapter, perhaps best describes the value of peer coaching: "Peer coaching is the first professional development experience that has resulted in real improvements in my classroom practices. Having the time and opportunity to focus on my classroom challenges with a colleague makes professional development relevant and empowering for the first time. I now feel like I have a way to be learning every year from the events that happen in my classroom."

12

Online Professional Development

An explosion of offerings and evolving methodologies make Web-based training an effective, viable professional development option for many schools and teachers.

—Chris Dede

Michelle and the other members of the middle school math team had spent time analyzing and discussing data from multiple sources (standardized test results, in-class test results, and teacher observations of students) to identify areas of student weakness. They all agreed that their students as a whole were not proficient in using critical-thinking skills to analyze a problem, and then apply learned math concepts to solve the problem. Mrs. Brennan, her principal, recommended that they all take an online course focused on helping middle school math teachers learn instructional approaches to enhance student critical-thinking and problem-solving skills.

Michelle was skeptical as she logged into her "class" for the first time. However, her thinking changed as she read posted materials and took part in online discussions, facilitated by an instructor with expertise on the topic, involving her school colleagues and teachers from other schools. She valued the ability to engage in dialogue when and where she wanted, and enjoyed having some degree of one-on-one interaction with the instructor. What was most helpful though, and what really transformed her skepticism into belief, was when the instructor had them attempt new strategies with their students and then reconnect with their online peers to discuss what did and didn't work. Being pushed to video segments of her classes, and then both share and receive feedback on her recorded lesson from her online instructor and peers, was an invaluable experience. Michelle and her colleagues were improving their instructional practices and were seeing real improvements in their students' thinking and their performance on tests and quizzes.

In reflecting on her experience, Michelle cited several significant benefits of her online course compared with traditional face-to-face workshops. First, she had more interaction, with both the instructor and her peers, allowing her to get her questions answered and reflect on the questions of others. Second, she had great flexibility regarding when she participated, permitting her to engage more fully in the content of the course. Finally, she felt she could express her worries, frustrations, and shortcomings more easily in an online discussion than during a crowded in-service workshop.

As I emphasized in earlier chapters, teacher professional development is key to educational improvement. Enhancing the effectiveness of professional learning is the leverage point with the greatest possibility for strengthening the knowledge and teaching practices of educators. For most teachers, professional learning is the most accessible avenue they have for developing the knowledge and skills required to enhance student learning. So we as a profession need to build teachers' capacity for improvement, but we must be sure that the time, energy, and resources are devoted to programs that teach with and about best practices. In short, we need professional development that improves teaching practices and student learning while being cost-effective. When implemented with care and foresight, online professional development can fit this prescription.

The Rationale for Online Professional Development

The need for professional development that is adapted to teachers' busy schedules, that draws on useful resources not available locally, and that provides job-embedded support has driven the establishment of many online professional development programs. Other online professional development programs have emerged as many schools have sought to provide quality professional learning opportunities for their teachers in a climate of professional development budget cuts.

Online professional development provides Web-based learning opportunities, including educational programs, courses, workshops, activities, resources, and online interactions with instructors, mentors, and colleagues. There are many different types of online learning, but the learning community model of online professional development is the most common and most effective (Fisher, Schumaker, & Culbertson, 2010). It combines readings, activities, and facilitated peer-to-peer collaborative discussions; is aligned with the Learning Forward standards of effective teacher professional learning; and has been shown to improve teacher knowledge and instructional practices (Dede, 2006).

In this model, participants access their course materials on the Web and complete a sequence of Web-based readings and activities. Activities include exploring a website or a computer-based simulation, experimenting with a new technology tool, viewing an online video clip, trying out a new technology-enhanced activity in the classroom, and sharing the results with others. The focal point is the online discussion, where learners participate asynchronously to share their reflections, ideas, comments, and questions in response to a focused discussion prompt posed by the instructor. Because participants and facilitators are able to take time to prepare comments and responses, online discussions can be more reflective than synchronous discussions or face-to-face workshops, and give all participants an opportunity to contribute to the discussion.

Eight benefits associated with online professional development provide a powerful rationale for engaging in this professional development approach (Treacy, Kleiman, & Peterson, 2002):

1. *Provides Improved Ability to Meet Teacher Learning Needs*

   Online professional development provides opportunities to engage in professional learning activities that might not be available locally.

2. *Allows Teachers to Experience Technology Use as a Learner*

   Online professional development does not require technical expertise. Rather, it gives teachers a chance to experience the utility of technology as a learner so they can be in a better position to use technology effectively with their own students.

3. *Offers the Ability to Meet a Variety of Learning Needs*

   The explosion of digital information and new media available on the Web offers abundant and engaging learning opportunities that can address a wide variety of teacher learning needs and styles. Further, it allows teachers to learn at a pace that is comfortable for them.

4. *Allows Learning When You Want, Where You Want*

   Online learning allows teachers to choose personally convenient meeting times, meaning they are more likely to be engaged with the material.

5. *Reduces Professional Development Costs*

   Online professional learning does not require costs such as class release time, space rental, speaker fees, conference fees, travel, and onsite equipment needed for face-to-face workshops.

6. *Provides Collaborative Learning Opportunities*

   Online professional learning connects teachers with educators and subject experts across time and place, and encourages them to become part of a global community of learning teachers.

7. *Impacts Instructional Practices*

   The ongoing nature of online professional learning opportunities allows them to include projects where teachers develop new lessons and apply new approaches, and share their experiences with peers in reflective discussions. The cycle of learning-applying-reflecting-sharing results in real instructional improvements.

8. *Facilitates Improved Follow-Up*

   Online professional development can extend learning beyond single in-service days and provide new ways for teachers to stay connected with colleagues after the end of a professional development experience.

A Framework for Implementing Online Professional Development

This chapter provides a framework school leaders can use to design and deliver online professional development to meet the learning needs of the teachers with whom they work. The framework combines what is known about effective professional learning, and the essential processes and resources needed to deliver it online. While the technologies used are a significant component of online professional development, there are many other factors that should also be considered to design and implement effective online professional development. Too often excessive attention is given to the technologies, with the result being an online professional development approach that is over budget, underutilized, and ineffective. So the framework presented here is intended to help school leaders keep the role of technology in perspective and to guide them through the steps of creating, nurturing, and maintaining an effective online professional development program.

Who Should Be Involved?

The simple and obvious answer is that everyone should be involved. It is essential when selecting online professional development opportunities to involve those who will be engaged in the online experiences and who will be affected by the outcomes. For teachers to be engaged in and committed to their online professional learning, they need to know about the options available to them and play a role in selecting them. When teachers are given a significant voice and choice in selecting and shaping professional learning strategies and activities, they find professional development more meaningful, are more committed to the success of professional development, and are more likely to seek out authentic applications of their learning (Wei et al., 2010).

Technology Considerations

Since you are going to deliver professional development online, before you get started be sure to assess whether or not your teachers can use the required technologies. Don't assume that all of your teachers have the knowledge and the skills to navigate a Learning Management System, participate in an online discussion board, or post a video of their classroom teaching. It's important to determine the proficiency of your faculty up front, perhaps through a survey or at faculty meetings. Then you can work with your technology staff to provide instruction and support to teachers who need it.

Of course, it's also important to make sure your teachers have access to a computer with a reliable Internet connection, ideally from both school and at home. Without easy and reliable access, the anywhere, anytime advantage of online professional development is diminished. It is also essential that your online professional development program have technical support available, both to help individuals with specific problems and adjust any filter or firewall settings that may interfere with teachers accessing essential online course materials.

Addressing Online Professional Development Myths

It is important that teachers approach their online learning experience with an accurate understanding of what online professional development is and what it isn't. "Many teachers misunderstand what online learning is all about. They think it's going to be easy like surfing the Web, so school leaders need to bust that myth from the outset" (Killion, 2000, p. 40). Here are some common myths about online professional development and the reality about each one (Ross, 2011):

- *Online professional development is easy.* As John Ross (2011) says, "just because you can shop online doesn't mean you're prepared for online learning" (p. 52). With high-quality content, facilitated discussions, and meaningful applications of learned concepts, teachers will be challenged by online professional development in a very good way.
- *Teaching online is like teaching face-to-face.* Quality online instructors go through an extensive training process. Instructors don't have the same visual and verbal cues in an online setting and must develop skills to facilitate online discussions and provide feedback to meet the needs of their students.
- *Online professional development is just a textbook online.* While there is online content composed of text and images, effective online professional development is much more than an online textbook. Effective online learning consists of meaningful interaction among participants and relevant application of learned concepts.
- *Online courses have teachers glued to the computer.* And face-to-face workshops don't have teachers glued to their chairs? Effective online courses have far less seat time and require teachers to get away from the computer to implement a new strategy or skill in the classroom and then share their experience with their online peers.
- *Online professional development is isolating.* It won't be if you align it with existing on-site collaborative learning groups. Through online professional development, teachers have an opportunity to be a part of two learning communities (one online and one onsite) that can complement and reinforce one another.

Connect Learning Goals With Specific Online Options

An essential aspect of any effective online professional development program is to establish specific learning goals for your teachers (Tracey, 2010). Once you have identified the specific knowledge, skills, and instructional practices to be acquired by teachers through professional development (using the procedures described in Chapter 4), it is important to determine which online option can best meet teacher learning needs. Some schools and school districts choose to build their own online courses. However, because building an online professional development experience in-house is such an expensive endeavor, both in terms of time and money, most schools turn to outside vendors to find online professional development that meets teacher learning needs.

Hundreds of facilitated learning community online professional development courses are available through established vendors like PBS TeacherLine, EdTech Leaders Online, and Teachscape. To help schools, school leaders, and teachers identify quality offerings, The National Education Association has recently created NEA Academy, an online repository that links educators to online courses that have passed a rigorous peer-review process. A quality review board scores online offerings from a variety of vendors using a rubric based on standards for quality online professional learning developed by the Southern Regional Education Board. In addition to using NEA Academy, educators should consider asking vendors questions in the following areas as they work to match online professional development with their specific teacher learning needs (Dede, 2006; Ross, 2011; Tracey, 2010):

1. Linked to Specific Student Learning Outcomes
   o What specific student learning outcomes are linked with each course?
   o Are courses linked with established standards?

2. Job-Embedded
   o In what ways does the professional development support the daily challenges of teachers?
   o What content or skills are addressed that are immediately applicable for teachers?

3. Ongoing With Follow-Up
   o What is the duration of the professional development experience? Is this flexible?
   o What find of follow-up is provided?

4. Authentic, Active Learning Experiences
   ○ What kinds of activities do teachers complete?
   ○ Can I get guest access to view the activities and learning prompts?

5. Includes Subject-Matter Content
   ○ What subject-matter content is included, and how is it used to help teachers develop new skills and knowledge?
   ○ Are the objectives of the course a good match for the learning needs of our teachers?
   ○ Do the content and skills emphasized in the course align with required content standards, or preferred pedagogies and philosophies?

6. Fosters Reflection on Content, Beliefs, and Pedagogy
   ○ What kinds of reflective activities are included, and how is deep reflection encouraged and assessed?

7. Collaborative
   ○ How is collaboration among participants promoted, and what technologies are used to do this?
   ○ Are my teachers ready, both in terms of technology skills and collaboration skills, to collaborate in the ways required by the course?

8. Support for Teachers
   ○ What kind and depth of content, program, and technical support is provided to teachers? Is the support provided enough for my teachers?

9. Evaluates Impact on Student Learning
   ○ What data are available regarding the impact of the course on instructional practices and student achievement?

Determine When Teachers Will Participate

Once you and your faculty have selected online professional development options that meet teacher learning needs, it is important to consider when teachers will engage in their online learning experiences. Contrary to popular perceptions, online professional learning is typically as rigorous as, if not more so than, many face-to-face approaches. Therefore, you should not expect to connect teachers with an online professional development option and just have them work it into their schedules on their own. Like the other approaches discussed in this book, time must be set aside for online professional learning to be effective. "We can't assume that teachers will engage in meaningful online learning at home in the evening" (Ross, 2011, p. 56).

One effective approach is to build time for online professional learning into the regular school day schedule. Harvard researcher Chris Dede (2006) emphasizes that "the schedule of the day must be restructured to provide teachers with focused opportunities to engage in meaningful online learning (p. 29)." Another way to create time for online professional learning is to schedule early dismissal days each month. A third approach is to provide stipends for work outside the school day and/or over summer. Finally, some of the time scheduled for faculty meetings can be used for online teacher professional learning. By providing and protecting the time needed for meaningful online professional learning, school leaders demonstrate in a powerful way their commitment to the ongoing learning of their teachers.

Align Online Professional Development With On-Site Professional Learning

It is important to connect the online professional learning at your school with the face-to-face professional learning at your school. Isolated online learning can be damaging to the collaborative learning culture in a school and is not likely to result in significant improvements in instructional practices (Dede, 2006). As noted educational researcher Joellen Killion emphasizes, "schools must be careful to purposefully connect online learning with collaborative on-site learning groups to prevent a deterioration of the school-based professional learning community that is at the heart of effective teacher learning" (2007, p. 22). Some schools intentionally have lesson study groups, Critical Friends groups, or action research groups take online courses together (Ross, 2011), or have mentoring and coaching pairs take online courses together (Feger & Zibit, 2006). Through doing this, the members of the groups come to feel they are part of two learning communities, one inside the school and one outside the school, both of which engage them in an ongoing effort to improve their own learning and the learning of their students.

Monitoring and Evaluating Online Professional Development

Many effective things are done in teacher professional development, but many ineffective, wasteful things are also done. It is important for educators to know the extent to which online professional development efforts are resulting in improved teacher knowledge and skills, and enhanced student learning. When you carefully specify teacher learning goals up front you can search for good evidence about whether you have achieved your goals. Quality evaluations involve collecting three types of information and provide useful and reliable information that can help you engage in an ongoing process of making your online teacher professional learning activities more effective:

1. Teacher Reflections

   While it should not be the only type of evaluation evidence gathered, teachers reflections are an important part of any evaluation. Did the online professional development meet their needs? Was it engaging and useful? Will it make a difference in their classroom teaching? Questionnaires and group interviews can help you answer these questions.

2. Teacher Learning

   Unfortunately, most evaluations do not go beyond gathering teacher reflections. Of course, it is also important to gather evidence about the extent to which teachers learned the intended knowledge and skills, and whether or not they are applying what they learned in their classrooms. Questionnaires and reflections provide limited information about what teachers learned. To provide more direct evidence that teachers have acquired specific knowledge and skills and understood them accurately, additional assessment methods should used. One way to do this is a simulation or demonstration, in which a teacher teaches a lesson involving the targeted knowledge and/or skills to a group of colleagues. Another way is to observe teachers attempting to apply the targeted knowledge and/or skills in an actual lesson with their own students. For both types of demonstrations, detailed checklists or rubrics should be developed in advance to keep observations focused on the application of specific knowledge and skills.

3. Student Learning

The most important, and most elusive, evidence to obtain pertains to student learning. Did the online professional development enhance student learning and achievement? Questionnaires, grades, standardized test scores, portfolios, and interviews can all be done to determine the extent to which student learning has been impacted.

Leading Online Professional Development Efforts

To implement an effective teacher professional development program, school leaders must realize that change takes time and that some teacher resistance is a normal, natural part of the implementation process. This is particularly true with teachers who are unfamiliar or uncomfortable with technology (Tracey, 2010). Rather than complaining about this resistance, it is more productive for school leaders to seek to understand it, acknowledge it, and be clear about what they will need to do to decrease it over time. When school leaders keep the focus of professional development on student learning, involve teachers in the selection of online professional development activities, provide ongoing support for teachers as they engage in their experiences, and provide time for teachers to engage in online professional development activities, resistance will be minimal. Further, school leaders build faculty support for implementation by frequently reiterating professional development goals, connecting online professional development experiences with collaborative on-site professional learning, and honestly discussing the complexities and challenges of significant change.

Summary

While online professional development is still relatively new for schools, evidence is growing that it can meet many teachers' needs as well or better than face-to-face approaches. An online approach to professional development offers an innovative means for teachers to plan instruction, obtain feedback, and exchange resources with colleagues. Expanding beyond a single location, an online professional learning community can form to meet the particular needs and interests of teachers around specific content or curriculum, connecting to their peers at a distance.

Online professional development has numerous advantages, particularly at a time when professional development budgets are shrinking. Online professional development provides access to content and instruction over time, and it allows contact with other teachers before and after the course has been completed. Online professional development accommodates a variety of learning styles. A typical online course may include written text, video clips, video meetings, face-to-face meetings, e-mail, discussion boards with other course participants, and group work. Some of the other advantages of online professional development include creating a learning community with statewide participation and communication, eliminating or reducing travel time and expense, allowing for flexibility in terms of when teachers can participate, allowing for benefits to both urban and rural areas, and providing large numbers of teachers with high-quality professional development within a specified time frame.

13

Personal Learning Networks

Personal learning networks provide teachers with access to global leaders and experts, bringing together communities, resources, and information that is impossible to access within one school's walls.

—Will Richardson

When Tracy first started teaching in the 1980s, there was the Internet but she wasn't on it. Most information was shared face-to-face. Her personal learning network (PLN), the people she learned from and shared with, was small—teachers at her school and a few colleagues from graduate school. When they gathered before or after classes, they occasionally would share a success or failure in the classroom, an article or a book they had read, or an idea they had picked up at a conference or a workshop. Books came from bookstores, journals came in the mail, and information from conferences came home in her suitcase. The really valuable stuff was organized in her filing cabinet for future reference.

Tracy's PLN expanded a bit in the 1990s. She communicated with people via e-mail, and bookmarked websites she liked, but most of her professional information sharing and gathering was still done face-to-face, and the amount of paper in her filing cabinet continued to grow. In the past decade, Tracy's PLN has changed dramatically. She orders books and journals online and downloads them to her computer. Updates from her various discussion groups await her each morning in her inbox, and she shares information daily with teachers around the globe using Twitter. Rather than printing out copies to file, she saves her valuable links on her favorite social bookmarking site, Diigo (www.diigo.com). Because she uses tags instead of file folders, she can easily search for specific items, and because teachers can search through one another's bookmarks, sharing is easy. Her PLN now consists of both teachers in her own school and teachers and experts from around the globe.

The sheer volume of information and possibilities is overwhelming, and Tracy is just beginning to manage and organize it with the help of Symbaloo (www.symbaloo.com), a personal web aggregator. If she has a question or concern connected to her discipline, her instructional practices, or her students, she is able to acquire knowledge, suggestions, and ideas quickly. She attends more conferences than she ever has in the past, but she travels much less due to online conference sessions and summaries. Her professional learning now consists of both the collaborative groups in her own school (for example, lesson study and Critical Friends), and the collaborative connections she creates and cultivates through modern digital tools and resources.

Modern digital tools and resources (for example, blogs, podcasts, social networking, and social bookmarking) are collaborative, mobile, and user driven. They include tools and platforms for connecting, sharing, publishing, and organizing. At their core, today's digital tools are about powerful, social, technologies connecting people and ideas. As PLN proponent Will Richardson (2011) states, "Blogs, social networking sites, and other digital tools aren't places to go, but rather are things to do, ways to express yourself, means to connect with others and extend your learning" (p. 17).

During a typical day, Tracy uses multiple digital tools to cultivate her PLN. She

- communicates via e-mail;
- uses Twitter and Classroom 2.0 to see what people are saying, blogging, what websites are being mentioned, and what webinars are available;
- visits the Educator's PLN Ning site (http://edupln.ning.com) to connect with educators from around the country and world;

- visits the Educational Wikis site, which focuses on best practices for using wikis to support instruction;
- visits bookmarks shared through the Diigo groups she belongs to;
- checks Facebook to see what personal and professional friends are saying;
- checks her blog, where she may post something new or respond to the postings of others;
- checks new posts on the blogs that she follows; and
- checks PodBean (www.podbean.com) to see podcasts posted by other educators.

Personal learning networks complement and expand on-site professional learning communities. Networks and partnerships external to schools can be a major conduit for teachers to improve their professional practice. For example, Tracy regularly uses her PLN to research best practices and discuss instructional ideas that she brings to her on-site lesson study group. In addition, she uses her blog, Twitter, and the Educator's PLN Ning to reflect on and share the work of her lesson study group. She feels she is part of both an on-site professional learning community and a larger learning community through her PLN. Both are important in helping her improve her knowledge base, share instructional ideas and challenges, and successfully address important problems of practice in her classroom.

Going Global

Educators in schools with effective professional development programs are involved in their school's professional learning community and have PLNs that enable them to connect with other educators and subject matter experts from around the globe. Individual teachers create PLNs specific to their needs to extend relevant learning connections to people with similar interests around the world. These connections need not occur face-to-face or in real time, nor does the learner have to personally know their knowledge collaborators. "PLNs provide teachers with access to global leaders and experts, bringing together communities, resources, and information that is impossible to access within one school's walls" (Richardson, 2011, p. 8). They are a terrific way for teachers to extend their knowledge and learning outside their classroom and school. In doing so, they are better prepared to scaffold this process with their students.

Educational researcher David Warlick (2009) says that building a PLN involves creating and cultivating three different types of connections (see Figure 13.1).

Figure 13.1   Three Types of Connections of a PLN

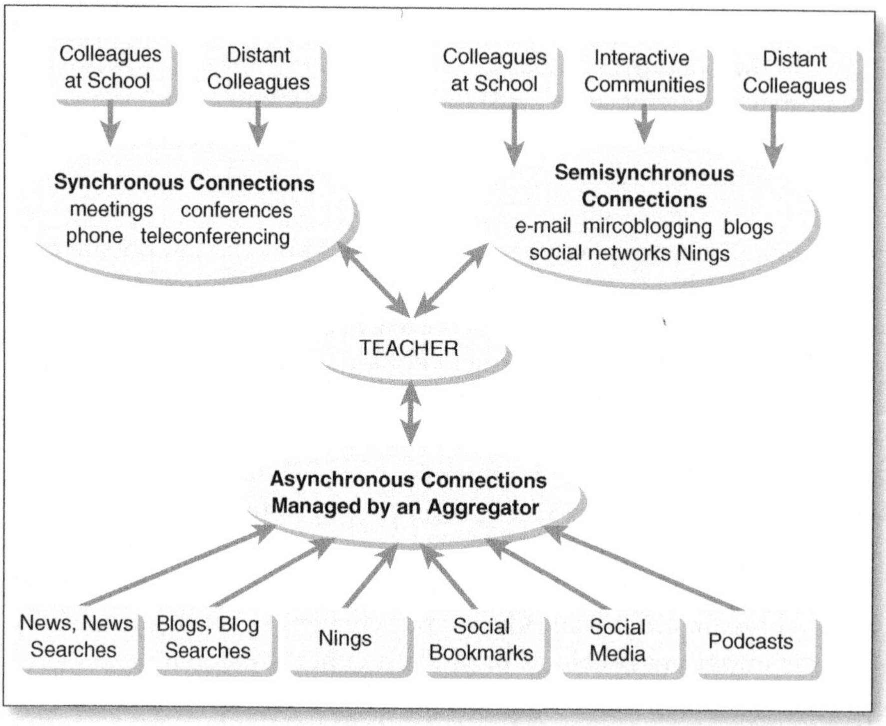

Source: Adapted from Warlick (2009).

1. Synchronous Connections

   This is the traditional network that includes the people and places teachers consult to answer questions, solve problems, and get things done. Today, however, teachers can expand this network with digital tools such as chat, instant and text messaging, teleconferencing, and microblogging. "It's like attending a meeting at school, only better, because the traditional barriers of geography, background, language, and culture become transparent" (Warlick, 2009, p. 13).

2. Semisynchronous Connections

   Semisynchronous refers to the idea that collaboration does not have to happen in real time. For networked teachers, these are conversations that are not like typical conversations. Questions can be directed toward a single friend or a colleague, but more likely they are sent out to a community of educators who, because of their interests, knowledge, skills, or perspectives, are in a position to help teachers solve problems of practice. Not only can collaborators be geographically distant, but educators can also join a discussion when it works best for their schedules, regardless of time zones or office hours. The tools educators can use to build and grow this type of network include Nings, social network sites, microblogging sites, group discussion boards, and commenting on blogs.

3. Asynchronous Connections

The first two types of connections connect teachers with other educators, while the third type most often connects teachers with content sources they have identified as particularly useful (Warlick, 2009). The primary tool for asynchronous connections is the RSS aggregator or feed reader. An aggregator is a digital tool that collects a specific type of information from multiple online sources. Aggregators such as Google Reader and Netvibes form the core of many educators' PLNs because they organize information that helps them do their jobs more efficiently and effectively.

When teachers subscribe to tagged Flickr photos, new videos from YouTube or TeacherTube, Google News searches, or podcasts, they are, in effect, training all this information to organize and deliver itself to them. For example, after finding an education blog a teacher can subscribe to its RSS feed using an aggregator. Then he or she just waits for the software to periodically check for new posts, retrieve them as they appear, and make them available for reading. Teachers can also subscribe to ongoing blog searches that will scan the entire Internet and automatically send to them new posts on a selected topic.

Other valuable asynchronous connections are social bookmarking services such as Diigo. As educators add new websites to their online bookmarks and categorize or tag them, that information becomes available to other people. What is the benefit here? If a teacher is looking for articles about gene therapy, for example, a Google search will return a list of approximately 12 million Web pages. Searching Diigo returns a smaller list of websites that are likely of higher quality, as someone thought enough of them to bookmark them for later use. In addition, teachers can subscribe to the RSS feed for the search so that all subsequently bookmarked websites tagged with *gene therapy* will be sent to them as well. This is a useful PLN tool because teachers are connecting to resources that are supported by a recommendation system.

The Power of PLNs

Personal learning networks are not really new. We have always depended on our families, friends, colleagues at work, and acquaintances to support and enhance our knowledge about our profession and the world. Further, we have been connecting with people and information through the Internet for decades. But things continue to change. Technologies have liberated content from the printed page, giving voice to the thoughts of individuals we have never had access to before and allowing us to reshape our information experiences to fit our learning needs (Warlick, 2009).

Using these new technologies to create and grow PLNs is critical for teachers who want to remain connected to the rapidly evolving world we must introduce to our students. Teachers can connect with communities of interest to find information sources, ideas for lesson plans, potential collaborators, current events and trends, new opportunities, resources, and a wide variety of additional answers and knowledge. PLNs provide access to sources of information that were not even available until quite recently. Thankfully, emerging technologies are making it possible to capture and make sense of the resulting information overload.

Both Will Richardson (2011) and Demetri Orlando (2010) have written extensively on why PLNs created with digital tools are so important for teachers' ongoing professional learning. This list represents a synthesis of their ideas and makes a case for teachers to create and cultivate PLNs to advance their own learning and the learning of their students:

- *PLNs are a powerful way to access, gather, and build content knowledge and pedagogical content knowledge (how to best teach specific content to a specific grade level).* The majority of communication that teachers have through their PLNs (for example, tweeted links, blog posts, wiki additions, Ning discussions, and Listserv messages) concerns teaching and learning resources. As they do this, they deepen their understanding of content and how to best teach it to their students. In addition, teachers become more skilled with the technological tools that are used to access, shape, and share digital content, preparing them to help their students develop the important 21st century ability to effectively access and manipulate digital information.
- *PLNs help teachers solve problems of practice and develop lifelong learning skills.* Teachers can use Twitter, Nings, Listserv messages, and blogs to ask questions to help them solve problems

of practice or just understand a concept or idea more deeply. A developed PLN enables a teacher to greatly expand the knowledge and experience he or she can draw upon to resolve problems and explore topics of interest. Being able to solve problems by tapping into networks using collaborative digital tools is a key skill for both teachers and students. As teachers cultivate their PLNs and become engaged in collaborative discussions, they participate in both asking and answering questions, and model the lifelong learning skills we want to help our students develop.

- *PLNs help teachers understand the ethical use of online information.* Students need to understand how to use the Web and the information on it safely and ethically. Teachers cultivating PLNs gain experience in this area, allowing them to more authentically teach and model the ethical use of online information to their students.

- *PLNs provide just-in-time learning for teachers.* As I have emphasized throughout this book, time is one of the biggest obstacles to establishing effective professional learning practices. Personal learning networks minimize the issue of time because they allow teachers to seek out information and answers anytime and anywhere. They eliminate the artificial constraints of the school building and school day. This just-in-time learning allows teachers to solve problems as they emerge, and helps them understand how best to best help their students reap the benefits of just-in-time learning by developing their own PLNs.

- *PLNs expose teachers to a global and extraordinarily diverse world.* Through PLNs, teachers interact with an incredible diversity of views, cultures, experiences, and ideas that help them expand their perspectives, deepen their understanding, and adjust their instruction to help their students better understand diverse peoples and viewpoints.

- *PLNs help teachers stay current and promote instructional innovation.* Many teachers find it less threatening to put their instructional ideas out there for critical review in the digital realm. As teachers collaborate and interact with educators and subject matter experts via digital tools, they stay current in their fields, are exposed to new instructional approaches, and are challenged and energized to develop new and better ways of teaching their own students.

- *PLNs help teachers sharpen their writing skills and critical reading skills.* Because of the seemingly endless amount of information available, teachers must evaluate content with a critical eye as they cultivate their PLNs. They must constantly assess content to determine if it is valid, reliable, and useful. Further, as teachers begin to participate through Listserv discussions, Twitter, Nings, and blog postings, their writing must be concise, clear, and persuasive for their ideas to be considered by others.

- *PLNs are fun and intrinsically rewarding.* The element of enjoyment makes PLNs more likely to "stick" as an effective approach to teacher professional development.

Effective professional development is defined as all of the formal and informal learning opportunities that result in improvements in teachers' knowledge and instruction as well as improvements in student learning. Personal learning networks meet the criteria for effective professional development in two ways. First, they enhance teacher knowledge and contribute to more effective instructional strategies, both of which improve student learning (Richardson, 2011).

Second, through creating and cultivating their PLNs teachers put themselves in a position to help their students develop the knowledge and skills to also become networked learners, which can enhance both student learning and student motivation (Orlando, 2010). Preparing children for an unpredictable future means helping them learn to teach themselves. That is why lifelong learning is such a crucial part of the education conversation and why modeling a learning lifestyle is one of the best things that teachers can do today. Being educators requires us to be learners ourselves. That's why we need convenient and unfettered access to new and emerging communication technologies and applications, as well as opportunities to gain and develop skills not only to operate these tools, but also to shape and even invent networks of learning.

Traditional professional development has failed to influence teacher instructional practices and student learning because teachers have been treated as passive recipients of information that is disconnected from the challenges they face in their classrooms. PLNs, in contrast, actively involve teachers in creating and receiving knowledge that is tailored to their specific needs and interests. Teachers become members of a collaborative community, where they are valued as participants in an ongoing effort to improve their own learning and the learning of their students.

Effective teacher professional development in the future will involve striking the right balance between on-site professional learning communities, on-site job-embedded collaborative approaches (discussed in Chapters 6–11), and PLNs. Our students are already developing PLNs on their own with such tools as Facebook, Twitter, Skype, and many others, but not all educators are leveraging this to teach them how to learn through these networks and do it safely, ethically, and effectively. Imagine if we could teach our students how to cultivate their PLNs more fully and use them in powerful ways to drive their learning. To do this we need to show them how powerful PLNs are in our learning, that we are not just engaged teachers but engaged learners, and that we face the future with confidence because we know how to learn with PLNs.

The Process of Creating and Cultivating PLNs

Personal learning networks may open up new worlds but the technologies that extend teachers' personal and professional learning beyond the school building can be difficult to understand and control. Teachers must develop skills and knowledge in six areas (Drexler, 2010) to tap fully into the promise of PLNs (see Figure 13.2). First, they must develop digital literacy, the basic knowledge and skills to get started exploring and using digital tools and resources. Second, they must know principles of digital responsibility to ensure they use tools safely and ethically. Third, they must learn how to effectively organize and manage the large volume of content they encounter. Fourth, they must develop skills to successfully socialize and collaborate across distances using digital tools. Fifth, they must learn how to synthesize and create things using digital tools. Finally, they must be able to use their PLNs to further their own learning and the learning of their students.

Getting Started

The goals in the early stages of establishing PLNs are to empower teachers to take control of their professional learning and to create a safe environment for them to explore how to use digital tools to create personal learning networks. To set up a useful PLN it is important to take incremental steps. Teachers, particularly those uncomfortable with modern technology, will become frustrated and overwhelmed if they try to do too many things at once. A skillful instructor (preferably on staff to increase comfort and be a consistent resource for follow-up questions) should introduce applications one at a time to

Figure 13.2   The Process of Constructing a PLN

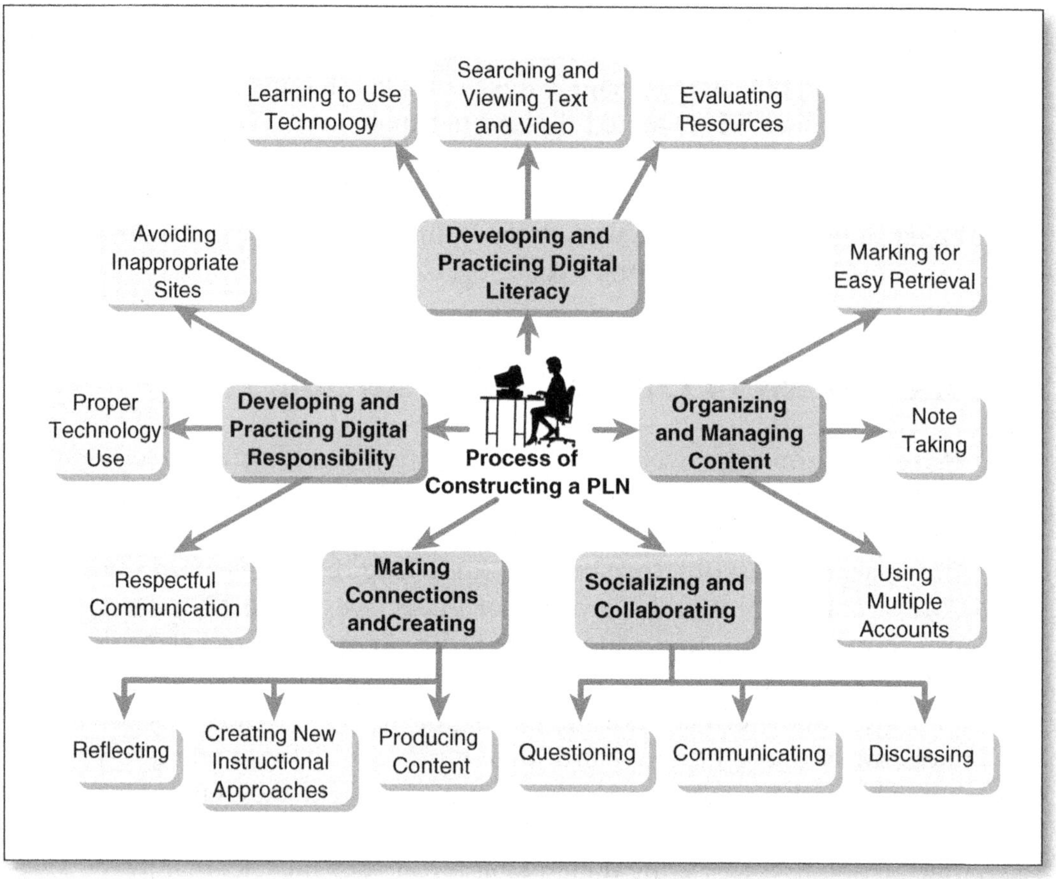

Source: Adapted from Drexler (2010).

give teachers an opportunity to become skilled with each tool. The instructor must work to strike the delicate balance between structure, guided instruction, and active teacher inquiry. They must be mindful that the goal is to guide and empower teachers to construct rich, effective PLNs in support of their unique learning needs. This initial start-up phase may take a semester or longer (it can be shorter if it is done over summer), as teachers will need opportunities to practice each application, get feedback from the instructor, and share reflections with colleagues. As teachers explore and master applications they develop digital literacy, learn digital responsibility, and share critiques with colleagues regarding what is most and least effective and useful.

Here is a sample of the digital tools and resources teachers may be asked to do during the start-up phase (see Figure 13.3).

Figure 13.3 Expanding Your PLN: Some of the Best Digital Tools

Category	Value
Social Networking	Connecting with and learning from educators who share specific interests and problems
Microblogging	Educators from around the globe share best practices and resources in short bursts
Professional Profiles	Locate other teachers and educators in your field
Blogs	Good sources of information for classroom best practices and personal opinions; blogs monitor new trends in education, and the commenting back and forth leads to many great ideas and relationships
RSS Aggregator or Feed Reader	RSS means "Real Simple Syndication"—an RSS aggregator or feed reader is a tool that allows you to keep up with your favorite sites and organize content in one place
Content Organizer	Allows teachers to save web content to a single location, manage and organize the content to fit their needs, permits annotated notes to be added to saved content, and allows the user to share their pages with friends and colleagues
Social Bookmarking	Share bookmarks with others, see what others are bookmarking; join groups and get e-mail updates on new bookmarks
Webinars	Live, online presentations or conferences, with real-time chat, hosted by experts on specific topics; a great way to learn about new things
Podcasting and Videosharing	Great sources of information on best practices and great instructional tools teachers can use with their students
Online Slideshows	Share ideas and approaches with others using photos, music, and voices—also is a great instructional tool teachers can use with their students

- *Join and participate in a professional social network.* The Educator's PLN Ning (a Ning is a community of people interested in similar topics and includes forums and messaging) is a good one to start with because it is an international networking site tailored to educators. It has approximately 60,000 members from approximately 200 countries, and groups are separated by subject area and grade level, making it easy to connect with educators who share specific problems and interests. Other excellent

Nings include Classroom 2.0 (www.classroom2.com) and Future of Education (www.futureofeducation.com). And while it is more often thought of as a strictly social network, Facebook can also be a useful way to connect and communicate with other educators about professional issues.

- *Pick several interesting education blogs and start reading them.* Technorati, Alltop, and EduBlogs are all excellent places to start. Blogs can be great sources of information about best practices, new trends in education, and new ideas and opinions to stimulate reflection and thought. Teachers can also create their own blogs (at EduBlogs), where they can begin posting their own ideas, thoughts, and reflections, and respond to the posting of visitors to their site.

- *Set up a feed reader or RSS aggregator.* With this tool teachers can begin to keep up with favorite blogs, news items, and journal articles all in one place.

- *Curate the Web with services such as EndNote, NoteFish, Symbaloo, or Diigo.* These services allow teachers to save Web content to a single location, manage and organize the content to fit their needs, permit annotated notes to be added to saved content, and allow the user to share their pages with friends and colleagues. In short, these services help teachers organize, share, and reflect on content that they deem valuable and useful.

- *Join the microblogging phenomena by posting and reading Tweets at Twitter.* A good place for teachers to start is to select several well-known Edubloggers to follow and watch all the great stuff they have to share. Then, once they feel comfortable, teachers can begin to respond to postings and share their own original postings with others.

- *Explore podcasting and videosharing.* A podcast—which stands for "portable on-demand broadcast"—resembles an online radio show, except the listeners get to decide when and where they want to listen. Audacity, iTunes, and Podbean can all be used to create podcasts. You don't need an iPod to listen to or create a podcast, but having an iPod (or similar portable device) makes listening to podcasts and other media really easy. The Education Podcast Network, with more than 2,000 education podcasts, is a great place to learn about how to use this technology. Teachers can also share ideas about teaching and learning through videosharing on YouTube and TeacherTube.

- *Create online slideshows.* Slideshows incorporating photos, music, and even narration by the person producing the slideshow can be created and shared online. (Animoto [http://animoto.com] and VoiceThread [http://voicethread.com] are two good places to begin.) Teachers can learn about new ideas by watching the slideshows of others and can add a valuable teaching approach to their instructional toolboxes by creating slideshows for their students on specific topics.

- *Follow several webinars.* Webinars are live online presentations with real-time chat, hosted by experts on specific topics, and are a great way to learn about new ideas and topics. Classroom 2.0 Live hosts regular webinars on a variety of topics, while the publication *Educational Weekly* at the University of Iowa also produces monthly webinars featuring nationally known educators.

A step-by-step guide can help teachers learn the basics without feeling overwhelmed so they can use these tools to create and cultivate their PLNs. While you can and should modify things based on your specific teacher and school needs and your instructor's preferences, the guide that follows (Paul, 2010) can be useful.

Step 1: Introduction to Digital Tools and Creating a Blog

- The instructor introduces digital tools, covers the types—blogs, social bookmarking, and so on—and explains and demonstrates their uses.
- Each teacher creates a personal blog and writes his or her first post.
- Each teacher selects and begins to follow two or three education blogs.
- Teachers follow one another's blogs.
- The instructor meets with teachers as a group so they can share frustrations and problems they are experiencing, what they like and don't like about the tools in this step, and potential professional uses of the tools in this step.

Step 2: Social Networking

- Each teacher selects and begins to participate in two education-related Nings.
- Each teacher uses a content organizer to store his or her favorite education-related sites and connect with other users to learn about their favorite sites.
- The instructor meets with teachers as a group so they can share frustrations and problems they are experiencing, what they like and don't like about the tools in this step, and potential professional uses of the tools in this step.

Step 3: Using an Aggregator

- Each teacher selects one or two RSS aggregators to keep up with his or her favorite news and information sites and to organize content in one place.
- Each teacher follows his or her RSS feeds.
- The instructor meets with teachers as a group so they can share frustrations and problems they are experiencing, what they like and don't like about the tools in this step, and potential professional uses of the tools in this step.

Step 4: Podcasting and Media Sharing

- Each teacher explores the educational uses of podcasts on the Education Podcast Network.
- Each teacher creates a podcast on an educational topic of his or her choice.
- Each teacher explores the educational uses of media-sharing sites.
- Each teacher creates and posts an educational video on TeacherTube.
- The instructor meets with teachers as a group so they can share frustrations and problems they are experiencing, what they like and don't like about the tools in this step, and potential professional uses of the tools in this step.

Step 5: Creating Online Slideshows

- Each teacher explores Flickr and learns how to share photos online.
- Each teacher explores Animoto and learns how to create, post, and share slideshows.
- Each teacher creates a slideshow on an educational topic of his or her choice.
- The instructor meets with teachers as a group so they can share frustrations and problems they are experiencing, what they like and don't like about the tools in this step, and potential professional uses of the tools in this step.

Step 6: Microblogging

- Each teacher creates a Twitter account and begins to follow several educators.
- Each teacher posts several tweets, and teachers follow one another's tweets.

- The instructor meets with teachers as a group so they can share frustrations and problems they are experiencing, what they like and don't like about the tools in this step, and potential professional uses of the tools in this step.

Step 7: Reflecting

- Each teacher reflects on the overall experience of learning the tools and using them to create a PLN.
- Each teacher identifies five tools he or she will continue to use to cultivate the PLN and specifies how each tool will be used.
- Teachers share their overall reflections and "top five" lists with one another.

Using Tools to Connect: Early PLN Formation

Direct instruction, guided inquiry, exposure to numerous digital tools and resources, and significant independent practice provide the foundation for this stage. By now, teachers will be comfortable with many digital applications and will be self-directed in how they use them to advance their learning. In the "getting started" stage, teachers primarily are consumers of learning materials, but in this stage they increasingly become producers of content as they create blogs and Twitter postings, contribute to Ning discussions, and post to media-sharing sites. A new term, *prosumer,* has emerged to refer to someone who is both a digital resources producer and consumer (Richardson, 2011). Teachers who are in the early stages of forming a useful, valuable PLN are moving from exploring tools and sites to being actively connected to educators outside their school, and are beginning to use these connections to further their learning and their ability to solve problems of practice.

In this stage, the role of the instructor changes to being a coach who engages in many one-on-one or small-group conversations (both in person and through e-mail) as questions and problems from teachers emerge. The instructor may create a blog where teachers can continue to share their questions, suggestions, successes, and failures with other teachers within their school who are working to build their PLNs. Some teachers will move from the "start-up" stage into the "early PLN formation" stage quickly, while others will take much longer to master the digital tools and feel comfortable using them.

Because PLN formation depends on the unique interests, learning needs, and problems of practice of each teacher, the structure and content of each PLN will be quite different. Instructors must be careful to allow teachers to form PLNs at their own pace and create them to serve their particular needs and interests. Whatever their pace, by the end of this stage teachers should be using digital tools and resources to connect across schools, should be starting to successfully organize and manage the large volume of content they encounter, and should be using some tools with students to help them develop PLNs of their own.

Advanced PLN Formation: What Does It Look Like?

Teachers in the advanced stage use their PLNs to help them solve immediate and pressing problems of practice and explore larger issues around how to best educate young people. They work to balance and connect inside knowledge, information, and ideas (from their collaborations within their school) with outside knowledge, information, and ideas (from their collaborations outside the school using their PLN). Like Tracy in the vignette at the beginning of this chapter, teachers become skilled prosumers in this stage, both creating and using content utilizing digital tools. They come to feel they are parts of two learning communities, one inside the school and one outside the school, both of which engage them in an ongoing effort to improve their own learning and the learning of their students.

Teachers with established PLNs use them to further their own learning and the learning of their students, and help their students cultivate their own PLNs. As they do these things, they occupy six different roles with their students (Nussbaum-Beach & Ritter Hall, 2011):

1. Learning Architect

   Teachers begin to see learning differently and work to redesign their instruction and their classrooms to connect their discipline with other disciplines and connect their students with ideas, concepts, and people outside of their school and classroom.

2. Modeler

   An important part of excellent teaching is modeling. As teachers use PLNs to further their learning, they model in a powerful way how their students can use the PLNs they create to advance their own learning.

3. Learning Coach

   Teachers begin to talk at students much less frequently and begin to work with them and beside them as they teach them how to make connections to solve authentic problems.

4. Change Agent

   Teachers are charged with preparing students for their future and to do that they must be part of changing some of the traditional practices in schools.

5. Network Guide

   Teachers must become adept with a variety of digital tools and resources so they can guide students in how to use these tools effectively to solve problems and further their learning.

6. Synthesizer

   Teachers must become skilled at sifting through large volumes of information to connect relevant things in a meaningful way for their students, and they must be able to help their students develop similar skills as they work with their PLNs.

The Challenges of PLNs

For all of the positive connections, links, and ideas that PLNs bring, they come with challenges and do not guarantee improved teacher knowledge, instructional practices, and student learning (Nussbaum-Beach, 2011). First, significant time, including both the span of time over which PLN formation occurs and the number of hours spent in PLN formation, is needed to develop the digital literacy required by this model. School leaders will need to make this time available and must be patient to allow teachers to develop their PLNs. Second, teacher resistance is common among teachers who are not comfortable with technology. School leaders and instructors teaching the digital tools will need to be firm, encouraging, and patient to help teachers work through their anxiety. As anxious teachers begin to experience some success using digital tools, their initial resistance is likely to give way to excitement about the possibilities the new tools bring with them. Third, the loose structure and variable pace of PLN formation makes supervision of the process messy. Establishing Nings and blogs for teachers to reflect on and share their experiences with the PLN formation process can inform instructors and school leaders about who is and who is not engaged in the process.

Because it is human nature to be pulled toward sources and websites that align with our own perspectives and opinions, school leaders must encourage teachers to be mindful to cultivate networks that challenge their thinking and worldviews. If teachers are only seeking out and connecting with educators and ideas consistent with their current views and practices, then little positive change will result. A final challenge is that teachers can unwittingly become passive with their PLNs, exchanging idea after idea and connecting with many people, but not taking the next step to put action to their ideas and actually change their instructional practices. If all a teacher does is network, then he or she does not take the extra step to go deep and actually learn by doing something with students. It takes both networking through a PLN and on-site communities of practice to result in deep, rich teacher learning that results in action in the classrooms.

Summary

As I have emphasized throughout this book, professional development needs to change because the way we "do" school in the 21st century must change to prepare our students for the realities of our "flat" world. We need to ask ourselves what changes should take place to allow us to remain relevant in the lives of our students and help them develop the knowledge and skills they will need to succeed in college and the workplace. Educators must accept and embrace the fact that the rate of change demands that we continuously unlearn, learn, and then relearn. The mantra of the school leader used to be that "change takes time," but that is not true of all types of change today. The challenge for school leaders is to adapt to the rapid pace of change—indeed, to become leaders of change—before we find ourselves and our institutions irrelevant in the lives of the students we seek to help.

With the advent of modern digital tools, learning is possible anywhere, anytime, and is both networked and collaborative. Our students are already learning this way, but most schools are not yet leveraging this reality to enhance student learning in our classrooms. As a teacher in the midst of developing her PLN recently told me, "I've come to realize is that by using digital tools to learn I am gaining exposure to the world that my students already inhabit easily, and learning in that environment is not neat and tidy." Policy makers and educators are calling for the teaching of 21st century skills and the transition to a learning community framework, but it has been difficult for teachers to understand how to be a co-learner with their students in this ever-changing learning landscape.

So how do school leaders work to prepare their teachers to produce critical, collaborative thinkers who understand how to use the Web in safe, ethical, useful ways? Providing the kind of job-embedded, collaborative teacher professional learning that results in sustainable learning and instructional improvement requires strong leadership that is distributed, collaborative, and connected. In today's environment, school leaders should work to understand and use a collaborative learning process first before expecting it of their teachers and students. This means that school leaders should learn together, construct meaning together, and grow in knowledge, skill, and understanding collaboratively and collectively before engaging teachers in this process. As a principal recently told me, "The more I use Web tools to connect and collaborate with colleagues, the more convinced I am that reflection and relationship building are the keys for school leaders and teachers striving to develop their practice and adapt to changing learning needs."

Through the development of on-site professional learning communities and personal learning networks, school leaders and teachers become learners who negotiate perceptions, values, information, and assumptions together. The critical inquiry and sharing of ideas in PLNs support the development and maintenance of a professional learning community within the school. A new term, *connected learning communities* (CLC), has been coined to refer to the powerful, systemic approach to teacher professional learning that combines learning in PLNs with learning in collaborative on-site professional learning communities. Schools with CLCs are characterized by teachers sharing ideas and asking questions of each other and their global networks. Giving teachers the time and support they need to learn from one another in connected communities, to reflect on shifts needed in their classrooms, and to grow as individuals and as members of a professional learning team will result in improved teacher morale, ongoing teacher learning, and enhanced student learning.

If teacher learning occurs within a context of a professional learning community that is nurtured and developed from both inside and outside of the school, our conception of teacher professional learning will be transformed and students will be better prepared for the realities of our modern world. As learning network researcher Dr. Sheryl Nussbaum-Beach (2011) emphasizes, "Enabling teachers to participate in creating both professional learning communities onsite at their schools and personal learning networks which stretch across schools, releases great power and energy to drive teacher learning, transform school culture, and enhance student learning" (p. 3).

14

The Challenges of Introducing New Forms of Teacher Professional Learning

We should anticipate that the enthusiastic embrace of change and the rapid transformation of values and norms will be rare.

—Rob Evans

"Okay, all the strategies you describe make sense, and I agree that we need to be implementing them—but what do we do about all those teachers who don't want to collaborate with colleagues and who don't want to change?" is the question I'm asked most often when I work with schools desiring to transform their professional learning programs.

When efforts to institute new professional development programs fail, teachers often end up getting blamed. School leaders lament that teachers were just resistant to the new approaches, were stuck in their old ways, and did not give the new strategies a chance to be successful. Rather than be surprised by teacher resistance, and blame them when things don't go as planned, it is more productive for school leaders to seek to understand why teacher resistance occurs and what they can do to make it easier for teachers to successfully implement new professional learning strategies (Miller & Rollnick, 2002). The tendency to hold onto the familiar and comfortable is a common human impulse, but teacher resistance to change efforts is best understood as a symptom of multiple underlying issues. The specific issues that are causing teacher resistance in your school often can be brought to the surface and understood by considering these six questions (Knight, 2009).

How Have Teachers Experienced Past Professional Development?

The degree to which teachers are resistant to your current professional development initiatives is inextricably linked to their prior professional learning experiences in your school. If past professional learning opportunities respected teachers' need for autonomy and input, connected to teacher and student needs, were thoroughly supported by school leadership, and involved opportunities to learn and collaborate during the school day, then teachers will approach your professional learning strategies with enthusiasm and little resistance.

However, teachers more typically have had poor experiences with traditional professional development practices and are skeptical that new initiatives will be any better. As one teacher said to me, "The professional development I have experienced for 10 years has been antithetical to professional growth and improvement, so why should I believe anything will be different now?" Educational consultant Dennis Sparks (1997) jokes that "teachers' skepticism about the latest staff development program is a sign that they are not brain dead" (p. 17).

School leaders should remember that most teachers have not been well served by past professional development efforts and that it makes perfect sense that numerous negative experiences would lead them to resist new professional development strategies. Not only have teachers typically experienced traditional workshops and speakers as fragmented, intellectually superficial, and ineffective in helping them address real problems of practice; many have also experienced a particularly destructive pattern of failed professional development initiatives that Jim Knight (2009) calls the "attempt, attack, abandon" cycle. In this cycle, a school leader introduces a new professional development approach but provides little or no follow-up for teachers. This leads to many teachers never trying to integrate the concept or method into their teaching, and leads others to *attempt* it with little success. Because the professional development approach produces few changes in teacher knowledge or instructional practices, both teachers and school leaders begin to *attack* the approach and eventually *abandon* it altogether. Not only does this cycle lead to little teacher professional growth and learning, but it also causes teachers to have little trust that future professional development initiatives will be worth their time, energy, and commitment.

Are Teacher Needs and Preferences Being Considered?

Professional development activities historically have been imposed on teachers with little consideration given to their specific needs and preferences. No wonder teachers have come to think of professional development as something done to them rather than something they participate in creating. Because past professional development experiences are linked with a sense of powerlessness and disregard of needs, ideas, and perspectives, new professional development initiatives will be viewed with caution. If the needs, experiences, and opinions of teachers are not considered when choosing and designing the mode and substance of professional learning opportunities, significant teacher resistance is sure to follow.

Are Teachers Treated With Respect?

Commenting on how another professional works is always delicate because we all have so much of our identity and sense of worth put into how we work. The issue is even more sensitive for educators because few professions are more personal than teaching (Finley & Hartman, 2004; Knight, 2009). Teachers may view a new professional development strategy as an assault on their current teaching strategies and respond with resistance to protect what is so personal to them. The wise school leader recognizes the personal nature of teaching and strives to respect it while also supporting learning opportunities that promote the ongoing development of teachers. One of the most frequent complaints I hear about traditional professional development approaches is that they fail to recognize and respect teacher experience and expertise. Bringing in an outside "expert" to give a lecture or conduct a workshop may communicate to teachers that their knowledge, skills, and experiences are not recognized and valued. Teachers can leave such sessions feeling patronized, disrespected, and frustrated, and unlikely to adopt any good ideas presented by the "expert." The following teacher's comment captures the views of many: "We have many teachers right here who already know these things and are doing great work, so why don't we tap into that expertise instead of having someone we don't know talk down to us for two hours?"

Of course, no school leader intends to make teachers feel disrespected, but what matters here is what teachers perceive. If teachers feel that their identity—their sense of how talented and competent they are—is under attack, resistance is likely (Finley & Hartman, 2004). School leaders need to listen respectfully and communicate appreciation so frequently and authentically that they foster an environment of ongoing regard. Rather than always bringing in outside experts, school leaders need to communicate recognition of and respect for the knowledge, experience, and expertise of faculty members by making collaborative work among teachers the foundation of the school's professional development program.

Are Teachers Being Asked to Collaborate, Think, and Innovate?

Teachers are what Thomas Davenport (2000) calls "knowledge workers." Knowledge workers "think for a living and regularly are called upon to make decisions, meet the needs of customers, collaborate and communicate with others in the course of doing their work, and innovate to create better solutions to the problems they face" (Davenport, 2000, p. 13). In fact, few people do more thinking on the job than a teacher in front of 20 students. Yet school professional development activities and school cultures typically have not treated teachers like knowledge workers. They have not encouraged innovation, experimentation, risk taking, and collaboration. Teachers may therefore be skeptical about professional development approaches favoring these things and/or may be unsure how to actively engage in strategies emphasizing collaborative experimentation. Resistance in this instance may be due to fear of the unknown, lack of clarity about how to do something, or distrust that new norms of teacher learning will be fully supported (Knight, 2009).

Do School Leaders Make the New Strategies Easy to Implement?

Many teachers experience what Michael Fullan (2007) calls the "press of immediacy." On an average day, teachers create and teach lessons, grade papers, attend meetings, speak with parents, and coach sports. They complete all of these tasks while doing work that demands significant emotional investment. So when they are asked to implement a new program or strategy on top of what they already do, it is understandable that they may feel overwhelmed and not fully commit to it. If teachers feel that professional development activities interfere with their ability to meet the press of immediacy of their jobs, then they will resist them. A common teacher frustration is that "Our professional development activities are always added on to everything else we are asked to do, so we never feel we have the time or energy to make the programs work and try new things in our classrooms." Furthermore, if they are asked to implement a new strategy without significant support to understand how and why to use it, then resistance is guaranteed. The wise school leader recognizes the press of immediacy and works to remove barriers impeding teacher commitment to professional development programs.

Are Professional Development Activities Linked to a Compelling Purpose?

Traditional professional development activities have not been linked with a compelling vision connected to the mission of the school or some other overarching purpose. Without a "why," teachers have seen little reason to endure the "how" and have come to feel that traditional professional development is disconnected from their work. Teachers will be more likely to fully engage with a new professional development strategy when it has been connected in a meaningful way to the mission of the school and the core work they do with students.

Breaking Down Barriers

It is important for school leaders to address the problem of teacher resistance by understanding its root causes. When school leaders carefully consider the questions posed above, "they often wonder why teachers do not resist new professional development strategies more vociferously than they do" (Knight, 2009, p. 52).

It helps to try to keep the problem in perspective. How many faculty members are active resisters compared to those who are sitting on the fence waiting to see if the change initiative persists over time? Very often a small number of faculty individuals who are persistent and vocal can be more influential than their numbers warrant. Their negativism has undue influence over the attitudes and hopefulness of their colleagues. Once you understand why teacher resistance is to be expected, and have worked to put teacher resistance at your school in perspective, you are ready to consider how to break down that resistance and make it easier for teachers to successfully implement new professional learning strategies. There are things school leaders can do to increase the likelihood that teachers will commit to and engage with the professional development strategies discussed in this book (Knight, 2009).

Involve Teachers in the Process

I have emphasized throughout this book that it is essential to involve your faculty in all important decisions about your professional development program. As I discussed in Chapter 3, this begins when they work to specify the new knowledge, understandings, and skills they need to acquire to effectively address current student needs and weaknesses. Once student and teacher learning goals have been set, school leaders earn teacher commitment by offering choices at other essential steps and valuing teacher voices and opinions. For example, teachers should be involved in deciding which professional strategy to adopt and how it will be adapted to the unique context of your school. The more teachers have a say in how and what new practices they implement, the more likely they will be to embrace new ways of doing things (Knight, 2009).

Help Teachers Experience Early Success

Because many teachers have had bad experiences with traditional professional development practices, and will be skeptical that new approaches will be more worthwhile, it is important to provide all the support you can to ensure that their earliest experiences with your new strategy will be positive. When someone has had persistent bad experiences with something, it will take more than words to persuade them to commit fully. As Michael Fullan (2007) has observed, "When it comes to teacher resistance, verbal persuasion rarely works" (p. 34). The key is to get teachers to stick with the new strategy long enough for them to experience that it is different from past professional development and to recognize that it can help them address their problems of practice in meaningful ways. When it comes to completely disposing of all resistance, teachers have to drink the water of success, so to speak, before they will commit to the new strategy. Thomas Guskey (1986) emphasizes this reality when he says, "Teachers will not commit until they have seen it work, and by work I mean when they see clear evidence of improvements in the learning of their students" (p. 7).

The implications for school leaders are clear. If it is known that teachers need to experience success to completely buy into a new professional development strategy, then school leaders should adjust how they communicate with their teachers. Trying to verbally persuade teachers to fully commit to a new strategy without providing successful experiences with it will be futile. A better approach is to be patient and support teachers' early attempts to experiment with the new strategy. If the strategy is powerful and leads to improved instruction and student learning, then teachers will jump on board.

Support Teacher Efforts

Because of the "press of immediacy," school leaders should do all they can to remove barriers that prevent teachers from engaging with new professional development strategies. Several types of support are particularly helpful. First, many teachers have told me that they benefit from seeing demonstrations of new strategies before they try to implement them. Similarly, they find it helpful when new strategies are broken down into clear steps. School leaders should carve out time, with at least some of it during the school day, for teachers to do the work connected with the new strategy. They should provide ongoing support to help teachers work through the early stages of learning how to collaborate with colleagues and implement the new strategy. And they should privately and publicly acknowledge and celebrate teacher efforts to engage with the new strategy. As school leaders provide ongoing support and recognition, and remove common barriers, teacher resistance will be likely to subside.

Attend to Context

Teachers will resist implementing the strategies discussed in this book unless a context supportive of adult learning is taking hold in your school. School leaders should constantly monitor school culture to make sure it fosters trust and promotes adult learning, risk taking, experimentation, and collaboration. Time should be available for learning and working with colleagues, and the level of trust and communication should be sufficiently high to enable the formation of a genuine community of learners. As Thomas Guskey (2000) has said, "The single most important factor in breaking down teacher resistance to new professional strategies is relational trust" (p. 46). Teaching is a personal endeavor, and teachers need to be able to trust that their principal and colleagues will focus on student learning and instructional best practices when they open up their classrooms to observation and feedback. The bottom line, according to Michael Fullan (2007), is that "when relational trust improves, teacher resistance wanes, and real progress can be made in improving the instructional practices in your school" (p. 78).

Keep the Focus on Student Learning

A common complaint I hear from teachers is that their professional development experiences lack any coherent purpose and are largely disconnected from the challenges they face in the classroom. If the reason for doing something is not clear, relevant, and alive, most people will not engage in the activity. When working with your faculty to choose and implement one of the strategies in this book, you will need to work tirelessly to keep the focus on student learning at all times. When the goal of professional development is clearly and consistently to improve student learning, and when professional development strategies address specific problems of practice identified by teachers, then teacher resistance is likely to dissipate (Knight, 2009). If you give teachers a "why" they will be much more likely to commit to your new strategies.

Summary

Professional development is supposed to contribute to lasting change in the classroom and when it doesn't we waste valuable time and resources, and compromise teachers' trust that time engaged in professional development is well spent. For many teachers, past professional learning opportunities have not respected their need for autonomy and input, have not been connected to teacher and student needs, have not been thoroughly supported by school leadership, and have not involved opportunities to learn and collaborate during the school day. It is not surprising that some teachers will approach professional learning strategies with skepticism and resistance.

Rather than complaining about this resistance, it is more productive for school leaders to seek to understand it, acknowledge it, and be clear about what they will need to do to decrease it over time. When school leaders keep the focus of professional development on student learning, involve teachers in the design and content of professional development activities, provide ongoing support for teachers as they learn new professional development strategies, help teachers experience early success with new strategies, and provide time for teachers to collaboratively engage in professional development activities, resistance will be minimal. School leaders would be wise to heed the words of Dennis Sparks (1997) when he advises that "Perhaps the most important thing to remember as a school leader facing teacher resistance is that you must model and embody the attitudes and behaviors you seek from your faculty" (p. 29).

15

A Call to Action

Teacher learning opportunities should be built into the daily work of teachers and involve teachers working collaboratively to discuss and solve problems directly related to their instruction and the students in their school.

—Rob Evans

Few school teachers and leaders would discount the eminently logical idea that teachers should be supported in the continuous improvement of their craft. In fact, millions of dollars and countless hours are spent on teacher professional development in American schools each year. Have professional development practices in our schools been effective in promoting the continuous growth and learning of their teachers? Does the money and time result in improved teacher knowledge and classroom instruction and in enhanced student learning?

A recent study I conducted indicated that most American teachers do not receive the kind of well-designed teacher professional development common in many other nations (Murray, 2011). As I have discussed in this book, professional learning in American schools in its current state is deeply flawed. Not only do most schools continue to rely upon fragmented, ineffective one-day or two-day activities, but relatively few learning opportunities for teachers also feature either the intense emphasis on content or the collegial work that has been found to positively influence teacher learning, teacher instructional practice, and student learning (Desimone, 2009).

Professional development is supposed to contribute to lasting change in the classroom and when it doesn't we waste valuable time and resources and compromise teachers' trust that time engaged in professional development is well spent. "The time and money spent on traditional professional development is frustratingly wasteful," says Mitchell Reed, a high school principal in Charlotte, North Carolina. "Workshops and conferences can raise awareness and enthusiasm, and can impart knowledge, but the opportunities for reflection, collegial discussions, and continued support that are needed to bring about instructional change are rarely provided."

Most schools lack the structures and/or cultures to support the kind of job-embedded, sustained, contextual, collaborative teacher professional learning that leads to substantive improvements in teaching and learning. Other professions in this country, from medicine to business to the military, do a much better job of providing effective learning opportunities and support for their professionals. In addition, the high-achieving nations of Finland, Sweden, Japan, South Korea, Australia, and the United Kingdom have established effective professional development for their teachers, characterized by teacher learning opportunities sustained over time; time for teacher professional learning built into their work hours; teacher learning opportunities involving active learning and collaboration; professional development activities that are embedded in teachers' contexts and focused on the specific content to be taught; and teachers who are involved in decisions about curriculum, assessment, and professional development.

The time has come for U.S. schools to engage their teachers in learning the way other professions do, and the way schools do in many other countries—continuously, collaboratively, and on the job—to address important problems and challenges in the workplace.

Why is there a gap between teacher professional learning practices in U.S. schools and professional development practices in high-achieving nations like Japan, Finland, and the United Kingdom? What barriers exist that should be overcome if our schools are to transform their professional development practices?

Professional development programs in our schools are typically based on the false assumption that significant teacher insight and learning requires external direction. This assumption leads to teachers being sent to conferences to learn from experts and to bringing the experts to the school to speak and conduct workshops. Because formal follow-up conversations to these events are rare, and because informal avenues for sharing and discussing what is learned are typically absent, these "outside" professional development events do not influence teacher instruction or student learning. More damaging, though, is that this false assumption leads to a reduction in collaboration and conversation among teachers—the very things schools most need to establish sustained effective professional learning.

The assumption that teacher learning should be externally driven must be challenged and changed for progress toward quality professional learning in schools to occur. Perhaps of greater importance, many of our schools have long been characterized by a culture in which teachers work in isolation and are insulated from opportunities to engage in and demonstrate professional learning and growth. The professional development activities that do exist are typically not even built into the regular work day, disconnecting them from the issues teachers face daily and communicating in a not so subtle way that professional learning is far down the list of priorities schools have for their teachers.

Efforts to close the gap between best practices and current practices should begin by creating a culture where continuous, job-embedded professional learning becomes part of the culture of schools. Other nations—our competitors—have made support for teachers and teacher learning a top priority with significant results. If we want our students to develop the higher-order thinking skills they need to succeed in the 21st century, we need teachers who possess higher-order teaching skills and deep content knowledge.

Ensuring student success necessitates new types of instruction, conducted by teachers who understand content, learning, and pedagogy; who can adapt to the diverse needs of their students; and who can build powerful connections between students' experiences and the goals of the curriculum. These types of changes require significant learning on the part of teachers and will not occur without support and guidance. Efforts to improve student achievement can succeed only by building the capacity of teachers to improve their instructional practice and the capacity of schools to promote teacher learning. For our students to develop to their fullest, their teachers should also be supported to succeed.

It is the responsibility of every school and every school leader to make teacher growth and development a priority and to possess a strong resolve to create and maintain the conditions and culture needed to build capacity in the individual and the school. Professional learning models and strategies are valuable tools, but the real learning happens in the cycle of conversations, actions, evaluation, and new actions that are supported through intentional leadership that gently pressures and nurtures teachers.

Effective professional learning involves reflective dialogue, observing and reacting to one another's teaching, working together to implement new strategies, sharing teaching approaches and materials, and engaging in collective action research focused on common issues of practice. My hope is that this book provides information and practical suggestions to help school leaders build and sustain effective teacher professional learning opportunities in their schools. Some of the strategies may seem more formidable than others, particularly if your school is in the early stages of becoming a learning community. But none of us can wait. Our students will be more engaged, and will learn more, when we create and sustain a context supportive of adult learning, when we intentionally focus the content of professional development on student needs, and when we carefully choose strategies that help teachers address them. It is time to support all teachers in an ongoing process of professional growth. The stakes are too important to ignore: our schools, our children, and our future.

References

Allen, D., & Leblanc, A. (2004). *Collaborative peer coaching that improves instruction.* Thousand Oaks, CA: Corwin.

Anderson, G., Herr, K., & Nihlen, A. (2007). *Studying your own school: An educator's guide to practitioner action research* (2nd ed.). Thousand Oaks, CA: Corwin.

Bambino, D. (2002). Critical friends. *Educational Leadership, 23*(3), 25–29.

Baranik, L. E., Roling, E. A., & Eby, L. T. (2010). Why does mentoring work? The role of perceived organizational support. *Journal of Vocational Behavior, 76*(3), 366–373.

Barbknecht, A. (2001). *Peer coaching: The learning teacher approach.* Thousand Oaks, CA: Sage.

Bartell, C. (2005). *Cultivating high-quality teaching through induction and mentoring.* Thousand Oaks, CA: Corwin.

Birman, B., LeFloch, K. C., Kletotka, A., Ludwig, M., Taylor, J., Walters, K., & Yoon, K. S. (2007). *State and local implementation of No Child Left Behind Act, Volume II–Teacher quality under NCLB: Interim report.* Washington, DC: U.S. Department of Education, Office of Planning, Evaluation and Policy Development, Policy and Program Studies Service.

Blanchard, K. (2007). *Leading at a higher level: Blanchard on leadership and creating high performing organizations.* Upper Saddle River, NJ: Prentice Hall.

Blank, R. K., de las Alas, N., & Smith, C. (2008). *Does teacher professional development have effects on teaching and learning? Analysis of evaluation findings from programs for mathematics and science teachers in 14 states.* Washington, DC: Council of Chief State School Officers.

Borg, W. (1981). *Applying educational research: A practical guide for teachers.* New York, NY: Longman.

Bransford, J., & Brown, A. (2002). *How people learn.* Washington, DC: National Academy Press.

Brighton, C. M., & Moon, T. R. (2007). Action research step-by-step: A tool for educators to change their worlds. *Gifted Child Today, 30*(2), 23–27.

Carmichael, L. (1995). Working with the authority pyramid: Principal as learner. *Education and Society, 17*(3), 311–323.

Caro-Bruce, C. (2000). *Action research facilitators' handbook.* Oxford, OH: Association for Supervision and Curriculum Development (ASCD).

Caro-Bruce, C. (2008). Action research. In L. B. Easton (Ed.), *Powerful designs for professional learning* (2nd ed., pp. 63–71). Oxford, OH: National Staff Development Council.

Caro-Bruce, C. (2008). School coaching. In L. B. Easton (Ed.), *Powerful designs for professional learning* (2nd ed., pp. 63–71). Oxford, OH: National Staff Development Council.

Chokshi, S., & Fernandez, C. (2004). Challenges to importing Japanese lesson study: Concerns, misconceptions, and nuances. *Phi Delta Kappan, 85*(7), 520–525.

Christie, K. (2010). Professional development worth paying for. *Phi Delta Kappan, 90*(7), 461–473.

City, E., Elmore, R., & Fiarman, S. (2009). *Instructional rounds in education: A network approach to improving teaching and learning.* Cambridge, MA: Harvard Education Press.

Corey, S. M. (1953). *Action research to improve school practices.* New York, NY: Teachers College Press.

Curry, M. (2008). Critical friends groups: The possibilities and limitations embedded in teacher professional communities aimed at instructional improvement and school reform. *Teachers College Record, 110*(4), 733–774.

Darling-Hammond, L. (2003). Keeping good teachers: Why it matters, what leaders can do. *Educational Leadership, 60*(8), 6–13.

Darling-Hammond, L. (2010). *The flat world and education: How America's commitment to equity will determine our future.* New York, NY: Teachers College Press.

Darling-Hammond, L., Wei, R. C., Andree, A., Richardson, N., & Orphanos, S. (2009). *Professional learning in the learning profession: A status report on teacher development in the United States and abroad.* Washington, DC: National Staff Development Council.

Davenport, T. (2000). *Working knowledge.* Cambridge, MA: Harvard Business School Press.

Dede, C. (2006). *Online professional development for teachers.* Cambridge, MA: Harvard Education Press.

Del Prete, T. (1990). *The Anna Maria College–Calvin Coolidge Professional Development School Guidebook.* Retrieved from ERIC database. (ED349266)

Del Prete, T. (1997). The rounds model of professional development. *From the Inside, 1*(1), 12–13.

Del Prete, T. (2010). *Improving the odds: Developing powerful teaching practice and a culture of learning in urban high schools.* New York, NY: Teachers College Press.

Del Prete, T. (2013). *Teacher rounds: A guide to collaborative learning in and from practice.* Thousand Oaks, CA: Corwin.

Desimone, L. (2009). Improving impact studies of teachers' professional development: Toward better conceptualizations and measures. *Educational Researcher, 38*(3), 181–199.

Desimone, L. M., Porter, A. C., Garet, M. S., Yoon, K. S., & Birman, B. F. (2002). Effects of professional development on teachers' instruction:

Results from a three-year longitudinal study. *Educational Evaluation and Policy Analysis, 24*, 81–112.

Drexler, W. (2010, May). *A networked learning model for construction of personal learning environments.* Paper presented at the annual meeting of the American Educational Research Association, Denver, CO.

DuFour, R. (2004). What is a "professional learning community"? *Educational Leadership, 61*(8), 6–11.

Dufour, R., & Eaker, R. (2004). *Professional learning communities at work.* Bloomington, IN: Solution Tree.

DuFour, R., Dufour, R., & Eaker, R. (2008). *Revisiting professional learning communities at work.* Bloomington, IN: Solution Tree.

DuFour, R., Eaker, R., & Many, T. (2006). *Learning by doing: Professional learning communities at work.* Bloomington, IN: Solution Tree.

Dunne, F., & Honts, F. (2000). *That group really makes me think: Critical Friends Groups and the development of reflective practitioners.* Paper presented at the American Educational Research Association annual meeting, San Diego, CA.

Dunne, F., & Nave, B. (2000). Critical Friends Groups: Teachers helping teachers to improve student learning. *Phi Delta Kappan, 28*(4), 31–37.

Easton, L. B. (2008). *Powerful designs for professional learning.* Oxford, OH: National Staff Development Council (NSDC).

Egodawatte, G., & McDougall, D. (2010). The effects of teacher collaboration. *Educational Research and Policy, 33*(2), 39–53.

Elmore, R. F. (2002). *Bridging the gap between standards and achievement: The imperative for professional development in education.* Washington, DC: Albert Shanker Institute.

Evans, R. (2002). *The human side of school change.* San Francisco, CA: Jossey-Bass.

Evans, R. (2005). *Family matters: How schools can cope with the crisis in childrearing.* San Francisco, CA: Jossey-Bass.

Evertson, C., & Smithey, M. (2000). Mentoring effects on protégés classroom practices. *Journal of Educational Research, 93*(5), 294–304.

Fairbanks, C., & LaGrone, D. (2006). Learning together: Constructing knowledge in a teacher research group. *Teacher Education Quarterly, 33*(3), 7–25.

Feger, S., & Zibit, M. (2006). *The role of facilitation in online professional development.* Providence, RI: Northeast Regional Education Laboratory.

Feiman-Nemser, S. (1999). *Creating a teacher mentoring program.* Washington, DC: National Foundation for the Improvement of Education. ERIC clearinghouse for teaching and teacher education.

Fernandez, C. (2003). Learning from Japanese approaches to professional development. *Journal of Teacher Education, 53*(5), 393–405.

Fernandez, C., & Chokshi, S. (2002). A practical guide to translating lesson study to a US setting. *Phi Delta Kappan, 84*(2), 128–135.

Fernandez, C., & Yoshida, M. (2004). *Lesson study: A Japanese approach to improving teaching and learning.* Mahwah, NJ: Erlbaum Publishing.

Ferrance, E. (2000). *Action research.* Providence, RI: LAB, Northeast and Island Regional Education Laboratory at Brown University.

Finley, L., & Hartman, D. (2004). Institutional change and resistance: Teacher preparatory faculty and technology integration. *Journal of Technology and Teacher Education, 12*(3), 319–337.

Fisher, J., Schumaker, J., & Culbertson, J. (2010). Effects of a computerized professional development program on teacher and student outcomes. *Teaching and Teacher Education, 61*(4), 302–312.

Fishman, B., Marx, R., Best, S., & Tal, R. (2003). Linking teacher and student learning to improve professional development in systemic reform. *Teaching and Teacher Education, 19*(6), 643–658.

Franzak, J. (2002). Developing a teacher identity: The impact of Critical Friends practice on the teacher. *English Education, 34*(4), 258–280.

Friedman, T. L. (2007). *The world is flat.* New York, NY: Picador Publishing.

Fullan, M. (2007). *The new meaning of educational change* (4th ed.). New York, NY: Teachers College Press.

Fullan. M. (2009). Instructional rounds comes of age. *Journal of Educational Change, 10*(2), 101–113.

Gareis, C., & Nussbaum-Beach, S. (2008). Mentoring to develop accomplished professional teachers. *Journal of Personnel Evaluation in Education, 20*(3), 227–246.

Garmston, R. J., & Wellman, B. M. (2009). *The adaptive school: A sourcebook for developing collaborative groups.* (2nd ed.). Norwood, MA: Christopher-Gordon Publishers.

Glanz, J. (2003). *Action research: An educational leader's guide to school improvement* (2nd ed.). Norwood, MA: Christopher-Gordon.

Glanz, J. (2005). Action research as instructional supervision: Suggestions for principals. *NASSP Bulletin, 89*(643), 17–27.

Goldschmidt, P., & Phelps, G. (2010). Does teacher professional development affect content and pedagogical content knowledge? *Economics of Education Review, 29*(3), 432–439.

Gottesman, B. (2000). *Peer coaching for educators.* Lanham, MD: Scarecrow.

Gratch, A. (1998). Beginning teacher and mentor relationships. *Journal of Teacher Education, 49*(2), 12–18.

Guskey, T. (1986). Staff development and the process of teacher change. *Educational Researcher, 15*(5), 5–12.

Guskey, T. (2002). Does it make a difference? Evaluating professional development. *Educational Leadership, 59*(6), 45–52.

Guskey, T., & Sparks, D. (2004). Linking professional development to improvements in student learning. In E. M. Guyton & J. R. Dangel (Eds.), *Research linking teacher preparation and student performance: Teacher education yearbook XII* (pp. 233–247). Dubuque, IA: Kendall Hunt.

Guskey, T. R. (2000). *Evaluating professional development.* Thousand Oaks, CA: Corwin.

Hampton, G., & Rhodes, C. (2004). *A practical guide to mentoring and peer-networking.* London, England: Routledge.

Harrison, J., Dymoke, S., & Pell, T. (2006). Mentoring beginning teachers in secondary schools: An analysis of practice. *Teaching and Teacher Education, 22*(8), 1055–1067.

Harwell, S. (2003). *Teacher professional development: It's not an event, it's a process.* Waco, TX: Council For Occupational Research and Development (CORD).

Heider, K. (2005). Teacher isolation: How peer mentoring can help. *Current Issues in Education, 8*(14), 1–7.

Hendricks, C. (2008). *Improving schools through action research.* New York, NY: Pearson.

Hewitt, R., & Little, M. (2005). *Leading action research in schools.* Tallahassee, FL: Florida Department of Education.

Hill, H. (2010). Fixing teacher professional development. *Phi Delta Kappan, 90*(7), 470–477.

Hollins, E., & McIntyre, L. (2004). Promoting a self-sustaining learning community: Investigating critical friends as a model for teacher development. *International Journal of Qualitative Studies in Education, 17*(2), 247–264.

Hord, S. (1997). *Professional learning communities: Communities of continuous inquiry and improvement.* Austin, TX: Southwest Educational Development Laboratory (SEDL).

Hord, S. (2008). Evolution of the professional learning community: A concept based on intentional collegial learning. *Journal of Staff Development, 29*(3), 10–15.

Hord, S., & Sommers, W. (2008). *Leading professional learning communities.* Thousand Oaks, CA: Corwin.

Huang, H. B. (2010). What is good action research? *Action Research, 8*(1), 93–109.

Jametz, K. (2002). *Isolation is the enemy of improvement: Instructional leadership to support standards-based practice.* San Francisco, CA: WestEd.

Jaquith, A., Mindich, D., & Darling-Hammond, L. (2011). *Teacher professional learning in the United States: Phase three.* Washington, DC: National Staff Development Council.

Johnson, C. (2007). Whole-school collaborative sustained professional development and science teacher change: Signs of progress. *Journal of Science Teacher Education, 18,* 629–661.

Johnson, C. (2011). School administrators and the importance of utilizing action research. *International Journal of Humanities and Social Science, 14*(1), 78–84.

Johnson, C., Kahle, J., & Fargo, J. (2006). A study of the effect of whole-school sustained professional development on student achievement. *Journal of Research in Science Teaching, 44*(6), 775–786.

Johnson, C., & Marx, S. (2009). Transformative professional development: A model for urban science education reform. *Journal of Science Teacher Education, 20*(3), 113–134.

Key, E. (2006, January). Do they make a difference? A review of research on the impact of critical friends groups. Paper presented at *The National School Reform Faculty Research Forum,* Denver, CO.

Killion, J. (2000). Online staff development: Promise or peril. *NASSP Bulletin, 84*(618), 38–46.

Killion, J. (2007). *Assessing impact: Evaluating staff development* (2nd ed.). Thousand Oaks, CA: Corwin.

Knight, J. (2009). What can we do about teacher resistance? *Phi Delta Kappan, 34*(3), 50–54.

Koshy, V. (2005). *Action research for improving practice: A practical guide.* Thousand Oaks, CA: Sage.

Learning Forward. (2011). *Standards for professional learning*. Oxford, OH: Author.

Levine, M. (2003). *A mind at a time*. New York, NY: Simon and Schuster.

Lewis, C. (2002). *Lesson study: A handbook of teacher-led instructional change*. Philadelphia, PA: RBS Publishing.

Lewis, C., & Perry, R. (2006). How should research contribute to instructional improvement? The case of lesson study. *Educational Researcher, 35*(3), 3–14.

Lewis, C., Perry, R., & Hurd, J. (2004). A deeper look at lesson study. *Educational Leadership, 61*(5), 18–25.

Lewis, C., & Tsuchida, I. (1998). A lesson is like a swiftly flowing river: Research lessons and the improvement of education. *American Educator, 22*(4), 12–19.

Lipton, L., & Wellman, B. (2001). *Mentoring matters: A practical guide to learning-centered relationships*. Sherman, CT: Miravia.

Marzano, R. (2007). Using action research to enhance teaching and learning. *Journal of Personnel Evaluation and Education, 20*(3), 117–128.

Marzano, R. (2011). Making the most of instructional rounds. *Educational Leadership, 68*(5), 80–84.

McLaughlin, M., & Talbert, J. (2006). *Building school-based teacher learning communities*. New York, NY: Teachers College Press.

McNeil, P., & Klink, S. (2004). School coaching. In L.B. Easton (Ed.), *Powerful designs for professional learning* (pp. 185–194). Oxford, OH: National Staff Development Council.

McNiff, J., & Whitehead, J. (2006). *Action research for teachers*. London, England: Fulton.

Meirink, J., & Meijer, P. (2007). Teacher learning in collaborative settings. *Teachers and Teaching, 17*(2), 145–164.

Miller, M., & Greenwood, D. (2003). Why action research? *Action Research, 1*(1), 9–28.

Miller, W., & Rollnick, S. (2002). *Motivational interviewing: Preparing people for change*. New York, NY: Guilford.

Morissey, M. (2000). *Professional learning communities: An ongoing exploration*. Austin, TX: Southwest Educational Development Laboratory (SEDL).

Murray, J. (2011). *Professional learning opportunities in U.S. independent schools*. London, England: Lambert Publishing.

National Education Association. (1999). *Creating a teacher mentoring program*. Washington, DC: National Foundation for the Improvement of Education.

Nave, B. (2000). *Critical friends groups: Their impact on students, teachers, and schools*. Evaluation Report submitted to the National School Reform Faculty, Bloomington, IN.

Nussbaum-Beach, S. (2011, May). Assessing 21st century learning: Digitally enhanced curriculum a core component for creating connected learners. *TechEdge*, pp. 11–13.

Nussbaum-Beach, S., & Ritter Hall, L. (2011). *The connected educator: Learning and leading in a digital age*. Bloomington, IN: Solution Tree.

Odden, A., & Archibald, S. (2002). A cost framework for professional development. *Journal of Education Finance 28*(2), 51–74.

Orlando, D. (2010). *Real reasons why social media matters for educators.* Retrieved from http://isenet.ning.com/profiles/blogs/real-reasons-why-social-media

Ormond, C. (2008). Tailoring mentoring for new teachers: An exploratory study. *Australian Journal of Teacher Education, 36*(4), 39–46.

Paul, S. (2010). *23 things for 21st century teaching and learning.* Retrieved from http://k12learning20.wikispaces.com/23Things_

Penuel, W., Fishman, B., Yamaguchi, R., & Gallagher, L. (2007). What makes professional development effective? Strategies that foster curriculum implementation. *American Educational Research Journal, 44*(4), 921–958.

Perry, R., & Lewis, C. (2008). What is successful adaptation of lesson study in the US? *Journal of Educational Change, 10*(4), 365–391.

Pitton, D. (2006). *Mentoring novice teachers.* Thousand Oaks, CA: Sage.

Portner, H. (2005). *Teacher mentoring and induction.* Thousand Oaks, CA: Corwin.

Qualters, D. (2009). Creating a pathway for teacher change. *Journal of Faculty Development, 23*(1), 5–13.

Quate, S. (2008). Critical Friends Groups. In L. B. Easton (Ed.), *Powerful designs for professional learning* (2nd ed., pp. 107–114). Oxford, OH: National Staff Development Council.

Richardson, W. (2011). *Personal learning networks: Using the power of connections to transform education.* Bloomington, IN: Solution Tree.

Robbins, P. (1997). *How to plan and implement a peer coaching program.* Alexandria, VA: Association for Supervision and Curriculum Development (ASCD).

Robbins, P. (1999). Mentoring. *Journal of Staff Development, 20*(3), 40–42.

Robbins, P. (2003). Designing a mentor program. *ASCD Education Update, 45*(1), 1–4.

Robbins, P. (2008). Mentoring. In L. B. Easton (Ed.), *Powerful designs for professional learning* (2nd ed., pp. 185–197). Oxford, OH: National Staff Development Council.

Roberts, S., & Pruitt, E. (2003). *Schools as professional learning communities: Collaborative activities and strategies for professional development.* Thousand Oaks, CA: Corwin.

Ross, J. (2011). *Online professional development.* Thousand Oaks, CA: Corwin.

Rowley, J. (2000). The good mentor: Supporting beginning teachers. *Educational Leadership, 56*(8), 20–22.

Sagor, R. (2000). *Guiding school improvement with action research.* Alexandria, VA: Association for Supervision and Curriculum Development (ASCD).

Sarason, S. (1996). *The culture of the school and the problem of change.* New York, NY: Teachers College Press.

Scherer, M. (1999). *A better beginning: Supporting and mentoring new teachers.* Alexandria, VA: Association for Supervision, Curriculum and Development (ASCD).

Schmuck, R. (2006). *Practical action research for change* (2nd ed.). Thousand Oaks, CA: Corwin.

Schulman, L. (1986). Knowledge and teaching. *Educational Researcher, 15*(2), 4–11.

Senge, P. (1999). Recapturing the spirit of learning through a systems approach. *School Administrator, 48*(9), 8–13.

Senge, P. (2006). *The fifth discipline: The art and practice of the learning organiza-tion.* New York, NY: Random House.

Silva, P. (2005). A day in the life of schoolwide CFGs. *Educational Horizons, 84*(1), 29–34.

Sisk-Hilton, S. (2011). *Teaching and learning in schools: Professional development through shared inquiry.* New York, NY: Teachers College Press.

Sizer, T. (1999). No two are exactly alike. *Educational Leadership, 57*(1), 6–11.

Sparks, D. (1997). *A new vision for staff development.* Alexandria, VA: Association for Supervision and Curriculum Development (ASCD).

Sparks, D. (1998). Reforming teaching and staff development. *Journal of Staff Development, 18*(4), 96–103.

Stepanek, J., Appel, G., Leong, M., Mangan, M., & Mitchell, M. (2007). *Leading lesson study.* Thousand Oaks, CA: Corwin.

Stewart, V. (2012). *A world-class education: Learning from international models of excellence and innovation.* Alexandria, VA: ASCD.

Stigler, J. W., & Hiebert, J. (1999). *The teaching gap.* New York, NY: Simon and Schuster.

Stringer, E. (2007). *Action research.* Thousand Oaks, CA: Sage.

Supovitz, J. (2002). Developing communities of instructional practice. *Teachers College Record, 104*(8), 1591–1626.

Supovitz, J., & Turner, H. (2000). The effects of professional development on science teaching practices and classroom culture. *Journal of Research in Science Teaching, 37*(9), 963–980.

The Teaching Commission. (2006). *Teaching at risk: Progress and potholes.* New York, NY: Author.

Teitel, L. (2010). Improving teaching and learning through instructional rounds. *Harvard Education Letter, 25*(3), 9–12.

Tracey, K. (2010). Leading online learning initiatives in adult education. *Journal of Adult Education, 39*(2), 36–49.

Treacy, B., Kleiman, G., & Peterson, K. (2002). Successful online professional development. *Learning and Leading with Technology, 30*(1), 42–48.

Tyler, R. (1949). *Basic principles of curriculum and instruction.* Chicago, IL: University of Chicago Press.

Veenman, S. (1984). Perceived problems of beginning teachers. *Review of Educational Research, 54*(1), 51–67.

Wagner, T. (2008). *The global achievement gap.* New York, NY: Perseus Books.

Warlick, D. (2009). Grow your personal learning network. *Learning and Leading with Technology, 36*(12), 12–16.

Webster-Wright, A. (2009). Reframing professional development through understanding authentic professional learning. *Review of Educational Research, 79*(2), 702–739.

Wechsler, M. E., Caspary, K., Humphrey, D. C., & Matsko, K. K. (2010). *Examining the effects of new teacher induction.* Menlo Park, CA: SRI International.

Wei, R. C., Darling-Hammond, L., & Adamson, F. (2010). *Professional develop-ment in the United States: Trends and challenges.* Washington, DC: National Staff Development Council.

Wiggins, G., & McTighe, J. (1998). *Understanding by design.* Alexandria, VA: Association for Supervision and Curriculum Development.

Wiburg, K., & Brown, S. (2007). *Lesson study communities: Increasing student achievement.* Thousand Oaks, CA: Corwin.

Wilson, K. G., & Daviss, B. (1996). *Redesigning education.* New York, NY: Teachers College Press.

York-Barr, J., & Duke, K. (2004). What do we know about teacher leadership? *Review of Educational Research, 74*(3), 255–316.

Zachary, L. J. (2000). *The mentor's guide: Facilitating effective learning relationships.* San Francisco, CA: Jossey-Bass.

Zachary, L. J. (2011). *Creating a mentoring culture: The organization's guide.* San Francisco, CA: Jossey-Bass.

Zepeda, S. (2007). *Professional development: What works.* Larchmont, NY: Eye on Education.

Zwart, R., Wubbels, T., Bolhuis, S., & Bergen, T. C. M. (2008, May). Teacher learning through reciprocal peer coaching: An analysis of activity sequences. *Teaching and Teacher Education, 24*(4), 982–1002.

Index

CORWIN

A SAGE Company

The Corwin logo—a raven striding across an open book—represents the union of courage and learning. Corwin is committed to improving education for all learners by publishing books and other professional development resources for those serving the field of PreK–12 education. By providing practical, hands-on materials, Corwin continues to carry out the promise of its motto: **"Helping Educators Do Their Work Better."**

Made in the USA
Middletown, DE
20 May 2023

30991019R00144